LEARNING RESOURCES CTR/NEW ENGLAND TECH.
GEN E302.5.F73 1986
Framers of the Constitutio
3 0147 0001 1665 0

W9-AQQ-056

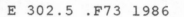

FRAMERS *of the* CONSTITUTION

FRAMERS *of the* CONSTITUTION

James H. Charleton
Robert G. Ferris
Mary C. Ryan
Editors

National Archives and Records Administration
Washington, DC

PUBLISHED FOR THE NATIONAL ARCHIVES AND RECORDS ADMINISTRATION
BY THE
NATIONAL ARCHIVES TRUST FUND BOARD
1986

A revised and updated edition of *Signers of the Constitution: Historic Places Commemorating the Signing of the Constitution*, published in 1976 by the National Park Service as Volume XXIX in the series *National Survey of Historic Sites and Buildings*, Robert G. Ferris, series editor. The volume was based on studies prepared by Prof. Charles H. McCormick, Fairmont State College, W. Va. James H. Charleton was the co-editor, and Dorothy Chatfield Buffmire was the photographic editor.

Library of Congress Cataloging-in-Publication Data

Framers of the Constitution.

Originally published under title: Signers of the Constitution. Washington: U.S. Dept. of the Interior, National Park Service, 1976.
Includes index.
1. United States. Constitution—Signers—Biography.
2. United States—Politics and government—1783–1789.
3. Statesmen—United States—Biography. I. National Archives Trust Fund Board. II. United States. National Park Service. Signers of the Constitution.
E302.5.F73 1986 973.3'13'0922 [B] 86-8413
ISBN 0-911333-43-6
Cover: Detail from Oil (1940) by Howard Chandler Christy. Courtesy Architect of the Capitol.

CONTENTS

Preface vii

Part I
Historical Background 1

Introduction, 3
Aims of the Founders, 4
Shortcomings of the Confederation, 9
The Mount Vernon and Annapolis Meetings, 19
The Delegates, 22
Convention Proceedings, 33
The Opening Days, 35 *The Virginia and New Jersey Plans, 38*
The Great Compromise, 44 *Writing the First Draft, 50*
Debates and Revisions, 56 *The Question of Presidential Election and Authority, 64* *The Final Draft, 66*
The Approved Document, 76
Ratification: Federalists vs. Antifederalists, 86
The First Presidential Election, 99
Amending the Constitution, 102
The Bill of Rights, 103 *Subsequent Amendments, 107*

Part II
Biographical Sketches 117

Political Experience, 119
Occupations, 119
Geographic and Educational Background, 120
Longevity and Family Life, 121
Post-Convention Careers, 122

Abraham Baldwin—*Georgia*, 123
Richard Bassett—*Delaware*, 124
Gunning Bedford, Jr.—*Delaware*, 125
John Blair—*Virginia*, 127
William Blount—*North Carolina*, 128
David Brearly—*New Jersey*, 129
Jacob Broom—*Delaware*, 131
Pierce Butler—*South Carolina*, 132
Daniel Carroll—*Maryland*, 133
George Clymer—*Pennsylvania*, 134
William Richardson Davie—*North Carolina*, 136
Jonathan Dayton—*New Jersey*, 138
John Dickinson—*Delaware*, 139
Oliver Ellsworth—*Connecticut*, 142
William Few—*Georgia*, 144
Thomas Fitzsimons—*Pennsylvania*, 145
Benjamin Franklin—*Pennsylvania*, 147
Elbridge Gerry—*Massachusetts*, 149
Nicholas Gilman—*New Hampshire*, 152
Nathaniel Gorham—*Massachusetts*, 153
Alexander Hamilton—*New York*, 154
William C. Houston—*New Jersey*, 157
William Houstoun—*Georgia*, 158
Jared Ingersoll—*Pennsylvania*, 159
Daniel of St. Thomas Jenifer—*Maryland*, 160

William Samuel Johnson—*Connecticut*, 161
Rufus King—*Massachusetts*, 163
John Langdon—*New Hampshire*, 165
John Lansing, Jr.—*New York*, 166
William Livingston—*New Jersey*, 168
James McClurg—*Virginia*, 170
James McHenry—*Maryland*, 171
James Madison—*Virginia*, 172
Alexander Martin—*North Carolina*, 175
Luther Martin—*Maryland*, 177
George Mason—*Virginia*, 179
John Francis Mercer—*Maryland*, 181
Thomas Mifflin—*Pennsylvania*, 182
Gouverneur Morris—*Pennsylvania*, 183
Robert Morris—*Pennsylvania*, 185
William Paterson—*New Jersey*, 187
William Leigh Pierce—*Georgia*, 189
Charles Pinckney—*South Carolina*, 190
Charles Cotesworth Pinckney—*South Carolina*, 192
Edmund Randolph—*Virginia*, 194
George Read—*Delaware*, 196
John Rutledge—*South Carolina*, 198
Roger Sherman—*Connecticut*, 200
Richard Dobbs Spaight, Sr.—*North Carolina*, 202
Caleb Strong—*Massachusetts*, 203
George Washington—*Virginia*, 204
Hugh Williamson—*North Carolina*, 208
James Wilson—*Pennsylvania*, 210
George Wythe—*Virginia*, 213
Robert Yates—*New York*, 215

Appendix
The Constitution and Its History, 217

Text of the Constitution and Amendments, 219
History of the Document, 235

Further Research in the National Archives, 242

Suggested Reading, 245

Art and Picture Credits, 247

Index, 251

PREFACE

Of all the documents in the care of the National Archives, the most famous are the Declaration of Independence and the Constitution of the United States. Ten years ago the Declaration was the focus of a grand nationwide celebration of two centuries of independence. Now we celebrate another bicentennial—the 200th anniversary of the framing of our Constitution.

Today we take the Constitution and the Bill of Rights for granted, but this landmark anniversary reminds us that our Constitution has both withstood and adapted to many challenges through the years. It has endured while the constitutions of other nations have fallen. Though amended 26 times, the basic document stands as it did when the delegates approved it at the Federal Convention. Throughout the summer of 1787 these men debated and resolved critical questions and made decisions that would shape the nation's future. The task the delegates set for themselves was not an easy one, and not all approved of the outcome. It is fitting, 200 years later, to reexamine the men and proceedings that framed the Constitution of the United States.

For the occasion, the National Archives and Records Administration has produced *Framers of the Constitution.* This book was first published by the National Park Service in 1976 under the title *Signers of the Constitution.* For this edition, the National Archives has added articles about the 16 delegates who did not sign the Constitution and has deleted the section on historic sites. With the exception of stylistic changes, the text prepared by the National Park Service has remained virtually the same. The great number of people who contributed to the original edition are again acknowledged, and special thanks to the Division of History at the National Park Service for their cooperation. At the National Archives, Mary C. Ryan was responsible for the revision. Shelby G. Bale, Ann Mohan, and Timothy Walch provided valuable advice and assistance, and Jan Danis edited for style. The book was designed by Wayne Pederson, and Richard Smith guided it through composition and printing.

As caretaker for the original documents of the Constitution and the Bill of Rights, the National Archives can take a unique part in the anniversary celebration. Among its vast resources are records particularly pertinent to constitutional analysis. These are reviewed in the final section of this book, "Further Research in the National Archives." *Framers of the Constitution*, it is hoped, will promote greater familiarity with one of our most treasured public documents and inspire readers to deeper study.

PART ONE

Framers of the Constitution: HISTORICAL BACKGROUND

For generations the people of the United States have revered the Constitution—and rightly so. It has provided an enduring and evolving framework for 200 years of national development. In some respects, it reflects the time of its creation, for it incorporates basic American tenets of the 18th century. These include the theory of the state as a compact between the people and the government and the idea that fundamental laws should be written. The Constitution also reaffirms the strong belief in the traditional rights of Englishmen to the protection of life, liberty, and property that Americans defended in their rebellion against Britain.

Above all, the document expresses, both in its provisions and in the process by which they were formulated, the Founding Fathers' abiding faith in man's willingness to reason—his ability to surmount political differences by means of rational discussion and compromise. Men sometimes disagree over the meaning of specific provisions of the instrument, but within its broad outlines and mechanisms for compromise lie means to reconcile disagreements. The Constitution expresses the concerns of a past age, yet it is the embodiment of a spirit and a wisdom as modern as tomorrow.

Introduction

Laboring at Philadephia from late spring until early fall in 1787, the 55 delegates to the Constitutional Convention created a new form of government for the United States. Few of them could likely have imagined how successful and enduring their efforts would be, for the flexible instrument they produced to replace the Articles of Confederation has persevered through the centuries as the foundation of our nation—though it has been buffeted by a civil war, two world wars, domestic conflicts, and economic depressions. During these years, amendments to and judicial clarifications of the Constitution have adapted it to a continually changing national mode of life. And today it serves as a symbol of democracy to the world, whose history it has immeasurably influenced.

The constitutional achievement is all the more remarkable when the vast social, economic, and political differences between the present age and the era of the framers are considered. While the country has evolved from a weak and basically agricultural collection of almost independent states into an industrial colossus that ranks high among the sovereign nations of the world, sweeping changes have occurred in American life, thought, and attitudes.

Living as they did in another day and serving far more restricted constituencies than our governmental representatives today, most of the Founding Fathers entertained some views that differed from our modern concept of democracy. These views reflected those of the aristocracy, the ruling-elite group to which the majority of them belonged. As legislators, politicians, lawyers, merchants, businessmen, planters, and landed gentry, for the most part they were predominantly conservative men of property.

Few of the Convention delegates would have acknowledged they were "democrats"; to most of them, "democracy" was virtually synonymous with "mob rule." They favored "republicanism," in which the aristocrats would be dominant. The framers were not truly seeking to establish a government under direct popular control.

Yet, though in some ways the Constitution originally demonstrated the self-interest of its creators, contained certain antidemocratic concepts, and sanctioned slavery, practically all the men who wrote it believed in the precepts of representative government and felt the people were its ultimate custodians. Thus, the document's underlying philosophy is essentially democratic.

To most of the founders, the issue was not simply "democracy" versus "republicanism" but national union versus disintegration. As pragmatic politicians rather than political theorists, they did not seek so much to impose a fixed governmental philosophy as to find a way to reconcile conflicting political and economic theories and realities within a framework that would facilitate the orderly and stable growth of the nation and ensure its security.

Aims of the Founders

Historians have long debated the motives and aims of the founders. Some scholars contend they were often guided by selfish or even sinister interests, particularly in the economic realm; others maintain that most of them were basically altruistic; members of a third group take positions somewhere in between the two extremes. Such a wide spectrum of opinion is at least partially explained by the diversities in personalities, backgrounds, and goals of the framers; incomplete biographical data; inadequacies in primary historical sources; historical semantic differences in the definition of the word "democracy"; the conflicting political and socioeconomic elements that went into the making of the Constitution; the pronounced differences between the modern and 18th-century milieus; and the biases of historians themselves.

Actually, the motivations of the framers were as diverse and complex as those of humanity. If most of them were committed to the preservation or improvement of their own economic situation, they also sought to better that of all citizens. Some of the makers of the Constitution stood to gain financially from the fiscal stability the new government would provide, but others stood to lose. On key issues, individuals often voted against or compromised their personal interests for what they believed to be the common good.

The delegates were also obviously swayed by their own political views and factions, the attitudes of their constituents, and the situations in their states. In a humanitarian vein, the Founding Fathers

Americans have always revered the basic documents of the Republic. The Constitution and the Bill of Rights, as well as the Declaration of Independence, are displayed in the Exhibition Hall of the National Archives.

strove to foster the general welfare and prevent tyranny from any source. Psychological factors were also apparent. Frayed tempers, jealousies, animosities, ambitions, and friendships had a major impact. Many of the framers also recognized they could likely attain positions of power in the new government. Finally, intellectual factors guided these men. They employed many logical premises and techniques, utilized rational dialogue, and drew on the lessons of history and political theory.

If the Founding Fathers had a contrary intent, they nevertheless devised an instrument that ultimately resulted in a democracy. As leaders of the day, they possessed the required education and political and economic experience to understand the needs of the nation and bring about the changes in government so necessary for its survival. Certainly it is unlikely that the framers would have been able or willing to transcend their background and experience and prepare a document surrendering the reins of power to and reflecting the needs and desires of another group.

Legitimate channels were followed in convoking the convention, which the Continental Congress had authorized. The only state not in attendance, Rhode Island, had rejected the invitation to take part. All the other 12 legislatures elected delegates in the approved manner. Most of these bodies, though they were not representative of the entire populace because of various voting and apportionment restrictions, were recently elected and broadly represented most areas and economic and social groups of the nation. Furthermore, the legislatures as a whole were more democratic than perhaps any other governmental assemblies in the world at the time.

The men at Philadelphia feared any form of tyranny. During their careers, a number of them had espoused human rights, protected economic and religious minorities, and sponsored antislavery legislation. The delegates were not alienated from the masses, with whom they had shoulder to shoulder recently overthrown British rule and with whom they identified in many other ways. Americans in mind and spirit, they were guided by a strong sense of public service.

Furthermore, the Founding Fathers based the proposed new government on popular, as well as state, sovereignty, though not all people were eligible to vote at the time. The Constitution left the determination of suffrage to the states, where this responsibility had been lodged. For federal officeholders, no property qualifications were imposed and religious tests were forbidden. Titles of nobility were also prohibited, on both the state and national level. And provisions for amendment of the instrument were far easier than in the Articles of Confederation.

Then, too, the founders were aware they would submit their work to Congress for whatever action it cared to take and specified that 9 of the 13 states would need to ratify the Constitution before it went into effect. Thus, opponents gained an opportunity to voice their objections. Had this group been better represented at the convention, perhaps the Constitution might not have been created. Some individuals in this category had been elected as delegates but chose not to participate. Had they done so, because voting was by state and most delegations were small, they could have made a substantial mark on the proceedings. One such person, Patrick Henry, was a spokesman for a group that had slight voice at Philadelphia, the small farmers.

Representation in a democracy is never perfect. At least one-third of the country's population today does not vote. Even those people who do can never be precisely represented because of a host of social, geographic, and political factors and the existence of individual shades of sentiment on particular issues.

How could the 55 delegates to the Constitutional Convention conceivably have spoken equitably for all the diverse elements of the nation? And, as a matter of fact, considering that the framers were apparently better educated, wealthier, and politically more experienced and powerful than most of their fellow aristocrats, they probably even imperfectly represented their own class. Also, some of the rich delegates had come from poor or humble backgrounds and thus likely possessed some understanding of the needs and problems of this group. No blacks attended the convention, yet some delegates vehemently argued against slavery.

The Founding Fathers were acutely aware that the fate of the nation would probably hinge on their success or failure at the convention. Heading a new and economically and militarily weak country that had few allies and was vulnerable to foreign intrigue and Indian attack, they were genuinely apprehensive about national security. Autonomous acts of some of the states in the field of foreign affairs threatened to involve the country in war. Further undermining international prestige was the lack of economic stability. For all these reasons, the framers granted control over foreign relations to the federal government and even went so far as to risk creating a standing army—in a country where such an institution was bitterly resented because of the recent experience with the British.

Critics of the founders have formulated numerous arguments. The principal ones, some of which reflect modern attitudes and retrospective judgments, are as follows: personal economic interests clearly guided some of the delegates; the majority of them were well-to-do aristocrats; fear of social radicalism and "democracy" spurred constitutional revision, especially after Shays' Rebellion; many of the framers felt a strong central government offered protection against majority rule; a large number doubted the stability and intelligence of the general populace; small farmers, workingmen, slaves, indentured servants, women, youth, and the poor were badly represented in Philadelphia or not at all; the Constitution did not outlaw slavery, reduce its effects, nor help blacks win the rights of citizenship; Rhode Island did not take part in the convention; New York and New Hampshire were not officially in attendance for extended periods; most creditors favored and most debtors opposed the Constitution; the bulk of the antinationalists who participated in the convention departed before it ended; and certain aspects of the Constitution are intentionally nondemocratic.

It is also true that, though public opinion polls were not conducted in 1787, a substantial number of Americans would likely have preferred continuance of the Confederation. The central government was only a distant and faint presence in the lives of most common men, who were inclined to resist any changes that might jeopardize their newly won freedom and whose basic allegiance was to their state governments. Furthermore, most of this group opposed any system resembling the British that would enjoy taxing power and maintain a standing army. Sharing this attitude were the state and local governments, which were not anxious to relinquish any of their powers.

WHATEVER their motivations, the Founding Fathers boldly and resourcefully created an instrument of government that fostered the growth of a democratic and prosperous nation. By so doing, they have earned the perpetual gratitude of the American people.

Many of the men at Philadelphia had played a key role in the Revolution, and in their view they were completing it. Even though they supplanted the Articles of Confederation, which had been its product, they firmly adhered to the republican ideals that lay at its heart and have attracted the allegiance of Americans ever since.

At the end of the grueling 4-month convention, perhaps none of the delegates was fully satisfied with their accomplishments. Yet posterity has learned, and continues to relearn, their true magnitude. Today the Constitution—an emblem of the viability of our Union and a beacon to all humanity—is enshrined at the National Archives Building in Washington, D.C.

Shortcomings of the Confederation

The Constitutional Convention met in a climate of national crisis, triggered by a series of governmental and economic problems—though historians have debated whether or not they were critical enough to warrant a drastic reorganization of the government. An anxious mixture of hope and despair gripped the minds of many leaders. Blessed with a huge territory stretching all the way to the Mississippi, the United States contained a wealth of natural resources. Its 3½ million inhabitants had demonstrated their industry and ingenuity. Only 4 years before, in the Treaty of Paris ending the War for Independence, they had won their freedom from Great Britain. Even earlier, they had taken their place among the nations of the world. And in 1781 a new government had been initiated under the Articles of Confederation, a constitution drawn up in 1777.

Yet, what if the experiment in self-government should fail? Such prominent men as George Washington, James Madison, and Alexander Hamilton feared it might. In many fields, the Confederation had proven to be ineffectual and its prestige had plummeted. The Continental Congress was unable to cope with all the country's problems.

The Articles of Confederation were a "firm league of friendship" among 13 semi-independent states; it did not provide for a truly sovereign national government. The principal governmental body was a single-house Congress, in which each state held one vote. No independent executive, to carry out the laws, or autonomous court system, to administer the legal and judicial system or to adjudicate disputes between the federal government and the states, was provided. The approval of a minimum of seven states, who elected and paid their delegates, was required for any legislation; nine, to wage war or pass certain other measures; and all 13, to alter or amend the Articles themselves. The Continental Congress was empowered to declare and wage war, raise an army and navy, make treaties and alliances, appoint and receive ambassadors, decide interstate disputes, negotiate loans, emit bills of credit, coin money, regulate weights and measures, manage Indian affairs, and operate a system of interstate post offices.

Severely inhibiting the effectiveness of Congress in carrying out its prerogatives were three major limitations. One was the lack of a most basic governmental power: the right to levy taxes, which would provide an independent source of revenue. Instead, Congress could only requisition money from the states and could not enforce payment. Suffering from the economic depression and saddled with their own war debts, states furnished only a small part of the money sought.

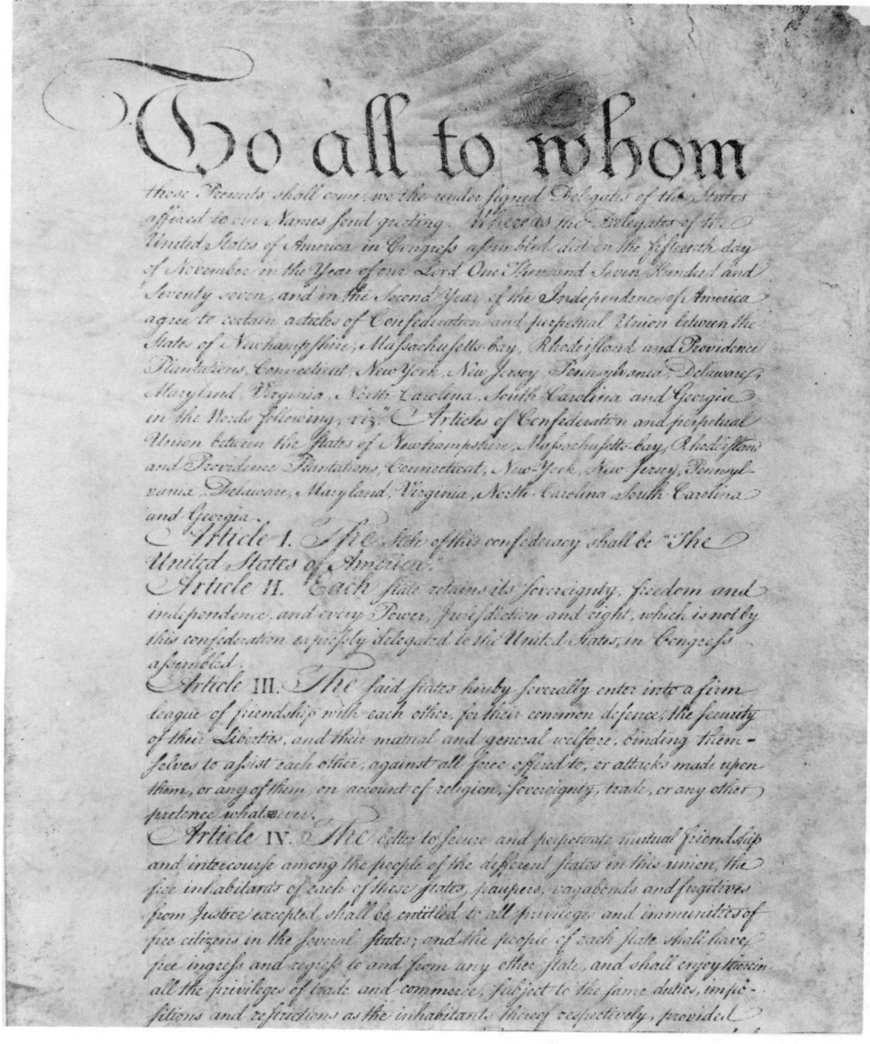

To all to whom these Presents shall come, we the under signed Delegates of the States affixed to our Names send greeting. Whereas the Delegates of the United States of America in Congress assembled did on the fifteenth day of November in the Year of our Lord One Thousand Seven Hundred and Seventy seven, and in the Second Year of the Independence of America agree to certain articles of Confederation and perpetual Union between the States of Newhampshire, Massachusetts-bay, Rhodeisland and Providence Plantations, Connecticut, New York, New Jersey, Pennsylvania, Delaware, Maryland, Virginia, North Carolina, South Carolina and Georgia in the Words following, viz. "Articles of Confederation and perpetual Union between the States of Newhampshire, Massachusetts-bay, Rhodeisland and Providence Plantations, Connecticut, New-York, New-Jersey, Pennsylvania, Delaware, Maryland, Virginia, North-Carolina, South Carolina and Georgia.

Article I. The Stile of this confederacy shall be "The United States of America."

Article II. Each state retains its sovereignty, freedom and independence, and every Power, Jurisdiction and right, which is not by this confederation expressly delegated to the United States, in Congress assembled.

Article III. The said states hereby severally enter into a firm league of friendship with each other, for their common defence, the security of their Liberties, and their mutual and general welfare, binding themselves to assist each other, against all force offered to, or attacks made upon them, or any of them, on account of religion, sovereignty, trade, or any other pretence whatever.

Article IV. The better to secure and perpetuate mutual friendship and intercourse among the people of the different states in this union, the free inhabitants of each of these states, paupers, vagabonds and fugitives from Justice excepted, shall be entitled to all privileges and immunities of free citizens in the several states; and the people of each state shall have free ingress and regress to and from any other state, and shall enjoy therein all the privileges of trade and commerce, subject to the same duties, impositions and restrictions as the inhabitants thereof respectively, provided

Dissatisfaction with the Articles of Confederation, whose opening paragraphs are reproduced here, gave rise to the movement that led to the creation of the Constitution.

The second serious congressional deficiency was absence of authority to regulate interstate and foreign commerce. The states negotiated separately with foreign powers on commercial matters to the detriment of the overall economy. And, when two states disagreed about trade matters, they dealt directly with each other much like countries did. Fortunately, to facilitate the conduct of legal business, at least the states had agreed to the mutual recognition of official acts.

Third, the Continental Congress could not properly exercise its treaty power because of the autonomy of the states. Their independent conduct of foreign relations and Indian policy not only hampered Congress in its dealings with other nations but also sometimes even jeopardized national security.

The Continental Congress had led the nation through the War for Independence, and in the Ordinances of 1784 and 1785 had established a plan to advance westward expansion by the addition of new states to the Confederation. But in financial matters, foreign affairs, national defense, mediation of interstate disputes, and protecting American sovereignty in the West it was less successful. After the war, the ramifications of political, social, and economic readjustment caught up with it. People blamed it for failure to solve problems that would have tried stronger governments. The deficiencies of Congress were real, however. By 1787 even its defenders recognized that it had fallen upon evil times.

Financially, the situation was chaotic. Congress could not pay its war debts, foreign or domestic, or meet current obligations. The private financial system of the country was feeble, and the nation lacked a stable and uniform currency. The central government was virtually powerless to correct the conditions.

Because much of the debt—federal, state, and private—was owed to foreign lenders, the future of the United States in international commerce was precarious. A nation that does not pay its debts cannot command respect from other countries. Furthermore, prosperity depended on trade with Europe and the Caribbean colonies, but Congress could not conclude suitable commercial treaties.

Another area where the Continental Congress had failed was foreign affairs. Other nations showed contempt for the United States. Many of them questioned the stability or even the continued existence of the Confederation. One British official remarked that it would be better to make 13 separate treaties with the individual states than to deal with the Continental Congress. American diplomats, whose efforts were hamstrung by the lack of a central authority that could formulate a unified foreign policy, made slight impress in world capitals. The prevailing mercantile system also prevented the opening up of markets for American agricultural produce.

Only a few European nations sent ministers to this country. In 1785 Great Britain received Minister John Adams, but not until 7 years later did she reciprocate with an exchange of diplomats. She also refused to grant trade concessions needed by the United States if prewar outlets for American goods were to be restored. And she did not evacuate a string of military and fur trading posts along the Great Lakes as called for in the Paris treaty of 1783. As grounds for refusal to do so, she contended that the United States had already violated it by failing to pay British and Loyalist claims. Congress could not solve the problem, lacking as it did the military power to drive the British out of the old Northwest or authority to force the states to settle the claims. Another source of English resentment was debts owed by individual Americans to British creditors.

France remained friendly, but trade with the United States was insignificant because the practical outlet for American raw materials was more industrialized Britain. Since the French foreign minister, the Comte de Vergennes, at the peace negotiations ending the War for Independence, had shown a willingness to sacrifice American claims to western territory to the interests of French diplomacy, relations between the two countries had cooled, though France remained the closest supporter of the United States.

During the Confederation period, domestic and foreign commerce languished. Scene at Philadelphia near the Arch Street Ferry.

Relations with Spain had never been cordial. Resenting U.S. acquisition of the vast Appalachian-Mississippi territory in 1783 and considering it a threat to her colonial empire, she did not recognize U.S. claims to parts of present Georgia, Alabama, and Mississippi, and she disputed the location of the boundary between Florida and the United States as defined by the Paris treaty. Spain also used her control of New Orleans and the mouth of the Mississippi to attempt to persuade American settlers in the West, who relied on the river to ship their produce to the East and Europe, to forswear the United States and join her. Seeking accommodation, Congress authorized John Jay to negotiate with the Spanish, but he met with little success.

Meantime, the Barbary States of North Africa plundered and exacted tribute from U.S. ships in the Mediterranean, and the Continental Congress could do nothing about it.

Vitally related to the debility in foreign affairs was the inadequacy of national defense. This was attributable to the Confederation's reliance on state militias and its financial difficulties. At the very time that westerners were clamoring for protection from the Indians and action against the British in the Northwest, the U.S. Army was in a moribund state. In 1783, in response to frontiersmen's pleas, the best Congress could do was call for an increase in the size of the army from 80 to 700 men. Before the adoption of the Constitution, even this modest goal was never reached, but enough state militiamen volunteered for U.S. Army service to erect and garrison a few forts in the Ohio country and provide token evidence of U.S. authority there. From 1784 until 1789, the army consisted only of these western garrisons, small detachments at West Point, N.Y., and the Springfield, Mass., and Pittsburgh supply depots. The "navy" of the War for Independence had disappeared. After the war, the few remaining ships were sold and the sailors discharged.

In disputes among the states, Congress was no more successful. Powerless to enforce its decisions, it hesitated to make many. It could not regulate interstate commerce or, for example, prevent states from passing restrictive measures against imports from one another. When the "State of Franklin" (1784–88) claimed independence from North Carolina and a faction within the state sought annexation to Spain, Congress was unable to resolve the issue. And it could not settle the conflicting claims of New Hampshire and New York to the Vermont area, at a time when Ethan, Ira, and Levi Allen, leaders of the semi-independent state, were said to be discussing with the British its possible annexation to Canada.

Crippled by its military and diplomatic shortcomings, the Continental Congress was unable to stop Indian raids along the frontier. The

Spaniards held sway over the natives in the old Southwest, machinated along the border, and threatened to close the Mississippi River to American trade. The British intrigued in the old Northwest and dominated the Indians there. All these conditions irritated western settlers, landowners, and speculators and threatened to lead them into alliances with foreign powers that would offer protection and create a climate hospitable to settlement. In response to these provocations, Congress could do little to reassure westerners, whose secession seemed possible. As Washington wrote, the West was "on a pivot," ready at the "touch of a feather" to turn to the nation that offered the most secure future.

Complicating the problems of the Confederation while at the same time revealing its impotence was the deplorable state of the economy. It was rocked not only by a postwar depression but also by rampant inflation, heavy British imports, and the loss of markets in Britain and the British West Indies. A logical move to counter the unfavorable balance of trade would have been imposition of a tariff to restrict imports or force Britain to make concessions in the West Indies, but the Confederation lacked authority to enact or apply such a measure. British merchants easily circumvented trade barriers erected by individual states by shipping their goods in through others. Another adverse factor was the great popularity of British products among consumers.

In the seaports of the East and on the farms of the South and West, export trade languished. In colonial times, certain products had enjoyed a guaranteed market under British mercantilism. Now, denied that favored status, or similar access to the trade of mercantilistic France and Spain, shippers and producers and all who depended on them felt the financial pinch. As a result, business failures and property foreclosures soared, and many people, particularly farmers, fell deeply into debt and lost their lands and homes.

The economic malaise affected most segments of society: merchants, shippers, planters, farmers, mechanics, artisans, and manufacturers. The farmers, who like manufacturers suffered from low prices for their products and the loss of markets, were also saddled with crippling taxes and property payments and in some regions faced crop failures. The lack of a uniform national currency, a shortage of gold and silver, and the fluctuating value of currency from state to state hampered interstate trade. State paper, bills of exchange, and foreign coins circulated freely. Economic rivalries, as well as currency and boundary disputes, were rife among the states.

The widespread indebtedness, coupled with the scarcity of hard money, generated pressures on state legislatures to pass laws

By the United States in Congreſs aſſembled,

October 12, 1785.

WHEREAS it is indiſpenſibly neceſſary, for the ſupport of the federal government, that the ſtates ſhould ſupply their quotas of money, for the purpoſes ſtated in the eſtimates of the ſubſiſting requiſitions of Congreſs.

And whereas certificates for the intereſt ariſing on loan-office certificates, and other certificates of liquidated debts, previouſly to the laſt day of December 1782, from the deficiencies of ſome of the ſtates to comply with the requiſition of the 4th September, 1782, and 27th and 28th of April, 1784, will, in purſuance of the requiſition of the 27th of September, 1785, be iſſued by the commiſſioners of the continental loan-offices in ſuch ſtates.

And whereas the extra certificates which the ſaid commiſſioners may iſſue for the payment of the ſaid intereſt, ſhould be called in or redeemed by the deficient ſtates in order to compleat their reſpective quotas of the intereſt of the domeſtic debt, ſpecified in the ſaid requiſitions of the 4th September, 1782, and 27th and 28th April, 1784.

RESOLVED,

That the ſeveral ſtates be earneſtly called on to compleat without delay the whole of their quotas of the requiſitions laſt mentioned, and that ſuch of the ſtates as may be deficient in paying their reſpective quotas of the intereſt of the domeſtic debt purſuant to the ſaid requiſitions, be required to collect and pay into the public treaſury the amount of ſuch deficiencies, either in certificates to be iſſued by the commiſſioners of the continental loan-offices, purſuant to the requiſition of the 27th September, 1785, for the payment of the ſaid intereſt, or in ſpecie, to be applied to the redemption of ſuch certificates; provided that the ſum ſo to be paid into the treaſury in intereſt certificates as part of the requiſition of the 27th and 28th April 1784, ſhall not at any time exceed the proportion of facilities to be paid into the treaſury, agreeably to the requiſition laſt mentioned.

Cha Thomson secy

Under the Articles of Confederation, the central government had no independent income and had difficulty collecting sufficient funds from the states.

favorable to debtors and to issue inflationary paper money, unbacked by gold or silver. This medium, which kept depreciating in value, made it easier for debtors to satisfy their creditors, often men of property who were outraged by the movement. But many debtors were too poor to pay in any kind of money. Soldiers returning from the war found their farms strapped with mortgages, which in some states were partly necessitated by heavy taxes.

As a result, debtor political factions arose that advocated not only the printing of more paper money and other antideflationary monetary policies but also laws to prevent foreclosures. In some places, while Congress stood by helplessly, relations between creditors and debtors deteriorated almost to the point of civil war. In Rhode Island and elsewhere, paper money flowed with the speed of the presses. In other states, like Massachusetts, the creditor and hard money interests prevailed.

It was in western Massachusetts that the debtor-creditor struggle peaked in 1786–87, and culminated in a resort to arms and bloodshed. The legislature, dominated by wealthy eastern creditors and commercial interests intent on paying off the governmental debt, levied land and poll taxes. These burdened small farmers, who were already deep in debt and suffering particularly from the drop in produce prices caused by the cessation of trade with the British West Indies. While the legislature ignored protests and petitions from the underrepresented agrarians for stay laws, the issuance of paper money, and constitutional changes, many honest men, their mortgages foreclosed and their property confiscated, went to prison.

Abandoning the traditional deference to authority of their class and demanding their right to express themselves on governmental matters, the farmers first harassed tax collectors, moneylenders, lawyers, courts, and officials who foreclosed mortgages. In September 1786 Daniel Shays, a former captain in the War for Independence, and some 600 of his followers marched on Springfield and forced the commonwealth's supreme court to disband. The following January, leading a force of more than 1,000 insurgents, he attacked the lightly guarded federal arsenal there. Militia defeated them, the revolt collapsed, and Shays fled to Vermont; later, the legislature lowered taxes. Although the uprising was quickly and rather easily quelled, it was only possible through the private subscriptions of various merchants. The response to pleas for help from Massachusetts by the Continental Congress, which lacked troops and money, was belated and ineffectual.

Shays' Rebellion, as well as similar disturbances elsewhere in New England and the possibilities of others in the country, raised the

PENNSYLVANIA, ſſ.

By the *Preſident* and the *Supreme Executive Council* of the Commonwealth of *Pennſylvania*,

A *PROCLAMATION*.

WHEREAS the General Aſſembly of this Commonwealth, by a law entituled "An act for co-operating with "the ſtate of Maſſachuſetts bay, agreeable to the articles of "confederation, in the apprehending of the proclaimed rebels "DANIEL SHAYS, LUKE DAY, ADAM WHEELER "and ELI PARSONS," have enacted, "that rewards additional to thoſe offered and promiſed to be paid by the ſtate "of Maſſachuſetts Bay, for the apprehending the aforeſaid "rebels, be offered by this ſtate;" WE do hereby offer the following rewards to any perſon or perſons who ſhall, within the limits of this ſtate, apprehend the rebels aforeſaid, and ecure them in the gaol of the city and county of Philadelphia, —— viz. For the apprehending of the ſaid Daniel Shays, and ſecuring him as aforeſaid, the reward of *One hundred and Fifty Pounds* lawful money of the ſtate of Maſſachuſetts Bay, and *One Hundred Pounds* lawful money of this ſtate; and for the apprehending the ſaid Luke Day, Adam Wheeler and Eli Parſons, and ſecuring them as aforeſaid, the reward (reſpectively) of *One Hundred Pounds* lawful money of Maſſachuſetts Bay and *Fifty Pounds* lawful money of this ſtate: And all judges, juſtices, ſheriffs and conſtables are hereby ſtrictly enjoined and required to make diligent ſearch and enquiry after, and to uſe their utmoſt endeavours to apprehend and ſecure the ſaid Daniel Shays, Luke Day, Adam Wheeler and Eli Parſons, their aiders, abettors and comforters, and every of them, ſo that they may be dealt with according to law.

GIVEN in Council, under the hand of the Preſident, and the Seal of the State, at Philadelphia, this tenth day of March, in the year of our Lord one thouſand ſeven hundred and eighty-ſeven.

BENJAMIN FRANKLIN.

ATTEST

JOHN ARMSTRONG, jun. Secretary.

Shays' Rebellion alarmed men of property and creditors across the land. This proclamation by the Commonwealth of Pennsylvania offered a reward for Daniel Shays and three other ringleaders.

specter of anarchy to businessmen, gentlemen of property, and the ruling class from New Hampshire to Georgia. To them, the Shays episode seemed to herald a period of demagogic mob rule that would destroy property rights—and with them the nation's future. This group feared that debt-ridden farmers in other states might take up arms, lamented congressional ineffectiveness in controlling the Shays outbreak, expressed shock at the violence, decried the attack on a federal arsenal and the intimidation of lawyers and courts, and resented agitation for the repudiation of debts and the issuance of paper money.

Many individuals in this category, some of whom even felt that British spies and sympathizers had fomented the uprising, exploited the issue politically. Although the states were already selecting delegates to the Constitutional Convention, the rebellion helped catalyze the desire for drastic remedial action. This led to the creation of a more nationalistic government at Philadelphia than would probably otherwise have been possible.

Many men of standing traced the rise of individuals like Shays to the apparent strength of "radical" elements within some of the states and the excessive power vested in the legislatures under the Confederation. This situation directly resulted from the Revolutionary upsurge of the 1760s and 1770s. In rebelling against distant British rule, Americans had rejected the monarchy, scorned the arbitrary exercise of executive authority, and placed their faith in their legislatures. All of them except those in Connecticut and Rhode Island, which merely modified their royal charters, had drawn up new written constitutions during the Revolution. Because the colonial assemblies had fought for the rights of Americans and the royal governors had been the principal exponents of British repression, most of these documents had granted extensive powers to the legislatures and few to the governors, who were reduced essentially to administrators.

Although the legislatures had guided the states through the war, these bodies had too often looked to their own parochial interests instead of those of the whole country. By the 1780s, in some states neighborly cooperation had almost ceased to exist and had given way to jealousy, mistrust, and opportunism.

Congressional effectiveness depended partly on national confidence, which by early 1787 had mostly evaporated. The people placed their faith in the state governments, which could levy taxes and duties, maintain militia, regulate commerce, and, when necessary, use force to maintain order. Members of the Continental Congress often did not even bother to attend its sessions. During one 4-month period in 1783–84, a quorum of states could be mustered only three times; only with difficulty could a sufficient number be assembled to ratify the Treaty of Paris ending the War for Independence. As the prestige of Congress continued to dim, the quality of its personnel as a whole declined. Many of the best men stayed at home near their legislatures, where the real power lay.

Despite the extent and seriousness of the problems, numerous attempts at overall revision or the correction of particular deficiencies in the Articles of Confederation had failed. Sometimes a majority of the states approved the changes, but the consent of the required 13 could never be obtained. Thus, chances for constitutional revision within prescribed governmental channels were virtually nonexistent. By 1787, the contention of thinkers of the day who held that republics were ineffective in large countries seemed accurate.

The Mount Vernon and Annapolis Meetings

Against this background, was it any wonder that a movement originated to revise the Articles of Confederation? Many leaders believed that the country required a more truly national government to replace the existing loose compact of states. Although many of the prevalent difficulties would probably be encountered by any new nation while establishing its sovereignty and authority over its people, most of them were attributed to weaknesses in the Confederation.

Maryland State House, where the Annapolis Convention met in September 1786.

DESPITE all the weaknesses of the Confederation that might have sparked reform, it was the congressional lack of power to regulate commerce that brought about the Mount Vernon Conference and the Annapolis Convention, two interstate meetings of limited scope. These led to the Constitutional Convention.

The Mount Vernon Conference, held in March 1785, began at Alexandria, Va., and concluded at George Washington's nearby estate. Representatives of the legislatures of Maryland and Virginia, who convened primarily for the purpose of discussing mutual navigation problems along the lower Potomac, also achieved agreement on maritime use of the Chesapeake Bay, fishing and harbor rights, criminal jurisdiction, import duties, currency control, and other matters. Although James Madison did not attend, he had been the prime mover behind the conference. Washington, whose canal-oriented Patowmack Company sought to develop east-west trade and who was concerned about foreign intrigue among western settlers, sympathized with the goals of the meeting even if he was not instrumental in convening it.

Spurred by the success of this interstate diplomacy, in January 1786 the Virginia legislature, acting on a resolution possibly drafted by Madison, invited all the states to another conference. This one was to deal with domestic and foreign trade and make recommendations for their improvement to the states and the Continental Congress.

The Annapolis Convention met in September 1786 at the Maryland State House. In attendance were 12 representatives of 5 states (Delaware, New Jersey, New York, Pennsylvania, and Virginia), including Chairman John Dickinson, Alexander Hamilton, Abraham Clark, William C. Houston, George Read, Richard Bassett, Edmund J. Randolph, and James Madison. Delegates from Massachusetts, New Hampshire, Rhode Island, and North Carolina either did not participate or arrived at the convention too late to take part; Maryland, Connecticut, South Carolina, and Georgia did not make any appointments.

Because of the sparse representation, the commissioners took no action on the announced topic. Hamilton and Madison, however, convinced them that they should exceed their limited mandate and recommend a national meeting to consider the adequacy of the Articles of Confederation. The carefully couched report, drafted by Hamilton, proposed that all the states and the Continental Congress endorse another conference to be convened at Philadelphia on the second Monday of May in 1787. Its purpose, in essence, would be the framing of measures to strengthen the Articles.

Annapolis in the State of Maryland
September 11th. 1786.

At a meeting of Commissioners from the States of New York New Jersey Pennsylvania Delaware and Virginia —

Present

Alexander Hamilton } New York
Egbert Benson

Abraham Clarke } New Jersey
William C. Houston
James Schuarman

Tench Coxe — Pennsylvania

George Read } — Delaware
John Dickinson
Richard Bassett

Edmund Randolph } — Virginia
James Madison Junior
Saint George Tucker

Mr. Dickinson was unanimously elected Chairman.

The Commissioners produced their Credentials from their respective States; which were read.

After a full communication of Sentiments, and deliberate consideration of what would be proper to be done by the Commissioners now assembled it was unanimously agreed: that a Committee be appointed to prepare a draft of a Report to be made to the States having Commissioners attending at this meeting — Adjourned till Wednesday Morning.

Wednesday September 13th 1786.

Met agreeable to Adjournment.

The Committee so, appointed for that purpose, reported the draft of the report, which being read the meeting proceeded to the consideration thereof, and after some time spent therein Adjourned till tomorrow Morning —

First page of the report of the Annapolis Convention, forerunner of the Constitutional Convention.

The Delegates

When the delegates rode away from Annapolis, they could not be sure that the proposed meeting would even take place. But the unfavorable national economic situation, among other factors, and possibly the outbreak of debtor disturbances in Massachusetts and New Hampshire, prompted the Continental Congress to act after seven states (Virginia, New Jersey, Pennsylvania, North Carolina, New Hampshire, Delaware, and Georgia) had already authorized delegations and named most of their representatives. On February 21, 1787, that body passed a resolution calling for the new convention:

> Whereas there is provision in the Articles of Confederation & perpetual Union for making alterations therein by the Assent of a Congress of the United States and of the legislatures of the several States; And whereas experience hath evinced that there are defects in the present Confederation, as a mean to remedy which several of the States and particularly the State of New York by express instructions to their delegates in Congress have suggested a convention for the purposes expressed in the following resolution and such Convention appearing to be the most probable mean of establishing in these states a firm national government
>
> Resolved that in the Opinion of Congress it is expedient that on the second Monday in May next a Convention of delegates who shall have been appointed by the several States be held at Philadelphia for the sole and express purpose of revising the Articles of Confederation and reporting to Congress and the several legislatures such alterations and provisions therein as shall when agreed to in Congress and confirmed by the States render the federal constitution adequate to the exigencies of Government & the preservation of the Union

ALL 13 states appointed delegates except Rhode Island, an insufficient number of whose leaders sympathized with the nationalistic goals of the convention. A total of more than 70 individuals were originally nominated, but a substantial number of them did not accept the assignment or did not attend. Their reasons included opposition to constitutional revision, poor health, family illness, and the press of personal or professional business.

Some of the men in this category were prominent, including Richard Henry Lee, Thomas Nelson, Jr., and Patrick Henry of Virginia; Abraham Clark of New Jersey; George Walton of Georgia; Henry Laurens of South Carolina; and Maryland's Thomas Stone and Charles Carroll of Carrollton. All these individuals except Henry and Laurens had signed the Declaration of Independence. Part of the group who rejected nomination or did not take part in the convention later favored the new frame of government and supported ratification of the Constitution; others opposed it.

Various national leaders and eminently qualified people were not even elected. Among these were such men as Thomas Jefferson and John Adams, who were on diplomatic duty in Europe; Samuel Adams, whose political fortunes were temporarily on the decline; and John Hancock, who was busy as governor of Massachusetts.

New York named the smallest delegation, three; Pennsylvania the largest, eight. Attendance ranged from New York, which for much of the time had only one unofficial representative (Hamilton) on hand, and New Hampshire, with two late arrivals, to Pennsylvania, whose eight delegates all participated throughout most of the convention. The states usually paid all or part of their representatives' expenses and apparently in some instances compensated them.

Each state specified what part of its delegation needed to be present to act for it and cast its vote. The credentials of all the delegates except those from thinly populated Delaware authorized them to approve such changes in the Articles of Confederation as they deemed desirable. Delaware directed its emmissaries not to agree to any changes in the basis of congressional representation from the one state–one vote system in the Continental Congress, though during the convention the Delawareans disregarded these instructions when the large and small states reached a compromise on this matter.

Among the prominent men who were not elected as delegates to the Constitutional Convention were Thomas Jefferson (left) and John Adams (right), who were on diplomatic service in Europe.

Four national leaders who did not attend the Constitutional Convention. Upper left, Richard Henry Lee; upper right, Patrick Henry; lower left, John Jay; lower right, Samuel Chase. The latter were not elected, and the first two declined to serve.

MANY of the delegates arrived at Philadelphia bone-weary and dusty or mud-splattered from their tedious journeys. The unpaved and rutted roads, dangerous bridges, treacherous fords, and unreliable ferries made cross-country travel hazardous, undependable, and unpleasant even in the best of weather. Stagelines, which frequently involved some boat travel, were the usual mode of transportation. Three lines connected Philadelphia with New York City, three with Baltimore, and one with Annapolis. Some of the framers, however, made the trip mainly by ship, and Washington drove up from Mount Vernon in his carriage. Delegates coming from New York City, including the sizable contingent from the Continental Congress, were among the most fortunate. That city, under favorable circumstances, was less than a day's journey away by stage or stage-boat combination. But travelers from Virginia and the southern part of New England required 4 days on the road and those from more distant points even longer.

Philadelphia, founded in 1682 by William Penn and the metropolis of the nation, had a population of more than 40,000. Cosmopolitan and sophisticated, it was a center of commerce, science, medicine, and culture. Fashionable gentlemen in powdered wigs and velvet and satin clothes and their elegant ladies ambled along the brick sidewalks in the prosperous downtown area among mechanics in leather aprons and buckskin breeches, visiting farmers in homespun and moccasins, black slaves and freedmen, foreign and domestic sailors, and an occasional Indian. The principal thoroughfares, often cleaned by prisoners from the city jail, were paved and lighted at night. More than 500 iron-handled pumps throughout the area provided the citizens with water.

By 1787 expansion had resulted in urban sprawl, and the initial grid pattern of broad streets and spacious lots had in some sections given way to narrow alleys and crowded houses. Sanitation problems plagued poor residents. Insects bred in the piles of trash, livery stables, and backyard privies. The din was distracting. The air reverberated with the sounds of construction, calls from street hawkers, church bells, and the "thundering of Coaches, Chariots, Chaises, Waggons, Drays, and the whole Fraternity of Noise."

Many Philadelphians sought refuge from the summer heat on their balconies and piazzas under awnings or in their shaded gardens. In the evenings, some people braved the mosquitoes to cool off on benches flanking the front doors. But by 11 o'clock most of them had retired, leaving the streets to members of the watch, who hourly until dawn called out the time and weather.

Blinds protected the convention members, sitting in the Pennsylvania State House (present Independence Hall), from the worst of the afternoon sun, but they were frequently uncomfortable in their close-fitting clothes and wigs, especially the New Englanders in their heavy woolen suits. When the windows were shut to reduce the noise, the air became oppressive; when they were opened, flies buzzed in.

Most of the delegates took accommodations near the State House. The majority lodged and boarded in hostelries or roominghouses, but Washington stayed at Robert Morris' elegant townhouse and Elbridge Gerry rented a house for himself and his family. Most of the framers, however, were separated from their loved ones. To reduce living costs and perhaps to quell any loneliness, some of them stayed two to a room. The Indian Queen Tavern, the city's most comfortable inn where many stayed, became an informal convention center and the management even provided them with a private common hall. Another popular spot was the City Tavern, furnished in the London mode. In addition to these inns, well-patronized dining and drinking spots were the George and the Black Horse.

The Pennsylvania State House (Independence Hall), where the delegates to the convention met to revise the Articles of Confederation.

Philadelphia, the site of the convention, was the national metropolis. Pictured here is a scene about a decade later, along Arch Street, showing the Second Presbyterian Church.

During their free time, when they were not discussing convention proceedings, visiting with one another, or writing letters home, the delegates found many diversions, particularly during the two adjournments. Social affairs were numerous, though some of the less sophisticated individuals disliked the excess of "etiquette and nonsense so fashionable." Some men were invited to dinner by Benjamin Franklin, Robert Morris, and other members of the Pennsylvania delegation, who all resided in the city or its environs.

Various framers visited John Bartram's botanical gardens across the Schuylkill River, heard a July 4 oration at a Lutheran church, dined at the splendid fish-eating clubs, and probably patronized Peale's Museum. A common pastime was likely reading, for which the Library Company collection in Carpenters' Hall, only a block from the State House, was conveniently located. The shops and twice-weekly farm markets offered an enticing assortment of food and imported goods. Some delegates went fishing. From time to time, others, particularly those from nearby states, took trips home to see their families or conduct personal and professional business. And, especially on weekends or during adjournments, a few went sightseeing to nearby areas.

Washington, the supreme national hero, was welcomed to town on May 13 by pealing bells, an artillery salute, and an escort of the City Light Horse Troop. Quickly swept up in a whirl of social affairs and ceremonies, he received the City Light Horse and infantry militiamen; attended a Roman Catholic mass; dined with the Society of the Cincinnati, the Sons of St. Patrick, and at the homes of various prominent people; visited several country estates, including those of Robert Morris and Thomas Mifflin; drank tea at different houses most every day; rode horses for exercise; sat for a portrait by Charles Willson Peale; and attended plays, concerts, and poetry readings. He also paid a nostalgic visit to Valley Forge and made an excursion to the Trenton Iron Works.

But, despite all the social hubbub, for most of the delegates it was a busy, lonely summer taken up with work, working dinners, and not much real leisure.

THE number of delegates who served at Philadelphia totaled 55, though they were not all on hand for the entire convention. Some arrived late, left early, or were temporarily absent for various lengths of time. The 55 men, 39 of whom subscribed to the Constitution, were as follows (nonsubscribers indicated by asterisks):

Baldwin, Abraham (Ga.)
Bassett (Basset), Richard (Del.)
Bedford, Gunning, Jr. (Del.)
Blair, John (Va.)
Blount, William (N.C.)
Brearly (Brearley), David (N.J.)
Broom, Jacob (Del.)
Butler, Pierce (S.C.)
Carroll, Daniel (Md.)
Clymer, George (Pa.)
Davie, William R. (N.C.)*
Dayton, Jonathan (N.J.)
Dickinson, John (Del.)
Ellsworth (Elsworth), Oliver (Conn.)*
Few, William (Ga.)
Fitzsimons (FitzSimons; Fitzsimmons), Thomas (Pa.)
Franklin, Benjamin (Pa.)
Gerry, Elbridge (Mass.)*
Gilman, Nicholas (N.H.)
Gorham, Nathaniel (Mass.)
Hamilton, Alexander (N.Y.)
Houston, William C. (N.J.)*
Houstoun, William (Ga.)*
Ingersoll, Jared (Pa.)
Jenifer, Daniel of St. Thomas (Md.)
Johnson, William S. (Conn.)
King, Rufus (Mass.)
Langdon, John (N.H.)
Lansing, John, Jr. (N.Y.)*
Livingston, William (N.J.)
McClurg, James (Va.)*
McHenry, James (Md.)
Madison, James (Va.)
Martin, Alexander (N.C.)*
Martin, Luther (Md.)*
Mason, George (Va.)*
Mercer, John F. (Md.)*
Mifflin, Thomas (Pa.)
Morris, Gouverneur (Pa.)

Morris, Robert (Pa.)
Paterson (Patterson), William (N.J.)
Pierce, William L. (Ga.)*
Pinckney, Charles (S.C.)
Pinckney, Charles Cotesworth (S.C.)
Randolph, Edmund J. (Va.)*
Read, George (Del.)
Rutledge, John (S.C.)
Sherman, Roger (Conn.)
Spaight, Richard D., Sr. (N.C.)
Strong, Caleb (Mass.)*
Washington, George (Va.)
Williamson, Hugh (N.C.)
Wilson, James (Pa.)
Wythe, George (Va.)*
Yates, Robert (N.Y.)*

Attending all or practically every session were 29 men: Bassett, Bedford, Blair, Brearly, Broom, Butler, Clymer, Fitzsimons, Franklin, Gerry, Gorham, Ingersoll, Jenifer, Johnson, King, Madison, Mason, Mifflin, Robert Morris, Charles Pinckney, Charles Cotesworth Pinckney, Randolph, Read, Rutledge, Sherman, Spaight, Washington, Williamson, and Wilson. Ten individuals missed only a few weeks: Baldwin, Davie, Dayton, Dickinson, Ellsworth, Livingston, Alexander Martin, Luther Martin, Gouverneur Morris, and Strong. Twelve persons were away for long periods: Blount, Carroll, Few, Gilman, Hamilton, Houstoun, Langdon, Lansing, McClurg, McHenry, Paterson, and Yates. Four men attended for extremely short stretches: Houston, Mercer, Pierce, and Wythe. Reasons for absences included personal and family illness, service in Congress, other professional or personal business, late appointment, early departure, boredom or a feeling of uselessness, faith in the views and actions of fellow state delegates, and opposition to the prevalent nationalism.

Although the group hardly matched Jefferson's characterization as an "assembly of demigods," it was a distinguished one. Statesmen, legislators, patriots, and leaders in commerce and agriculture for the most part, the men were as a whole highly talented and well educated. They also enjoyed extensive political and worldly experience.

Nearly all of the body had much at stake in the experiment in government that was called the United States, and they were determined to see that experiment succeed. Four-fifths, or 44, of the 55 individuals were serving in or had been members of the Continental Congress. Most of them had heartily backed the rebellion against Great Britain, and about half had fought in the Continental Army or state militia. Eight (Clymer, Franklin, Gerry, Robert Morris, Read, Sherman, Wilson, and Wythe) had signed the Declaration of Independence. All but a few had participated in or were at the time actively involved in colonial, state, and local governments—from minor county offices to governorships. Many had helped draft the constitutions of their states or had codified their laws. And a large number were to assume important posts, including the presidency (Washington and Madison), under the government they were to establish.

A considerable number of the Founding Fathers were friends or acquaintances. Many had attended college together or been political or business colleagues. Most of the men were wealthy or well-to-do and lived under comfortable circumstances. Land, slaves, and commerce were the principal sources of wealth. Almost a third of the group sprang from aristocratic families; practically all the rest came from families that were respectable and substantial. Not many more than a handful of individuals were of humble origins or of modest means.

By profession, the law predominated. This was the pursuit of more than half the delegates, though a substantial number were businessmen, merchants, planters, and large-scale farmers. In numerous cases, because of multiple occupations, overlapping occurred. Only two owned small farms. At least 12 men received their major incomes in the form of salaries from public office. Three were physicians, and the same number had retired from active economic pursuits.

As a group, the framers were relatively youthful. The average age was 43. The youngest was Jonathan Dayton at 26. The eldest was 81-year-old Franklin, who was so infirm that prisoners from the city jail usually had to carry him from his nearby home to the sessions in his sedan chair, which had been made specially for him after his return from France.

About half the delegates had attended college, principally at William and Mary, Harvard, Yale, College of New Jersey (present Princeton), King's College (Columbia), and the College of Philadelphia (University of Pennsylvania). Several men had studied abroad and held or were to hold graduate and honorary degrees. A considerable number were privately educated or self-taught.

The best known and respected were Washington of Virginia and Franklin of Pennsylvania. Their presence not only cooled passions but also lent dignity and authority to the proceedings and helped to assure their success. Madison of Virginia, a political genius, was an excellent debater and a keen student and practitioner of government. The first to arrive in Philadelphia, on May 3, he had carefully prepared himself by studying various forms of governments since ancient times and had formed a realistic conception of what a government should be. He was to play a predominant role at the convention.

Other outstanding delegates included Randolph, Mason, and Wythe of Virginia; Gerry, King, and Gorham of Massachusetts; Sherman, Ellsworth, and Johnson of Connecticut; Hamilton of New York;

Gouverneur Morris, Robert Morris, Mifflin, and Wilson of Pennsylvania; Dickinson of Delaware; Luther Martin of Maryland; Williamson of North Carolina; Livingston of New Jersey; and Charles Pinckney, Charles Cotesworth Pinckney, and Rutledge of South Carolina.

City Tavern, where many of the delegates to the convention stayed, as it appeared around 1800.

Despite wide differences in temperament and political views, most of the framers were nationalists and believed that the Articles of Confederation needed substantive revision. Based on their experience with the inadequacies of the Confederation, practically all of them were united in the belief that the United States should be a single, unified nation, not an agglomeration of semi-independent states, and they transferred that faith to the Constitution.

A correſpondent obſerves, that as the time approaches for opening the buſineſs of the fœderal convention, it is natural that every lover of his country ſhould experience ſome anxiety for the fate of an expedient ſo neceſſary, yet ſo precarious. Upon the event of this great council, indeed, depends every thing that can be eſſential to the dignity and ſtability of the national character, The Veteran who has toiled in the field, the Stateſman who has laboured in the cabinet, and every man who participates in the bleſſings of American Independence, muſt feel that all the glory of the paſt, and all the fortune of the future, are involved in this momentous undertaking. The imperfections and debility of the league, framed during a ſtruggle for liberty and political exiſtence, were obſcured and concealed by the ardor of enterprize, and the proximity of danger. The feelings of the people were then more obligatory than the poſitive injunction of law; and men, in the purſuit of an important object, required no conſideration to diſcharge their duty, but their intereſts and their paſſions. Though the fœderal compact, therefore, thus fortified, might be adequate to the *acquiſition*, yet from the nature and diſpoſition of human affairs, it becomes inadequate to the *preſervation* of ſovereign power. Unleſs ſome rule is preſcribed, ſome motive introduced, which in a ſtate of tranquility will enforce a regard to the general intereſt, equal to the voluntary enthuſiaſm ariſing from common ſufferings and apprehenſions, we have only exchanged tyranny for anarchy——we have

This extract from a Philadelphia newspaper on the eve of the convention reveals how concerned some Americans were about its success.

Probably few of the group would really have considered a monarchy or the abolition of the states, nor would more than two or three have considered the elimination of the central government and the division of the country into three or four confederacies. All the men were fully aware that their work was unprecedented and complex. Major common concerns were the preservation and prosperity of the Union, establishment of a suitable national defense, fear of tyranny, protection of property rights, and the prevention of domestic discord.

Sometimes torn between the wishes of their constituents or states and their vision of the new nation, concerned for posterity yet respectful of the past, and united in purpose, the delegates embarked upon their task.

Convention Proceedings

During a 4-month period between May 25 and September 17, 1787, the "Federal" or "Grand" Convention, as the newspapers called it, created a new frame of government for the United States. On the scheduled opening date, May 14, the conferees who were on hand

Robert Morris' townhouse on High (present Market) Street, where Washington stayed during the convention and later as President. In 1787 he had originally planned to reside at Mrs. House's rooming place, but Morris persuaded him to change his mind.

convened in the Pennsylvania State House's assembly, or east, room—the same one where the Declaration of Independence had been approved and signed. But, because of bad weather, travel difficulties, and other reasons, only about 10 were present, apparently just from Pennsylvania and Virginia—but in sufficient numbers for state quorums.

During the 11-day interim while awaiting a quorum of states and while other delegates kept reporting, many of the attendees held private discussions and exchanged opinions. But the Virginia delegation, led by Gov. Edmund J. Randolph and spurred by Madison, met daily to prepare for the convention. Its early arrival and thorough planning were to place it in a position of leadership.

On May 25 the daily official meetings of the main body yielded the necessary quorum of seven states. On that date, 29 delegates were present in sufficient numbers from Delaware, New Jersey, New York, North Carolina, Pennsylvania, South Carolina, and Virginia, plus one each from Massachusetts and Georgia.

Not until July 23, however, when the two New Hampshire emissaries arrived, were all 12 states that were to attend represented.

PORTSMOUTH, (New Hampſhire) May 19.

We are authoriſed to inform our readers that the probability of the honorable delegates from this ſtate not attending the convention at Philadelphia, cauſes great uneaſineſs in the minds of the true whigs of New Hampſhire, and will occaſion a conſiderable inſpection into the ſtate of our finances.

Near one quarter part of the towns in this ſtate have reſolved not to ſend any repreſentatives to the enſuing General Court. A correſpondent ſuppoſes this circumſtance will greatly accelerate public buſineſs.

B O S T O N, May 19.

The legiſlature of Connecticut having laſt week appointed its deputies, twelve ſtates will be repreſented in the grand federal Convention, now ſitting in Philadelphia.—Rhode Iſland is the delinquent ſtate—but, obſerves a correſpondent, this is a circumſtance far more joyous than grievous; for her

Because New Hampshire did not provide funds, its two delegates, John Langdon and Nicholas Gilman, did not arrive at the convention until July 23, 1787, and had to pay their own way. Rhode Island was the only state not represented, as this extract from a Philadelphia newspaper also indicates.

Claiming financial distress but possibly also evidencing inertia or suspicion of the goals of the convention, New Hampshire had not provided funds for its delegates, one of whom paid for both of them. Meanwhile, though, on July 10, two of the three New York representatives had departed. This left only Alexander Hamilton from that state in an unofficial capacity and 10 states officially taking part until July 23, after which 11 did so for the duration of the convention.

Between May 25 and September 17, except for Saturday May 26 and during the two adjournments (July 3–4 and July 26–August 6), sessions were held 6 days a week. The hours usually ranged between 10 or 11 a.m. and 3 or 4 p.m., though sometimes they were shorter or longer. But the expenditure of time in sitting on committees, drafting papers and speeches, and otherwise preparing for the sessions made for long days for most of the group.

In April, before the convention, the Continental Congress had extended the franking privilege to the delegates. How other costs were to be defrayed was not clear at the time of the meeting; many of the representatives thought they would need to do so out of their own pockets. Later in 1787, however, after the convention, the Continental Congress was to pay the salaries of the secretary, doorkeeper, messenger, and the clerks who transcribed and engrossed the Constitution, as well as stationery charges; the Second U.S. Congress was to pay the printing bill in 1793.

The Opening Days

Most of the first week's business was devoted to organization. On the first day, Friday, in a fateful move, Washington was unanimously chosen as presiding officer. Although he was not to say much during the deliberations, he guided them smoothly and his presence helped make the work of the convention acceptable to the nation.

Maj. William Jackson was designated as secretary. Unfortunately, he performed his recordkeeping duties indifferently. Had it not been for a few individuals who kept journals or notes—especially Madison, but also Yates, Lansing, King, McHenry, Paterson, Hamilton, and Pierce—not much would be known about the details of creation of the Constitution.

Credentials were accepted and read. Most of the rules that were adopted for the conduct of business followed those of the Continental Congress. As in that body, voting was to be recorded in geographical order north to south from New Hampshire to Georgia and be by state rather than individual delegate. Decisions of the majority could be reconsidered during the life of the convention and were to be revocable.

Finally, it was quickly decided to keep the deliberations secret. Nothing "spoken in the House," was to be "printed, or otherwise published or communicated without leave." Doormen stood at the entrances of the meeting room throughout the sessions, and the public remained essentially uninformed about the deliberations. As a result, only gradually over the course of many years did the basic story of the formulation of the Constitution emerge.

Many of the delegates believed that only an atmosphere free of publicity and external pressures would ensure the free and frank exchange of ideas and allow the participants to speak their hearts with candor and sincerity. At the same time, because they could change their minds and bargain with their colleagues, compromise would be facilitated. Temporary rashnesses would not appear on the public record, and outsiders would be prevented from becoming aroused over any disputes.

Yet, whatever the justifications, the secrecy did demonstrate a certain mistrust of the people; some of the delegates would never have dared deliver their convention speeches, which contradicted things they said in public, to their constituents. Opponents of the secrecy rule claimed it would arouse public suspicion of the motives of the conferees.

William Jackson, secretary of the convention.

In federal-Convention. page 1

On monday the 14th of may. a.D. 1787. and in the eleventh year of the independence of the united States of america, at the State-House in the city of Philadelphia - in virtue of appointments from their respective States, sundry deputies to the federal-Convention appeared - but, a majority of the States not being represented, the members present adjourned from day to day until friday the 25th of the said month, when, in virtue of the said appointments appeared from the States of

Massachusetts. ... The honorable Rufus King Esquire.

New-York. ... -- The honorable Robert Yates, and Alexander Hamilton Esquires.

New-Jersey. ... The honorable David Brearly, William Churchill Houston, and William Patterson Esquires.

Pennsylvania -- The honorable Robert Morris, Thomas Fitz Simmons, James Wilson, and Gouverneur Morris Esquires.

Delaware .. The honorable George Read, Richard Basset, and Jacob Broom Esquires.

Virginia ... His Excellency George Washington Esquire, His Excellency Edmund Randolph Esquire. The honorable John Blair, James Madison, George Mason, George Wythe, and James McClurg Esquires.

North-Carolina The honorable Alexander Martin, William Richardson Davie, Richard Dobbs Spaight, and Hugh Williamson Esquires.

First page of Secretary Jackson's journal, May 25, 1787, date of the first full-quorum meeting of the Constitutional Convention.

The Virginia and New Jersey Plans

The first substantive business was conducted May 29–30. On those days, evincing the planning and initiative of the Virginia delegation, Randolph presented a speech outlining the weaknesses of the Confederation and offering a series of 15 resolutions to remedy them. These came to be known collectively as the Virginia Plan. It resulted in the first major conflict and compromise: the large versus small state issue. Despite its prominence at the time, this controversy was to have almost no bearing on the evolution of the constitutional system; rather, the great disputes were to be intersectional in nature.

Because Virginia had been one of the leaders in calling the convention and was the most populous and in many ways the most powerful state, she played a major role in the proceedings. The Virginia Plan was the product of several minds, but preeminently that of Madison. By conceiving a relatively simple and clear plan and arranging for its early introduction, he seized a commanding position for the nationalists, who were never to relinquish it.

Far more than an attempt to revise the Articles of Confederation, the plan represented nothing less than a call for a new constitution. As such, it exceeded the desires of a number of the delegates, many of whom also felt it violated congressional and constituent instructions. Considering the extent of this opposition, surprisingly the plan was not seriously challenged as a whole until June 15. Nevertheless, it was a key point of debate throughout the proceedings and became the partial basis of the Constitution.

Reducing the states to a clearly subordinate position, the Virginia Plan called for a strong central government, which would, unlike that of the Confederation, consist of three separate branches: executive, legislative, and judicial. The number of persons who would constitute the executive office was not specified. The legislature was to elect the executive, which was eligible for only one term. The single-house Continental Congress would be replaced by a two-house, or bicameral, legislature. The plan suggested that the people elect the lower house; from lists of persons nominated by the state legislatures, the lower house would elect the upper. In both cases, representation would be based upon "quotas of contributions" [state monetary contributions] or the "number of free inhabitants," rather than upon state parity as under the Articles of Confederation, where Virginia held no more voting power than tiny Delaware.

A second sharp departure from the Articles was the vesting of broad authority in the proposed national legislature. It was authorized to pass laws on all matters "to which the separate States are incompetent, or in which the harmony of the United States may be

State of the resolutions submitted to the consideration of the House by the honorable Mr. Randolph, as altered, amended, and agreed to in a Committee of the whole House.

1. Resolved that it is the opinion of this Committee that a national government ought to be established consisting of a Supreme Legislative, Judiciary, and Executive.

2 Resolved. that the national Legislature ought to consist of Two Branches.

3 Resolved that the members of the first branch of the national Legislature ought to be elected by the People of the several States for the term of Three years. to receive fixed Stipends, by which they may be compensated for the devotion of their time to public service to be paid out of the National Treasury. to be ineligible to any Office established by a particular State or under the authority of the United States (except those peculiarly belonging to the functions of the first branch) during the term of service, and under the national government for the space of one year after its expiration.

4 Resolved. that the members of the second Branch of the national Legislature ought to be chosen by the individual Legislatures. to be of the age of thirty years at least. to hold their offices for a term sufficient to ensure their independency, namely seven years. to receive fixed stipends, by which they may be compensated for the devotion of their time to public service — to be paid out of the National Treasury to be ineligible to any Office established by a particular State, or under the authority of the United States (except those peculiarly belonging to the functions of the second branch) during the term of service, and under the national government, for the space of One year after its expiration.

First page of the Virginia Plan as amended by the committee of the whole and recorded on June 13, 1787.

interrupted by the exercise of individual [State] Legislation." The legislature was also empowered to negate state laws that in its opinion contravened the constitution and to force obedience.

A "council of revision," made up of the executive and a number of judges, could veto legislative acts. The plan also proposed that the legislature would choose and pay a separate judiciary. Because the legislature would elect both the executive and the judges, the three branches lacked the independence ultimately granted them in the Constitution.

The remainder of the proposals were less startling. New states were to be admitted with less than a unanimous vote of the legislature, and each state and territory was to have a republican form of government, as were the old ones. The Continental Congress was to continue until the new government took over. State officers were to take an oath to support the new constitution. Finally, the Continental Congress and then state conventions, "expressly chosen by the people," were to approve the new frame of government.

The plan was not a proposal for a "federal" or "confederated" union as those words were understood in 1787. Instead, it called for a consolidated "national" government. This was bound to provoke controversy. The delegates resolved to refer the plan and one offered by Charles Pinckney of South Carolina for a "federal government" to a committee of the whole, where less stringent rules would stimulate informal debate and allow the formulation of special proposals for consideration of the convention. Daily, Washington called the meeting to order and surrendered the chair to Nathaniel Gorham of Massachusetts. Although the former took no part in the debates, he voted on all motions made by the committee of the whole; at other times when the Virginia vote was divided, he cast his vote, usually in accordance with Madison's views.

Ignoring the Pinckney proposal for the most part, the committee would debate the Virginia Plan from May 30 through June 13.

ON May 30, by a vote of six (Delaware, Massachusetts, North Carolina, Pennsylvania, South Carolina, and Virginia) to one (Connecticut), with New York divided, the delegates resolved to proceed toward the establishment of a "*national* Government . . . consisting of a *supreme* Legislative, Executive, & Judiciary." Randolph had suggested this wording as a substitute for the first resolution of the Virginia Plan, which had stressed amendment of the Articles of Confederation. This action in effect represented a commitment almost from the beginning to scrap the Articles and focus attention on a totally new frame and form of government.

Over the next 2 weeks, the committee of the whole debated the implications of this resolution and the various provisions of the Virginia Plan. Many disagreements arose over various points, but the deepest and most persistent was over the matter of representation in the proposed legislature. For obvious reasons, most of the delegates of states with large populations or wealth or those such as Georgia with sizable areas that might be expected to be populous in the future favored representation based upon those factors.

But many ardent nationalists from the small states—Paterson of New Jersey and Sherman of Connecticut, for example—resented the loss of equal power they enjoyed under the Articles of Confederation and feared they would be dominated or even swallowed up by the large states. Some of these men felt their credentials did not authorize them to support such a proposal or that their states would not approve such an action. This group insisted that representation in at least one house should be by state as it was in the Continental Congress. At first, it appeared that the large states would prevail, but by mid-June it had become clear that the small ones would not budge and that some form of compromise was imperative.

On Wednesday, June 13, the initial debate ended, and the committee reported out 19 resolutions. The Virginia Plan had undergone some modifications. Madison's treasured "council of revision" had been thrown out. So had the authority of the national government to use force against intractable states. A 3-year term was specified for the lower house and a 7-year term for the upper. The minimum age for both was 30. The central government, instead of the states, was to pay members of the two houses—an important step in making Congress responsible to the national rather than to the state governments. The executive, now defined as one person, was to be elected by the national legislature for a single 7-year term. To balance the executive's dependence upon the legislature, he was given the power to veto legislative acts unless overridden by two-thirds of both houses. Finally, the upper house would choose a "supreme Tribunal" of judges. Most other provisions were virtually identical with the original Virginia Plan.

A key element of that plan retained in the committee report was the principle of variable representation based upon the relative population and wealth of the states. Determination of the ratios involved was to be a major point in the continuing debate.

Despite serious disagreements remaining among the delegates, it became clear that most of them sought a national government and that an increasing number favored granting some form of sovereignty to the people at large as well as the states. This contradicted classical political theory, which held that sovereignty could have only a single source and the body politic a single head.

IN mid-June, however, the sovereignty issue still needed to be settled. Several features of the revised Virginia Plan continued to alienate small-state delegates. They countered with their own plan. On June 14 Paterson asked for a day's delay so that he might submit a "purely federal" scheme as an alternative to the Virginia Plan. The fruit of his labor and that of Sherman and others was the New Jersey, or Paterson, Plan, introduced on June 15.

This proposal consisted of a set of nine resolutions designed to revise and strengthen the Articles of Confederation without abandoning them or changing their character as a league of states focused around the Continental Congress—which was all that many of the delegates felt they were authorized to do. New and expanded powers were proposed for Congress, in which each state was still to hold one vote. Included were the power to raise revenue through import

Restored Assembly Room, where the Constitution and the Declaration of Independence were debated, adopted, and signed.

duties, stamp taxes, and postage; the power to regulate commerce among the states and with foreign nations; the authority to force the states, when approved by an unspecified number of them, to support the government financially and militarily; and the right to use armed force to compel obedience to federal law by individuals as well as states.

Dividing the federal authority into legislative, executive, and judicial branches like the Virginia Plan, the New Jersey Plan proposed a plural executive, elected by Congress for a single term and subject to removal by a majority of the state executives. The executive would have authority to appoint a supreme court.

The New Jersey Plan was surely less radical than the nationalistic Virginia Plan, but it was not "purely federal." The sixth resolution clearly established the primacy of congressional acts and treaties—a provision hardly in keeping with the notion of a voluntary compact of 13 separate but equal states.

On June 16 and 19 the committee of the whole debated the New Jersey Plan. Arguing in its favor, Lansing of New York and Paterson of New Jersey asserted that the Virginia Plan must be rejected because the delegates lacked authority to create a government not based upon the existing Confederation and because the states and people would never approve such a plan. Wilson of Pennsylvania replied that the convention was authorized to propose whatever it chose. South Carolina's Charles Pinckney tartly observed that if national representation were made equal by states New Jersey would readily assent to the Virginia Plan. Randolph of Virginia claimed the national crisis was severe enough to warrant a departure from the Confederation system.

At this point, on June 18, Hamilton of New York, who attended irregularly, gave one of his rare speeches—a long one. "Continental" in nature and monarchical in spirit, the supreme central government he proposed would make all the laws and appoint all state executives. The president would be responsible for executing laws enacted by the legislature and would enjoy veto power over their passage, as well as extensive appointment and treaty-making powers. Although the members of the lower house would be elected to 3-year terms by popular vote, the upper as well as the president would be chosen indirectly by electors and would hold office for life during good behavior. Not only would the power of the states be quashed, but also governmental control would be placed in the hands of the wealthy and participation of the populace at large minimized. The plan was clearly unacceptable to the majority of the delegates and they ignored it.

Part of the reason for Hamilton's surprisingly small role in the debates was his extreme nationalism, which put him out of step with his fellows. Another factor was undoubtedly the frustrating effect of his minority position vis-à-vis the two other New York delegates, Lansing and Yates, who usually outvoted him to cast the state's vote. For this reason, until they departed on July 10, he spent some time at home in New York City attending to his law practice; after they left, he had little more reason to participate because, as the sole delegate present from his state, he could not cast its vote.

The day after Hamilton presented his plan, the delegates finished discussion of the New Jersey Plan. Madison made an extended address on the weakness of the proposal and sought to appeal to the self-interest of the small states in forming a strong union. Then, by a vote of seven states (Connecticut, Georgia, Massachusetts, North Carolina, Pennsylvania, South Carolina, and Virginia) to three (Delaware, New Jersey, and New York), with Maryland divided, the framers accepted the Virginia Plan. It was clear, however, that the idea of proportional representation in both houses was continuing to be strongly opposed. The convention adjourned the committee of the whole and went back into regular session to consider the resolutions that had been passed during the preceding weeks.

During the period June 20–27, when the resolutions on the amended Virginia Plan began to be considered, the debates touched on a variety of subjects: the nature of representation, corruption of legislatures, and the purposes and functions of the upper and lower houses. The nationalists yielded on certain minor points. Several compromises were struck. Madison, Randolph, and others in their camp agreed to drop the word "national" from the committee's first and third resolutions since that word had offended many.

Other changes included the approval of a 6-year term for members of the upper house, one-third of whom were to be elected every 2 years. Because this provision made no mention of the source of legislators' pay, it retreated from the controversial stipulation in the resolution that they were to be paid out of the national treasury. Agreement was also reached that members of the legislature would not be simultaneously eligible for state and national offices.

The Great Compromise

By this time, despite such temporary harmony, feeling had grown so intense on the issue of representation that the convention seemed on the brink of dissolution. Some members began to talk about going home, but fortunately most were not willing to abandon hope of compromise. In a long and bitter speech on June 27 and 28, Luther

Martin, a late arrival from Maryland who consistently opposed majority programs, took the floor and denounced Virginia, Massachusetts, and Pennsylvania for seeking to control the other states. He upheld the principle of one vote for each state. In a forceful rebuttal, Madison stated that these three large states had not made common cause against the others under the Confederation. What the small states really had to fear, he insisted, was a continuation of the existing system, where they were really at the mercy of their large-state neighbors.

Franklin, apparently believing that passions needed to be cooled, proposed that the daily sessions be opened with prayers offered by a local clergyman. Sherman seconded the motion, but Hamilton opposed it. The latter feared the presence of a minister might cause the public to believe the convention was torn with dissension. Others argued that reason—not heavenly help—was what was needed. In any case, Franklin's proposal died after Williamson raised the embarrassing question of where the money would be obtained to pay the clergyman.

AT this point, bitter debate began. It would last until mid-July. The subject was still representation in the national legislature. The result was the "Great" or "Connecticut" Compromise. The prolonged contention arose largely from the central position of the legislature in the proposed new scheme of government. Under the Virginia Plan, as revised, which the convention had accepted, the legislature would be virtually supreme. Not only would it elect the executive and the judiciary and have authority to annul all state laws, but also its overall authority in national affairs was extremely broad.

On June 29 the convention voted six (Georgia, Massachusetts, North Carolina, Pennsylvania, South Carolina, and Virginia) to four (Connecticut, Delaware, New Jersey, and New York), with Maryland divided, to base representation in the lower house upon some system different from that used in the Confederation; this was almost precisely the same vote as on the same issue in the committee of the whole nearly 3 weeks earlier. Succeeding days brought continued discussion of the question of representation—but in the upper house. Franklin even made a complicated proposal for variable voting depending on the type of legislation.

On July 2 a deadlock occurred on a vote to allow each state an equal voice in the upper house. Five states (Connecticut, Delaware, Maryland, New Jersey, and New York) were in favor and five (Massachusetts, North Carolina, Pennsylvania, South Carolina, and Virginia) were opposed; Georgia was divided. This key vote was determined partially by chance because one Maryland delegate was absent, which permitted Martin to cast the state's vote, and Baldwin changed his stand and divided Georgia's vote. The issue between the large and small states was joined. To break the impasse, a committee of one member from each of the 11 states present was appointed.

The main body adjourned for July 3–4 to celebrate independence and to allow time for the committee to deliberate. It consisted of Gerry of Massachusetts, Sherman of Connecticut (sitting in for Ellsworth), Yates of New York, Paterson of New Jersey, Franklin of Pennsylvania, Bedford of Delaware, Luther Martin of Maryland, Mason of Virginia, Davie of North Carolina, Rutledge of South Carolina, and Baldwin of Georgia.

The membership was notably weak in nationalists of the Madison and Wilson stripe, both of whom opposed establishment of the committee, and strong in states-rights men and moderate nationalists. The basic idea of a compromise had been suggested as early as June 2 by Dickinson, and reiterated later by several others, notably Sherman and Ellsworth. Thus, the decision of the committee came as no surprise. On July 5 Gerry brought in the report. It based representation in the lower house on the free population and three-fifths of the slaves, and in the upper by state. In neither case was an exact total specified, nor was distribution made by state in the lower house. As a concession to the large states, it was further proposed that the lower house should possess exclusive power to initiate money bills without changes or amendments by the upper house. In the lower house, every 40,000 inhabitants were to be represented by one member; states having less population were each guaranteed one.

This compromise solution still did not please most of the delegates, many of whom remained angry over the bitter debates that had preceded appointment of the committee. Its recommendations, however, provided a basis for action and steered the convention away from complete deadlock. On July 6 the part of the committee report giving special powers to the lower house was approved.

That same day, another committee, dominated by large-state nationalists and made up of Gorham and King of Massachusetts, Randolph of Virginia, Rutledge of South Carolina, and Gouverneur Morris of Pennsylvania, was created to iron out the numerical formula for state representation in the proposed lower house. The next day, the convention approved equality of votes in the upper. Two days later, on July 9, Morris presented the committee's report. It recommended that the first assembly of the lower house consist of 56 seats. These had been hastily and subjectively broken down among the 13 states (ranging from one to nine each), mainly on the basis of population but also to some degree on wealth. Subsequently, the national legislature was to vary apportionment of the seats based upon future alterations in the same elements.

Yet an additional committee immediately came into being to prepare a more satisfactory distribution of seats in the lower house. The members were King, Sherman, Yates, Brearly, Gouverneur Morris, Read, Carroll, Madison, Williamson, Rutledge, and Houston. The next day, King delivered the report, which raised the number of seats to 65, an increase of 1 for most of the states. This undoubtedly was attractive to the small ones. Efforts by Madison to double the number and by Charles Cotesworth Pinckney to increase by one the seats for North Carolina, South Carolina, and Georgia were both defeated. Finally, the second committee's formula was approved.

The following day, July 11, was one of the most contentious of the summer. Debate focused on the role of slaves in the scheme of representation and the need for and mechanisms of a national census; the latter subject had first arisen the day before. Slavery was the second major controversial issue to arise during the representation conflict and to require compromise. Unlike the large–small state clash, which was to have but slight later impact, this one, which revealed not only the different economic interests of the North and South but also presented a moral dilemma, was to lead to disunion and civil war.

The crux of the problem was that most northern sentiment favored the counting of slaves in deciding each state's share of direct federal taxes but not for representation. Most of the emissaries from southern states wanted to exclude slaves from the tax computation but to include them for the purpose of representation in the lower house, though they had no intention of permitting them to vote. Charles Cotesworth Pinckney and Butler of South Carolina proposed that slaves be counted equally with freemen, but the motion failed by a vote of seven states to three (Delaware, Georgia, and South Carolina).

New York was not registered on this or any subsequent tallies during the convention because the majority of its delegates, Yates and Lansing, had headed home after the previous day's session. Followers of states-rights advocate Gov. George Clinton and at odds with their colleague, Hamilton, by this time they were probably sure that ultimately the convention would advocate a highly centralized type of government. They also had pressing legal and judicial business in New York. Apparently at the end of August they decided not to return to Philadelphia. After they left, Hamilton's status was reduced to an unofficial one, and only 10 states voted until July 23, when New Hampshire's representatives finally arrived.

Later on July 11, six states to four voted in favor of taking a census of free inhabitants to determine representation. By the same numerical margin, a proposal was rejected to count three-fifths of the slaves, a formula that the Continental Congress had frequently utilized in making requisitions on the states and that had been discussed earlier in the convention. At the close of the session, the resolution on the census was annulled and the decision was made to adjourn. There was hope of progress on the morrow.

That session began with a resolution by Gouverneur Morris to correlate representation, based on wealth and population, with taxation. After discussion and amendment to "direct" taxation, the measure passed unanimously. A separate motion, as amended, provided that a census was to be taken within 6 years of the adoption of the new government and thereafter once every decade (decennially) to determine the respective wealth and population of the states. As for the matter of slaves, representation and taxation were both to be computed by counting five of them as equal to three free inhabitants. A concession by the northern states, this assured southerners that all slaves would not be taxed as such and that their region would also gain some representational advantage. Some southern delegates once more tried to amend the motion to count slaves equally with free inhabitants, but the motion met defeat by a vote of

The Indian Queen Tavern as it appeared about 1833.

eight states to two. A divisive issue had been bridged and the way to the Great Compromise lay open.

The most significant action on Friday, July 13, was a vote to eliminate wealth as a basis for representation in the lower house of the national legislature. Wilson and Randolph brought nine states with them in this tally, despite the vigorous protests of Gouverneur Morris. Population was thus established as the sole criterion for the apportionment of representation. When new states were admitted, representation of the old would be adjusted at the time of the succeeding census.

The next day, Saturday, July 14, the large-state nationalists again tried to improve their position. Charles Pinckney proposed a specific apportionment scheme for the upper house, based generally upon population. Despite the support of Wilson and Madison, the resolution failed six states to four. The compromise was holding.

On Monday, the 16th, the body reconvened to consider the Great Compromise as a whole in its final form. The vote was close: five states (Connecticut, Delaware, Maryland, New Jersey, and North Carolina) in favor, four (Georgia, Pennsylvania, South Carolina, and Virginia) opposed, and Massachusetts split.

That night, July 16—not convinced by the slim 5-4-1 vote of the need or the desirability of surrender—representatives of the large states met informally at the Indian Queen Tavern to consider the situation. The next morning, before the convention proceedings resumed, they caucused formally. Had the large states surrendered too much to the small? Should they continue to attend the convention? Should they continue to oppose the Great Compromise? After much discussion, they could not agree. This irresolution did not satisfy the diehards among them, but it cleared the way for continuation of the business of writing the new constitution because the large-state delegates no longer presented a united front.

The most controversial issue was now essentially resolved, but much remained to be done. Many details were still vague and undefined. A document incorporating the decisions of the convention to that point still needed to be written. But the principal obstacle sharply dividing men who agreed that the Articles of Confederation needed a complete overhaul had been overcome. In the lower house of the proposed national legislature, representation would be adjusted in relation to population, as revealed by a decennial census, and three-fifths of the slaves would be counted. In the upper house, each state would enjoy equal representation.

The Great Compromise, by correlating representation with population in the lower house and providing for equality by state in the upper, confirmed the existence of the states and gave Congress both federal and national attributes. The fears of many small-state delegates that the large states would control the Union, if not put totally to rest, were measurably assuaged. On the whole, the compromise was a victory for the small states, though on other matters their delegates tended to follow the Virginia Plan, which provided for a strong central government. Although Madison and other large-state delegates had opposed the compromise right up to the last, they recognized it was the price they had to pay for a consolidated Union. The small states, by yielding on equal representation in the lower house, had abandoned their hopes for a mere league of states like that provided for by the Articles of Confederation. The large states, by accepting equality of voting power in the Senate, signaled the end of their attempts to dominate the government.

On the other hand, from this point on the small states, recognizing they would have a greater share of power in the central government than their population or wealth warranted, were no less desirous of strengthening the central government than the large ones.

Writing the First Draft

With the most severe crisis of the convention behind them, during the period from July 17 to July 26 the delegates discussed and more easily settled a number of specifics of the proposed constitution. It was agreed that the national legislature would "enjoy the Legislative rights vested in Congress by the Confederation, and moreover to legislate in all cases for the general interests of the Union, and also in those to which the States are separately incompetent, or in which the harmony of the United States may be interrupted by the exercise of individual legislation." But the proposed capability of the national legislature to negate state laws was dropped. In the upper house, each state was to have two representatives, who would vote as individuals rather than as a unit. The national court system was granted jurisdiction over cases stemming from laws passed by the legislature and over questions related to national peace and harmony.

Many other issues reached the floor but did not result in changes to the emerging constitution. These included efforts to empower state legislatures to ratify the instrument, to remove the provision for impeachment of the executive, and to strike appointment by the upper house of judges of the "supreme tribunal."

The matters that proved the most difficult to resolve, even tentatively, in this comparatively harmonious phase of the convention were those dealing with election of the executive, the length of his

54. Journal of the federal Convention Monday July 16. 1787

The question being taken on the whole of the report from the grand Committee as amended

it passed in the affirmative

and is as follows, namely.

Resolved — That in the original formation of the Legislature of the United States the first Branch thereof shall consist of sixty five members. of which number

New Hampshire shall send — Three
Massachusetts — Eight
Rhode Island — One
Connecticut — Five
New York — Six
New Jersey — four
Pennsylvania — Eight
Delaware — One
Maryland — Six
Virginia — Ten
North Carolina — Five
South Carolina — Five
Georgia — Three

But as the present situation of the States may probably alter in the number of their inhabitants the Legislature of the United States shall be authorised from time to time to apportion the number of representatives: and in case any of the States shall hereafter be divided, or enlarged by addition of territory, or any two or more States united, or any new States created within the limits of the United States the Legislature of the United States shall possess authority to regulate the number of representatives: ~~and~~ in ~~case~~ any of the foregoing cases upon the principle of their number of inhabitants,

according

The Great Compromise of July 16, 1787, as recorded by Secretary Jackson on the first of two pages in the official convention journal.

term, and his eligibility for reelection. Proposals were entertained and then voted down for election by the people at large, electors chosen by the legislatures, the governors or electors picked by them, the national legislature, and electors chosen by lot from the legislature. Some delegates suggested that the executive should be eligible for reelection. Others questioned the proposed 7-year term of office. After extensive debate, on July 26 the decision was made to retain the original resolution. The national legislature was to elect the executive for a single 7-year nonrenewable term.

ON July 26 the convention adjourned until August 6 to allow a five-member "committee of detail," which had been appointed on July 24, to prepare a draft instrument incorporating the sense of what had been decided upon over many weeks. While some of the delegates went home and others rested and relaxed in or near Philadelphia, the committee (Rutledge of South Carolina, Randolph of Virginia, Wilson of Pennsylvania, Ellsworth of Connecticut, and Gorham of Massachusetts) went about its work. Within a few days, a draft of the constitution was sent to Dunlap & Claypoole, the firm on Market Street that handled printing for the Continental Congress, which was meeting in New York City. The compositor for most of the convention's work was likely David C. Claypoole because his partner, John Dunlap, was apparently away most of the time coordinating congressional printing.

About August 1 a seven-page set of proofs was returned to the committee. After its deliberations, a corrected copy bearing Randolph's emendations, a dozen in number, was sent back to the printer, who incorporated them. By August 6 a first draft of the constitution had been printed, numbering probably 60 copies; it was the first printed rendition of the instrument in any form. The seven-page folio draft, which provided ample left-hand margins for notes and comments, consisted of a preamble and 23 articles. Randolph had apparently prepared a rough draft, which Rutledge and Wilson thoroughly reworked.

The committee conscientiously tried to express the will of the convention, but it also made some modifications and changes that provoked considerable debate. In selecting provisions and phrases, the conferees borrowed extensively from a variety of sources. Of course, the approved resolutions that had sprung from the Virginia Plan provided the basic ideas. But state constitutions, particularly that of New York (1777), and the Articles of Confederation were leaned on heavily, as was also to a lesser degree Charles Pinckney's long-ignored plan. Certain state papers of the Confederation and the rejected New Jersey Plan also provided some of the wording and substance.

The committee necessarily filled in many specifics that various resolutions had left vague or unexpressed. For the first time, names, largely derived from the state constitutions, were given to the members and branches of the national government: President, Congress, House of Representatives, Speaker, Senate, and Supreme Court. The famous opening phrase of the final Constitution's preamble, "We the People," appeared for the first time, as did such others as the "privileges and immunities" of citizens and the presidential "state of the Union" message.

Instead of the broad general authority voted to the courts and Congress before the recess, significantly the draft enumerated 18 congressional powers and also areas of jurisdiction for the federal courts. It likewise listed powers for the chief executive, though the convention's resolutions had laid a precedent for that.

The last and most sweeping of the congressional authorities was the right to make all laws "necessary and proper" to carry out the enumerated powers and all others vested in the central government by the Constitution. Essentially all the old powers of the Continental Congress under the Articles of Confederation were retained. To them were added new ones, which the majority of delegates felt were essential to correct the defects in the old frame of government.

Among the new congressional mandates was the most vital one missing under the old system: authority to impose and collect direct taxes of several kinds. Other new powers conferred were the regulation of domestic and foreign commerce, establishment of nationwide rules for the naturalization of citizens, coining and borrowing of money, organization of a national army and navy, authority to call up the state militias, election of a national treasurer, and the quashing of rebellion in the states, with the permission of the appropriate legislatures. Directly contrary to a resolution of the convention, however, the committee draft specified that the states would pay the congressmen.

Particular prerogatives of the House of Representatives and the Senate were specified, the principles of their parliamentary organization were outlined, and the privileges of their members were listed. Some of these provisions were modeled on similar ones in state constitutions. The Senate would appoint ambassadors and Supreme Court judges, make treaties, and participate in the settlement of interstate disputes. The House alone could impeach errant high federal officials, including the President, and originate money bills.

Each house would enjoy a virtual veto on the other, for bills would need to pass both to become law.

In its attempt to define the areas of national authority more precisely, presumably to allay the fears of the less nationalistic delegates, the committee of detail included express restrictions on certain actions by the legislature. Three of these, apparently reflecting the sentiments of Chairman John Rutledge of South Carolina, were designed to protect the interests of the southern states. One prohibited the national government from passing any "navigation act" or tariff without a two-thirds majority of members present in both houses of Congress. Another, without employing the word "slaves," forbade the legislature from taxing or prohibiting the import of slaves or their migration. The third provided that it could pass no law taxing exports. It would also be unable to approve personal capitation taxes except in proportion to the census. The government as a whole was barred from creating titles of nobility and was limited in the definition it could give to treason.

The legislature would elect the President for a single 7-year term. His powers were somewhat more carefully spelled out than previously, though not significantly augmented. The most important of these was the veto, though this could be overriden by a two-thirds vote of both houses of Congress. The chief executive would exercise general executive powers for the enforcement of all national laws, appoint key officials except for ambassadors and judges, enjoy the right to pardon, and serve as commander in chief. His responsibilities of informing the legislature about state matters, making recommendations to it, receiving ambassadors, and corresponding with state executives involved him directly in the formulation of legislative programs and foreign relations. The provisions relating to the presidency were strongly influenced by state constitutions, especially that of New York.

The committee of detail outlined new prohibitions upon the rights of the states that went far toward establishing national dominance. They were not to coin money or grant letters of marque and reprisal. Without the consent of Congress, they could not emit bills of credit, issue paper money, tax imports or exports, or make agreements with other states. Reiterated were the old Articles of Confederation provisions preventing any of them from entering into independent treaties, alliances, or confederations, waging war independently, or granting titles of nobility.

Relations among the states would be governed by principles of equality, including recognition of the "privileges and immunities" of each other's citizens and "full faith and credit" for official actions.

WE the People of the States of New-Hampſhire, Maſſachuſetts, Rhode-Iſland and Providence Plantations, Connecticut, New-York, New-Jerſey, Pennſylvania, Delaware, Maryland, Virginia, North-Carolina, South-Carolina, and Georgia, do ordain, declare and eſtabliſh the following Conſtitution for the Government of Ourſelves and our Poſterity.

ARTICLE I.

The ſtile of this Government ſhall be, "The United States of America."

II.

The Government ſhall conſiſt of ſupreme legiſlative, executive and judicial powers.

III.

The legiſlative power ſhall be veſted in a Congreſs, to conſiſt of two ſeparate and diſtinct bodies of men, a Houſe of Repreſentatives, and a Senate; ~~each of which ſhall, in all caſes, have a negative on the other. The Legiſlature ſhall meet on the firſt Monday in December in every year.~~

The legislature shall meet at least once in every year and that meeting shall be on the first Monday in December unless a different day shall be appointed by Law.

IV.

Sect. 1. The Members of the Houſe of Repreſentatives ſhall be choſen every ſecond year, by the people of the ſeveral States comprehended within this Union. The qualifications of the electors ſhall be the ſame, from time to time, as thoſe of the electors in the ſeveral States, of the moſt numerous branch of their own legiſlatures.

Sect. 2. Every Member of the Houſe of Repreſentatives ſhall be of the age of twenty-five years at leaſt; ſhall have been a citizen ~~in~~ *of* the United States for at leaſt [illegible] years before his election; and ſhall be, at the time of his election, [illegible] *an inhabitant* of the State in which he ſhall be choſen.

Sect. 3. The Houſe of Repreſentatives ſhall, at its firſt formation, and until the number of citizens and inhabitants ſhall be taken in the manner herein after deſcribed, conſiſt of ſixty-five Members, of whom three ſhall be choſen in New-Hampſhire, eight in Maſſachuſetts, one in Rhode-Iſland and Providence Plantations, five in Connecticut, ſix in New-York, four in New-Jerſey, eight in Pennſylvania, one in Delaware, ſix in Maryland, ten in Virginia, five in North-Carolina, five in South-Carolina, and three in Georgia.

Sect. 4. As the proportions of numbers in the different States will alter from time to time; as ſome of the States may hereafter be divided; as others may be enlarged by addition of territory; as two or more States may be united; as new States will be erected within the limits of the United States, the Legiſlature ſhall, in each of theſe caſes, regulate the number of repreſentatives by the number of inhabitants, according to the [illegible] the rate of one for every forty thouſand. *Provided that every State shall have at least One representative.*

Sect. 5. All bills for raiſing or appropriating money, and for fixing the ſalaries of the officers of government, ſhall originate in the Houſe of Repreſentatives, and ſhall not be altered or amended by the Senate. No money ſhall be drawn from the public Treaſury, but in purſuance of appropriations that ſhall originate in the Houſe of Repreſentatives.

reconsidered or struck out

Sect. 6. The Houſe of Repreſentatives ſhall have the ſole power of impeachment. It ſhall chooſe its Speaker and other officers.

Sect. 7. Vacancies in the Houſe of Repreſentatives ſhall be ſupplied by writs of election from the executive authority of the State, in the repreſentation from which they ſhall happen.

V.

George Washington's annotated copy of the committee of detail draft of the Constitution. The first printed version, it was distributed to the delegates shortly after the convention reconvened on August 6, 1787.

Arrangements were to be made for the extradition of criminals. These measures were virtually identical with similar ones in effect under the Articles, though they had not really ameliorated interstate conflicts. The federal judiciary now would be in a position to apply these provisions under the new government.

Another problem the Confederation had not resolved, the admission of new states, was to be handled by admitting them on an equal basis with the original ones, by a two-thirds vote of those present in each house of Congress.

The jurisdiction of the Supreme Court, now also more precisely defined, would include cases arising under U.S. laws, those affecting public officials, maritime and admiralty matters, interstate disputes, and legal contests among citizens of more than one state, between states, and when other countries or aliens were involved. The Court would also try impeachments brought by the House of Representatives.

Although instructed to report property qualifications for Members of Congress, the committee directed Congress to do so itself. A further specification was that qualifications for voting to elect members of the House of Representatives were to be tied to state law; people who could vote for the more numerous house of the state legislatures were to constitute the electorate for the House of Representatives. In practice, the state regulations on this subject had varied widely and a uniform formula would have not only been difficult to devise but might also have seemed to intrude too much on state authority. In the vexing matter of the number of states required to approve the Constitution before it became the law of the land, the committee simply left a blank. The convention would have to decide.

Demonstrating considerable skill and energy, the committee of detail had performed creditably, though the degree of the changes and innovations it had made apparently surprised the delegates. Its services were not completely done, and it reported to the convention from time to time later on, when difficult matters were referred for its consideration.

The convention reconvened on August 6. Either on that day or the next the delegates received individual printed copies and began to consider the first draft of their handiwork.

Debates and Revisions

Five weeks of intensive discussion were required to revise the draft constitution. These weeks were tedious and debilitating for the delegates. The weather, in a day of no air conditioning, was miserable. Many of those in attendance had been away from their families and professional duties since May. All wanted to finish and go home. In fact, as time passed, the pressure of personal business and other factors, including dissatisfaction with the course of the proceedings, lured a few more individuals away from Philadelphia beyond those who had already departed.

Those who stayed became increasingly anxious to finish their work. In mid-August lengthened sessions were briefly experimented with, but this proved to be unsatisfactory, for they interfered with the dinner hour. Speeches tended to become more concise and the spirit of compromise intensified. And more and more the strong nationalists—Madison, Wilson, and Gouverneur Morris among the leaders—gained the dominant voice. As the draft constitution was studied article by article and line by line, much debate occurred, mostly on a high level, though some of it was tedious and inconsequential. The process had to be endured, however, and many significant changes emerged from it.

The question of the number of representatives proved to be a source of difficulty. The committee of detail had specified one in the lower house for each 40,000 inhabitants. Madison, objecting, contended that as population increased that body would grow to an unwieldy size. The states voted unanimously to change the wording of the provision to read "not exceeding the rate of one for every forty thousand."

Another matter attracting much attention was the citizenship and minimum residency requirements for senators and representatives. The committee of detail had proposed 3 years of citizenship for members of the House and 4 years for the Senate. Fearing new residents might be too much influenced by their foreign background, the delegates increased the figures to 7 and 9 years, respectively.

Countering its earlier instructions to the committee of detail, the convention refused to prescribe property qualifications of any sort (either land or capital) for federal officeholders, though most states specified such requirements for both voting and officeholding. Although Charles Pinckney and Gerry argued for such restrictions, the convention accepted Franklin's reasoning that they would debase the "spirit of the common people." Pinckney, however, was responsible for the motion barring religious tests for officeholding; these were also a common feature of state laws.

The committee of detail had revived the question of who should pay congressmen. By a large majority, its suggestion that the states do so was revoked, and the convention's earlier resolution that they be compensated from the national treasury was reinserted.

Added to the congressional powers granted by the committee draft was the vesting of the legislature with authority to declare war. Gouverneur Morris argued strenuously against the provision giving the national government power to "borrow money and emit bills." He held that the "Monied interest" in the nation would oppose the Constitution if paper money were not prohibited. Because the government would enjoy the capability to borrow money and presumably to use public notes, the delegates heeded Morris' objections and struck out the phrase. A limit on congressional tariff powers also won approval. It specified that tariffs would need to be uniformly and equally applied throughout the country.

The Great Compromise had included a clause stating that money bills should originate in the House of Representatives and not be subject to Senate amendment. Many delegates had entertained serious reservations about this provision. It had been borrowed from colonial and state procedures, which had not always worked well. The issue came up twice in early August during debates in which many delegates participated, but the convention, after tentatively resolving it twice again, found it so dangerous that it threatened to overturn the entire Great Compromise. Final consideration of it was postponed until the powers of the Senate might be considered.

Several delegates argued vociferously that the national government must assume the state, as well as national, or Confederation, war debts, on the grounds that they had all been incurred for the common good during the Revolution. Opponents of this proposal contended it would benefit speculators rather than legitimate debt holders. Some controversy also arose between some of the states that had paid off substantial parts of their war debts and some of those that had not. The question was hotly disputed because it involved Congress taking over the states' power to tax imports, a major source of their income. An assumption of state debts would lessen the reluctance of creditor interests in the states to support the new Constitution. The matter was referred to a special committee, composed of one member from each state.

After that group reported a compromise, which was followed by another frustrating debate, the delegates approved an amended version that merely stated that "all debts contracted and engagements entered into, by or under the authority of Congress shall be as valid against the United States under this constitution as under the confederation." This ambiguous wording avoided the difficult question of exactly what debts were valid against the Confederation.

A recommendation to give the national government power over the state militias touched on the vital matter of states rights and on the Continental Army's troubled dealing with the militias during the Revolution. The dispute was so grievous that a committee was instructed to bring in a solution. It was proposed that the national government be empowered to pass laws requiring uniform militia organization from state to state and comparability of arms and discipline. The government also gained the power to control units called into federal service. The states retained the right to train their own militias and appoint their own officers. These recommendations were accepted without amendment.

One of the sharpest exchanges of the convention occurred toward the end of August over slavery and the committee of detail's plan to protect the import slave trade and prohibit federal taxation of it. This was an explosive issue. Some northern delegates and Mason of Virginia objected to slavery or the slave trade on moral grounds; others saw more practical considerations. Luther Martin pointed out that prohibition of an import tax on slaves meant lack of national control over the traffic and provided a possible incentive to the southern states to augment their representation by adding to their slave populations. The power to tax could, on the other hand, be used to discourage or prevent the import of slaves, and southerners tended to oppose this. Mixed into this debate and into that on the regulation of foreign trade was the matter of divergent economic interests in the states. A related problem involving southern–northern conflict was the specification in the draft constitution that a two-thirds vote would be necessary to pass navigation acts.

After many delegates had expressed their opinions, the unresolved matters of slave import regulation, federal taxation of it, and the navigation acts were turned over to another special committee, consisting of one member from each state. Complicating solution of this issue further was the Northwest Ordinance, which the Continental Congress had passed the preceding month. By providing that states formed north of the Ohio would be free of slavery, the ordinance touched on an argument that later would be of great significance, the status of that institution in new territories and states. Any compromise would presumably need to heed this new legislation.

The committee presented a complicated compromise. Congress could not act to prohibit the import of slaves before 1800 into states that had existed in 1787, but it might tax such importation at an average rate compared to that for other imports. The committee also suggested that a simple congressional majority should be sufficient to pass navigation acts.

The part of the compromise dealing with the trade in slaves underwent modification. Congress was instructed not to forbid the traffic prior to 1808 (again for those states existing in 1787) and a specific limit was set on the taxes that might be imposed on it. Over

New Brunswick,
23d August, 1787.

Dear Sir,

In looking over some Papers a few Days ago, I met with your Note against Niles, which I enclose. I hope you will be able to recover the Money due upon it.

What are the Convention about? When will they rise? will they agree upon a System energetick and effectual, or will they break up without doing any Thing to the Purpose? Full of Disputation and noisy as the Wind, it is said, that you are afraid of the very Windows, and have a Man planted under them to prevent the Secrets and Doings from flying out. The Business, however, is

As the summer dragged on, many delegates questioned whether or not the convention would ever reach agreement. In this extract from a letter written on August 23, 1787, by William Paterson from his home in New Jersey to fellow-delegate Oliver Ellsworth (Connecticut), the former wonders: "What are the Convention about? When will they rise? Will they agree upon a System energetick and effectual, or will they break up without doing any Thing to the Purpose?"

the objections of Delaware, New Jersey, Pennsylvania, and Virginia, the part of the compromise concerning slavery was accepted. Both sides probably privately considered the result a victory. Antislavery delegates felt they had succeeded in writing into the Constitution a provision that could ultimately end the importation of slaves. Proslavery delegates hoped that agitation against the slave trade might disappear after a moratorium of two decades.

Simply to have made it possible to act against the slave trade at that future time was as substantial a victory as the antislavery men at Philadelphia could win in view of existing political realities. The southern states would have rejected any major restrictions on slavery, and the northern would compromise no further, though they soon accepted without protest a provision for the return of fugitive slaves. The stipulation that abolition of the slave trade could be considered after 1808 at least demonstrated that the founders were not all immutably subscribing to the system and that future action against it was not precluded.

Indicative of the gingerly manner in which the topic was treated in the convention, the words "slave" and "slavery" do not even appear in the final Constitution, where slaves are referred to by such euphemisms as "other persons." As a matter of fact, the subject is touched on in only a few places. Articles I and II prevent Congress from outlawing the import trade in slaves until 1808. And existence of the institution is acknowledged in the "three-fifths" clause dealing with representation (Article I) as well as in the stipulation for extradition of an escaped "Person held to Service or Labour" (Article IV).

Had the delegates not handled the issue so carefully and obtained the support of all sections, the convention would probably have dissolved over it. On the other hand, the compromise brought the moral price of the Constitution to a high level.

The second part of the compromise dropped the two-thirds requirement for adoption of navigation acts by Congress. In some ways, acceptance of this provision represented a greater potential sacrifice for the South than most other compromises of the summer. As a region producing an abundance of staple crops and needing to export surpluses, it was fearful of granting the general government power to tax imports and exports. Randolph and Mason of Virginia were worried, prophetically as it turned out, that if northern commercial and manufacturing centers gained in population and power they would enact taxes and other measures destructive of the southern economy.

A number of southern delegates, however, failed to heed their two colleagues and voted for the compromise. The southern states were probably conciliatory on this issue because they had earlier won exemption of exports from federal taxation. Many southerners also believed that the future would bring rapid expansion to the agricultural sections of the country and that the South and West, as economic allies, would be able to prevent the commercial states of the Northeast from dominating the government. The future would prove them wrong. The northern states were content with this part of the complex compromise because it would allow them to pass commerce legislation more easily than they had anticipated.

New prohibitions on congressional action suggested and approved by the full convention while reviewing the draft of the committee of detail included ones against bills of attainder, *ex post facto* laws, and suspension of the writ of *habeas corpus* in peacetime. Troubles in trying to agree on the powers of the Senate caused postponement of action on this matter. The delegates did strike out its role in the settlement of interstate disputes and passed this to the Supreme Court. The authorities of the House of Representatives gave rise to little controversy during this period of the debates.

The veto power of the President was also enhanced. Williamson moved, and the delegates endorsed, a three-fourths vote of each house to override the veto of the executive. This move was undoubtedly motivated by a desire to increase his independence from the legislature, which was at this point still slated to elect him.

Late in August the convention once again debated election of the President. Misunderstanding arose over the method of casting the legislative ballot. The delegates proceeded to approve a joint vote by the two houses, rather than separate ballots by each of them. The small states protested because they felt this decision would virtually give the power of election to the large states, whose contingents in the lower House were strong.

Unable to resolve this problem readily, the convention returned to discussion of the President's powers, largely going along with the original committee of detail's proposals. Adopted from a supplementary committee report, on August 22, were provisions that the President should be 35 years of age and a resident for 21 years. A suggestion in this same report that the President enjoy the advice of a privy council of cabinet members and top legislators died without formal consideration.

Occasioning only brief discussion was jurisdiction of the federal courts. It was extended far beyond what had been granted by the committee of detail, which had given them power only over cases arising under federal legislative acts. This was now amended to include all cases arising under the Constitution, which was to be the "supreme law."

Curiously, the right of the Supreme Court to pass finally on the constitutionality of laws, treaties, and executive actions was not explicitly stated, though many of the delegates apparently understood that it would exercise such authority. On one matter previously assigned to it, the trying of impeachments, the committee postponed a decision.

Anxious to assert exclusive national authority over what they deemed to be vital matters, the delegates not only approved committee limitations on the states, but also imposed certain additional ones, especially a prohibition on the issuance of paper money.

The admission of new states was also a provocative issue. The committee of detail had proposed that they be admitted as equals with the older ones by a two-thirds vote in each house. Gouverneur Morris, who had previously argued that the preponderance of power must remain with the original seaboard states, renewed his objections. Despite cogent rebuttals from Madison, Mason, and Sherman, he persuaded the convention to alter the committee's proposal. The statement "New States may be admitted by the Legislature into the Union" was then unanimously substituted. Morris long remained convinced that it really meant the eastern states would govern much of the West. So noncommittal was the language, however, that future Congresses were to interpret it to mean that a virtually unlimited number of new states could be brought into the Union as equals of the original ones.

Provisions relating to interstate relations, which the committee of detail had largely adapted from the Articles of Confederation, met approval with minor changes. Included were the extradition of criminals and the return of fugitive slaves, as well as state recognition of each other's legislative and judicial actions and the "privileges and immunities" of citizens. Also adopted was the committee of detail proposal that when two-thirds of the state legislatures applied to Congress for an amendment to the Constitution a convention would be called to consider it.

As for the number of states required to ratify the completed Constitution, the committee of detail had left the number blank. Ideas on this issue ranged from proposals that all 13 must express their approval, as the Articles of Confederation required, to suggestions from Madison, Wilson, and Washington that a bare majority, 7, would be sufficient. Nine was finally chosen as the proper number. This action demonstrated a crucial break with the Articles of Confederation. The delicate matter of the role of the Continental Congress in the ratifying process also caused debate. The delegates boldly resolved to submit the Constitution to it with the recommendation that the instrument simply be forwarded to conventions in the states.

The Question of Presidential Election and Authority

By August 31 the delegates had considered practically all the recommendations of the committee of detail word by word. They were fatigued, restless, and wanted to go home, but a number of loose ends remained. The most important of these "postponed matters" were the method of election of the President, the locus of appointive powers and treatymaking, the organ of government that would try impeachments, and the method of originating money bills.

Because the procedure seemed to have worked so well before, the convention appointed a committee on postponed matters. Representing each of the 11 states officially in attendance, it was chaired by Brearly of New Jersey and included Sherman of Connecticut, Dickinson of Delaware, Baldwin of Georgia, Carroll of Maryland, King of Massachusetts, Gilman of New Hampshire, Williamson of North Carolina, Gouverneur Morris of Pennsylvania, Butler of South Carolina, and Madison of Virginia.

The committee, which reported on several days in early September, modified the draft constitution extensively, largely to the satisfaction of the convention. Details of the qualifications of the President were changed somewhat. His term was reduced from 7 years to 4, and no limit was set on reeligibility. The minimum residence requirement was reduced from 21 to 14 years, but the President was required to be either native born or a U.S. citizen at the time of the adoption of the Constitution. His powers were augmented considerably. He gained authority to make treaties, which would need to be approved by two-thirds of the Senators, and to appoint ambassadors, judges, and other officials, including members of the Supreme Court. Appointees would be subject to the endorsement of a Senate majority.

The committee also proposed that power to try impeachments of high officials be transferred from the Supreme Court to the Senate and that conviction require a two-thirds majority.

The most difficult "postponed matter" was election of the President. From the beginning of the convention there had been little dispute about his importance, but agreement could never be reached on how he would be elected. So long as a consensus prevailed that he be chosen by the legislature, most delegates felt he should serve a rather long term and be ineligible for reelection to prevent undue legislative influence on him. Madison, Wilson, and some other leaders favored, at least in theory, direct or indirect election by the people. But a direct popular vote seemed impractical. There was no uniform national franchise, and the convention had not even attempted to create one. Many of the delegates and other national leaders shared a conviction that the people at large were incapable of making a wise selection. In addition, no system existed to limit candidates to a reasonable number. Finally, some accommodation to the federal character of the Union was imperative.

The committee on postponed matters offered an ingenious and complex method of election that met widespread approval. Electors would be selected in each state, according to a method chosen by the legislature. The number of electors would equal the state's total of senators and representatives. The electors would ballot for two persons, at least one of whom could not be a resident of their state. The votes would be dispatched to the Senate. The person holding a majority of the votes would become President. But what if no candidate received a majority? The Senate would then choose the President from the five candidates who had won the most votes.

The person holding the second highest number of electoral votes would become Vice President; in case of a tie, the Senate would make a choice. This was a new office that many delegates only grudgingly accepted. Its occupant would preside over the Senate, cast the deciding vote there in case of ties, and occupy the presidency in the event the incumbent died, resigned, or was otherwise unable to fill the office.

The committee on postponed matters carefully avoided an electoral scheme that would grant absolute power to the people at large to elect the President. Few delegates would allow that, and those who supported the idea knew that most of the states would not. On the other hand, the committee left the way open to the evolution of a form of popular election by allowing the states to determine the method of choosing electors. The small and large states were both pleased with the formula of adding each state's representatives and senators to arrive at its electoral vote.

Objections led to some modification of the committee's proposals. Many of the founders feared for the future. They were reasonably certain Washington would be the first President, but they foresaw that it might be difficult to agree upon his successor and the Senate might thus need to make the choice. This would allow it to exercise undue, perhaps even oligarchic, influence. The committee, trying to anticipate this fear, had already stripped the Senate of much of its treatymaking and appointive powers by shifting basic authority in these areas to the President.

Now, after a vigorous debate, the Senate lost its prerogative of choosing the President in cases where no candidate had a majority. The convention was in a quandary again because the small states bitterly opposed election by the House. At Sherman's suggestion, a fresh crisis was avoided by obtaining agreement that the House of Representatives would indeed choose the President in the event none of the five leading candidates had won a majority. Each state, however, would have only one vote regardless of its number of representatives.

The trying issue of the authority and election of the President was at last resolved. The committee on postponed matters had given him larger powers and reduced his dependence on the legislature. Although rumors outside the statehouse reported the convention was considering the establishment of a monarchy, no such thing was in the minds of the majority. Instead, it was determined to balance the three branches of government so that no one would dominate the others. A strong, independent executive was sought, not a too-powerful Senate. The intent was to achieve a balance between the executive and legislature.

One last compromise remained. The matter of originating money bills had been debated and tentatively resolved several times. The large states, which would enjoy stronger representation in the lower House, were determined that money bills be initiated there without amendment by the upper. The small states hoped that the Senate, where they would be more powerful, would play a role. It was finally agreed that such bills would originate in the House of Representatives but would be subject to senatorial amendment.

The Final Draft

By the close of business on September 8, review of the work of the committee on postponed matters had been essentially finished. It remained to put the emerging constitution into its final form, approve, and sign it. To this end, another committee, of style, or revision, to put the finishing touches on the work of the convention, was selected. It consisted of five talented and distinguished members: Chairman William Samuel Johnson, Gouverneur Morris, Madison, King, and Hamilton. These men worked from September 8 to 12. Little is known about their procedures or day-to-day workings. The preponderance of evidence, however, suggests that Gouverneur Morris was the actual "penman," or drafter, of the Constitution.

Meantime, the rest of the delegates had made a few last-minute adjustments in their handiwork. Amendments could be initiated by two-thirds of the Congress or by a constitutional convention if two-thirds of the state legislatures so requested. Proposed amendments would have to be approved by three-fourths of the states, acting through their legislatures or conventions. Some delegates were concerned that the amending process might undo the work of the convention, but the only specific limitation put on the process at this time was a provision to prevent interference with the slavery compromise so painfully agreed to earlier. Sherman later won a proviso to protect equality of state suffrage in the Senate. Randolph sought in vain to authorize a second convention before the new government went into effect to consider amendments the states might offer during the ratification process.

The convention adjourned on September 10 to await the report of the committee of style and met again the next day, but the report was not ready so another adjournment occurred. The following day, the delegates reassembled, and the committee submitted its draft, which was read and sent to the printer. All that remained was to compare the work of the committee with the amended draft given to it and make final corrections.

During the printing process, the rest of the 12th was devoted to discussion of final modifications. By the close vote of six states to four, with one divided, it was decided to reduce the congressional margin needed to override the President's veto from three-fourths to two-thirds.

The absence of a bill of rights came up once again. Mason, author of the Virginia Declaration of Rights, pleaded that such a bill should preface the completed Constitution. Gerry of Massachusetts moved that a committee be appointed to prepare one. But Sherman of Connecticut, objecting, contended that the Constitution did not repeal the state bills of rights, which he felt were sufficient guarantees. Mason responded that the laws of the United States under the Constitution were to be supreme and might therefore negate state enactments. Despite this argument, the delegates, as a whole, seemed to fear that, though only a few hours might be required to write such a bill, weeks of debate would be needed to obtain its approval. So, by a vote of 10 states to none, with Massachusetts absent, a bill of rights was rejected.

This proved to be the most serious mistake made during the convention. When debates over the ratification began, objections were raised everywhere to the absence of a bill of rights, and several states considered making their ratification contingent upon the speedy addition of one. They contented themselves with suggesting amendments, however, and the First Congress moved rapidly to remedy this defect.

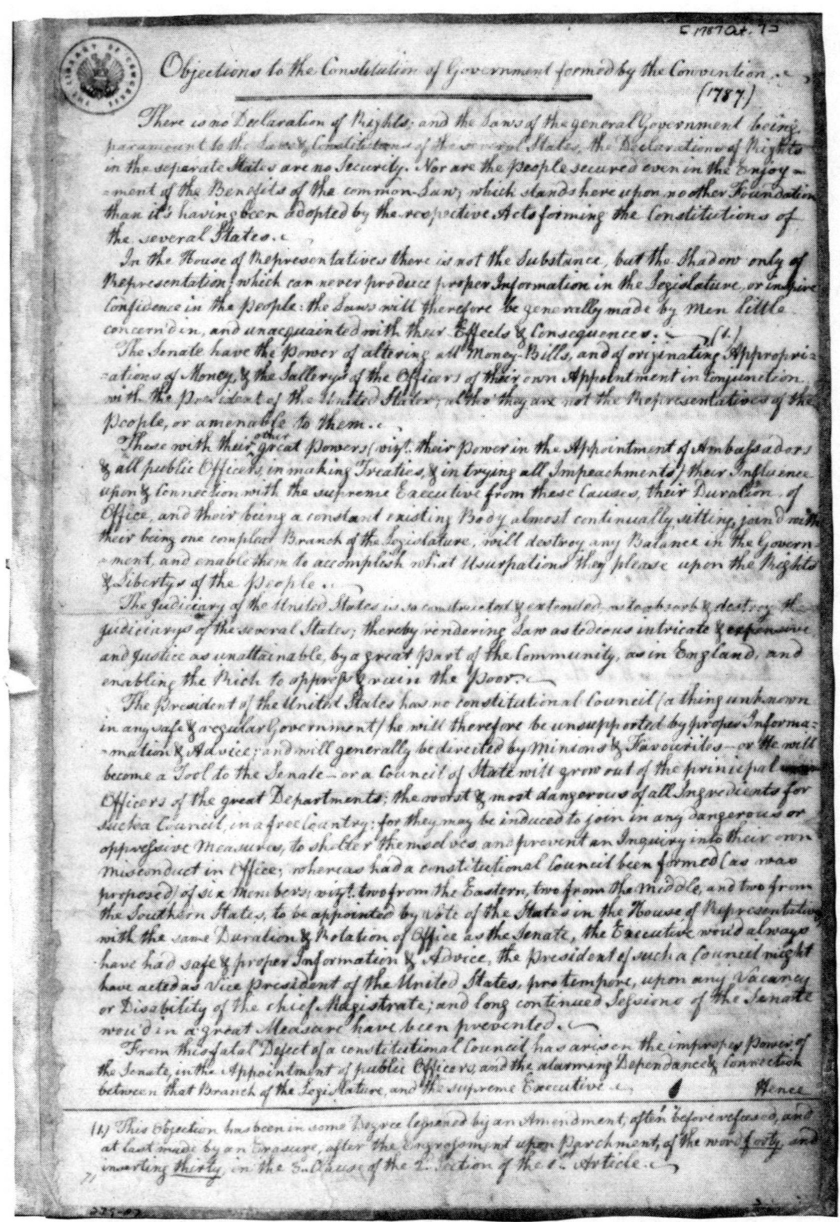

[1787 Oct. 7]

Objections to the Constitution of Government formed by the Convention. (1787)

There is no Declaration of Rights; and the Laws of the general Government being paramount to the Laws & Constitutions of the several States, the Declarations of Rights in the separate States are no Security. Nor are the People secured even in the Enjoyment of the Benefits of the common-Law; which stands here upon no other Foundation than it's having been adopted by the respective Acts forming the Constitutions of the several States.

In the House of Representatives there is not the Substance, but the Shadow only of Representation; which can never produce proper Information in the Legislature, or inspire Confidence in the People: the Laws will therefore be generally made by Men little concern'd in, and unacquainted with their Effects & Consequences. (1.)

The Senate have the Power of altering all Money-Bills, and of originating Appropriations of Money, & the Sallerys of the Officers of their own Appointment in Conjunction with the President of the United States; altho' they are not the Representatives of the People, or amenable to them.

These with their other great Powers (viz. their Power in the Appointment of Ambassadors & all public Officers, in making Treaties, & in trying all Impeachments) their Influence upon & Connection with the supreme Executive from these Causes, their Duration of Office, and their being a constant existing Body almost continually sitting, join'd with their being one compleat Branch of the Legislature, will destroy any Balance in the Government, and enable them to accomplish what Usurpations they please upon the Rights & Libertys of the People.

The Judiciary of the United States is so constructed & extended, as to absorb & destroy the Judiciarys of the several States; thereby rendering Law as tedious intricate & expensive, and Justice as unattainable, by a great Part of the Community, as in England, and enabling the Rich to oppress & ruin the Poor.

The President of the United States has no Constitutional Council (a thing unknown in any safe & regular Government) he will therefore be unsupported by proper Information & Advice; and will generally be directed by Minions & Favourites — or He will become a Tool to the Senate — or a Council of State will grow out of the principal Officers of the great Departments; the worst & most dangerous of all Ingredients for such a Council, in a free Country; for they may be induced to join in any dangerous or oppressive Measures, to shelter themselves and prevent an Inquiry into their own Misconduct in Office; whereas had a constitutional Council been formed (as was proposed) of six Members; viz. two from the Eastern, two from the Middle, and two from the Southern States, to be appointed by Vote of the States in the House of Representatives with the same Duration & Rotation of Office as the Senate, the Executive wou'd always have had safe & proper Information & Advice, the President of such a Council might have acted as Vice President of the United States, pro tempore, upon any Vacancy or Disability of the chief Magistrate; and long continued Sessions of the Senate wou'd in a great Measure have been prevented.

From this fatal Defect of a constitutional Council has arisen the improper Power of the Senate, in the Appointment of public Officers, and the alarming Dependance & Connection between that Branch of the Legislature, and the supreme Executive.

Hence

(1.) This Objection has been in some Degree lessened by an Amendment, often before refused, and at last made by an Erasure, after the Engrossment upon Parchment, of the word forty, and inserting thirty, in the 3d Clause of the 2d Section of the 1st Article.

George Mason, although he had an almost perfect attendence record at the convention, refused to sign the Constitution. He formally stated his reasons, the first being a lack of a bill of rights, in "Objections to the Constitution."

From September 13 to 15 the delegates carefully reviewed the finished document and made some changes, many editorial in nature. Some 60 copies, in pages, had been returned by the printer; it was the second printed version of the Constitution. Ably performing its assignment, the committee of style had reduced 23 articles to 7 and smoothed wording here and there but had made only two substantive modifications.

Fatefully, but unintentionally, the opening phrase of the preamble had been revamped so that it spurred the cause of nationalism. The committee of detail's version, approved by the Convention earlier, had read "We the People of the States . . ." and then had listed each of the 13 states. The committee of style had altered it to read as follows: "We the People of the United States. . . ." The phrase ". . . in order to form a more perfect Union" was also added. The states were not specified.

The new phrase had the effect of making it seem to appear that sovereignty was placed in the people of the United States rather than in the states. But this was not the actual reason for the change. The earlier version had been predicated on the assumption that all the states of the Confederation would need to approve the new government before it could be established and they were therefore named in the preamble. But, after the convention's momentous decision to rely on ratification by nine states, it was not known if all the states would ratify. Furthermore, the delegates could hardly speak for the two states not present.

The second alteration made by the committee of style was at the urging of King of Massachusetts. Seeking to guard property rights, it forbade the states from passing laws that might impair the obligation of contracts.

Although the committee made only these two basic changes, the convention made several dozen, most of them minor clarifications or changes of wording. Aside from those, the delegates shifted the power to appoint a national treasurer from Congress to the President. They also prohibited the chief executive from receiving any emolument except his salary from the national government. As with the earlier provision specifying that the treasury would pay congressmen, this one was designed to lessen any dependence national officials might have on the states of their origin. In addition, the amending process was revised to provide that future constitutional conventions might be held should two-thirds of the state legislatures so request.

Other modifications were rejected during the last 3 days. Among these were Franklin's proposal that the government should have the express power to build canals; Madison and Charles Pinckney's

WE, the People of the United States, in order to form a more perfect union, to eſtabliſh juſtice, inſure domeſtic tranquility, provide for the common defence, promote the general welfare, and ſecure the bleſſings of liberty to ourſelves and our poſterity, do ordain and eſtabliſh this Conſtitution for the United States of America.

ARTICLE I.

Sect. 1. ALL legiſlative powers herein granted ſhall be veſted in a Congreſs of the United States, which ſhall conſiſt of a Senate and Houſe of Repreſentatives.

Sect. 2. The Houſe of Repreſentatives ſhall be compoſed of members choſen every ſecond year by the people of the ſeveral ſtates, and the electors in each ſtate ſhall have the qualifications requiſite for electors of the moſt numerous branch of the ſtate legiſlature.

No perſon ſhall be a repreſentative who ſhall not have attained to the age of twenty-five years, and been ſeven years a citizen of the United States, and who ſhall not, when elected, be an inhabitant of that ſtate in which he ſhall be choſen.

Repreſentatives and direct taxes ſhall be apportioned among the ſeveral ſtates which may be included within this Union, according to their reſpective numbers, which ſhall be determined by adding to the whole number of free perſons, including thoſe bound to ſervitude for a term of years, and excluding Indians not taxed, three-fifths of all other perſons. The actual enumeration ſhall be made within three years after the firſt meeting of the Congreſs of the United States, and within every ſubſequent term of ten years, in ſuch manner as they ſhall by law direct. The number of repreſentatives ſhall not exceed one for every forty thouſand, but each ſtate ſhall have at leaſt one repreſentative: and until ſuch enumeration ſhall be made, the ſtate of New-Hampſhire ſhall be entitled to chuſe three, Maſſachuſetts eight, Rhode-Iſland and Providence Plantations one, Connecticut five, New-York ſix, New-Jerſey four, Pennſylvania eight, Delaware one, Maryland ſix, Virginia ten, North-Carolina five, South-Carolina five, and Georgia three.

When vacancies happen in the repreſentation from any ſtate, the Executive authority thereof ſhall iſſue writs of election to fill ſuch vacancies.

The Houſe of Repreſentatives ſhall chooſe their Speaker and other officers; and they ſhall have the ſole power of impeachment.

Sect. 3. The Senate of the United States ſhall be compoſed of two ſenators from each ſtate, choſen by the legiſlature thereof, for ſix years: and each ſenator ſhall have one vote.

Immediately after they ſhall be aſſembled in conſequence of the firſt election, they ſhall be divided as equally as may be into three claſſes. The ſeats of the ſenators of the firſt claſs ſhall be vacated at the expiration of the ſecond year, of the ſecond claſs at the expiration of the fourth year, and of the third claſs at the expiration of the ſixth year, ſo that one-third may be choſen every ſecond year: and if vacancies happen by reſignation, or otherwiſe, during the receſs of the Legiſlature of any ſtate, the Executive thereof may make temporary appointments until the next meeting of the Legiſlature.

No perſon ſhall be a ſenator who ſhall not have attained to the age of thirty years, and been nine years a citizen of the United States, and who ſhall not, when elected, be an inhabitant of that ſtate for which he ſhall be choſen.

The Vice-Preſident of the United States ſhall be, ~~ex officio~~, Preſident of the ſenate, but ſhall have no vote, unleſs they be equally divided.

The Senate ſhall chooſe their other officers, and alſo a Preſident pro tempore, in the abſence of the Vice-Preſident, or when he ſhall exerciſe the office of Preſident of the United States.

The Senate ſhall have the ſole power to try all impeachments. When ſitting for that purpoſe, they ſhall be on oath. When the Preſident of the United States is tried, the Chief Juſtice ſhall preſide: And no perſon ſhall be convicted without the concurrence of two-thirds of the members preſent.

Judgment in caſes of impeachment ſhall not extend further than to removal from office, and diſqualification to hold and enjoy any office of honor, truſt or profit under the United States: but the party convicted ſhall nevertheleſs be liable and ſubject to indictment, trial, judgment and puniſhment, according to law.

Sect. 4. The times, places and manner of holding elections for ſenators and repreſentatives, ſhall be preſcribed in each ſtate by the legiſlature thereof: but the Congreſs may at any time by law make or alter ſuch regulations.

The Congreſs ſhall aſſemble at leaſt once in every year, and ſuch meeting ſhall be on the firſt Monday in December, unleſs they ſhall by law appoint a different day.

Sect. 5. Each houſe ſhall be the judge of the elections, returns and qualifications of its own members, and a majority of each ſhall conſtitute a quorum to do buſineſs: but a ſmaller number may adjourn from day to day, and may be authoriſed to compel the attendance of abſent members, in ſuch manner, and under ſuch penalties as each houſe may provide.

Each houſe may determine the rules of its proceedings; puniſh its members for diſorderly behaviour, and, with the concurrence of two-thirds, expel a member.

Each houſe ſhall keep a journal of its proceedings, and from time to time publiſh the ſame, excepting ſuch parts as may in their judgment require ſecrecy; and the yeas and nays of the members of either houſe on any queſtion ſhall, at the deſire of one-fifth of thoſe preſent, be entered on the journal.

Neither houſe, during the ſeſſion of Congreſs, ſhall, without the conſent of the other, adjourn for more than three days, nor to any other place than that in which the two houſes ſhall be ſitting.

Sect. 6. The ſenators and repreſentatives ſhall receive a compenſation for their ſervices, to be aſcertained by law, and paid out of the treaſury of the United States. They ſhall in all caſes, except treaſon, felony and breach of the peace, be privileged from arreſt during their attendance at the ſeſſion of their reſpective houſes, and in going to and returning from the ſame; and for any ſpeech or debate in either houſe, they ſhall not be queſtioned in any other place.

No ſenator or repreſentative ſhall, during the time for which he was elected, be appointed to any civil office under the authority of the United States, which ſhall have been created, or the emoluments

James Madison's annotated copy of the first page of the committee of style printing of the Constitution. The second printed version, it was received from Dunlap & Claypoole on September 13, 1787.

suggestion that it be empowered to establish a national university; an effort to reinsert a two-thirds vote requirement for the passage of navigation laws; and Madison's recommendation that the government have the power to incorporate businesses for the purpose of supporting internal improvements. An attempt to insert the principle of the freedom of the press was set aside as unnecessary. Randolph repeated his call for a second constitutional convention to consider amendments that might be offered by the states, but he met deaf ears.

Late in the afternoon of Saturday, September 15, the states voted unanimously to accept the Constitution, directed the printer to make the appropriate revisions in the type that had been set on September 13, and ordered the engrossing of the finished product.

Late Saturday evening or Sunday it was undoubtedly Secretary Jackson who obtained the engrossing services of Jacob Shallus, assistant clerk of the Pennsylvania General Assembly, which had been meeting since September 4 in the room above that used by the convention. Shallus was apparently provided with a corrected copy of the report of the committee of style and a revised text of the last two articles (dealing with ratification) of the report of the committee of detail. These two articles appeared as the fifth, or last, page ("resolution of transmittal" or the "ratification notice") of the Constitution. Shallus worked hurriedly over the remaining part of the weekend and apparently received $30 for his effort. Possibly some unidentified person prepared the decorative lettering "We the People" and the numbered "Article" heads.

ON Monday, September 17, the convention reconvened for the signing. That morning, 41 of the 55 delegates who had participated were present. After someone, probably Secretary Jackson, read the document aloud, Franklin obtained permission to speak. Because of his infirmity, however, Wilson read his speech for him. It sought to conciliate the delegates and unite them all in signing the instrument. Franklin admitted he did not approve of several parts of it but averred that in the fullness of time he might come to favor them. In any case, no one would be completely satisfied and the document was the best that could be achieved. Furthermore, the public good required its acceptance.

At the end of his speech, Franklin offered a motion, conceived by Gouverneur Morris, that was intended to cajole some dissenting members to sign—on behalf of their states, not as individuals. For this purpose, the resolution suggested the following wording for the closing block of the Constitution: "Done in Convention by the unanimous consent of the States present the seventeenth day of

New Hampshire	Massachusetts	Rhode Island	Connecticut	New York	New Jersey	Pennsylvania	Delaware	Maryland	Virginia	North Carolina	South Carolina	Georgia	Questions	ayes	noes	divided
no	aye		no		no	no	aye	no	no	no	no	no				
dd	aye		aye		aye	no	no	no	no	no	no	no				
no	no		aye		no	no	no	no	no	no	no	no		1	10	–
no	no		aye		aye	no	aye	no	no	no	no	no		3	8	–
no	no		aye		aye	no	dd	no	no	no	no	no		2	8	1
dd	no		no		no	no	aye	aye	no	aye	no	no		3	7	1
no	no	[illegible]	no		no	no	aye	no	no		no	no				
dd	no		no		aye	no	aye	aye	no		no	no				
no	no		no		no	no	no	aye	aye		no	aye	~~The [illegible]~~	3	7	–
no	no		no		no	no	no	no	no		no	no				
aye	aye		aye		aye	aye	aye	aye	aye		aye	aye				
aye	aye		aye		aye	aye	aye	aye	aye		aye	aye	The Constitution unanimously agreed to			
aye	aye		aye		aye	aye	aye	aye	aye	aye	aye	aye	The Constitution unanimously agreed to.			
aye	aye		aye		aye	aye	aye	aye	aye	aye	dd	aye				
no	aye		aye		aye	aye	aye	no	aye	aye	aye	aye	To deliver over the Journals and papers to the President			

Secretary Jackson's official record of the last day's voting.

September. . . ." Before the vote could be taken, Gorham moved that the stipulation providing for representation in the House not to exceed one representative for each 40,000 inhabitants be changed to one for each 30,000. King and Carroll offered seconds. Washington rose to give his only speech of the convention, in favor of Gorham's proposal, which passed unanimously.

Attention was again turned to Franklin's resolution. But, prior to the vote, one final bit of debate occurred. Randolph and Gerry reiterated their objections to the Constitution and explained they would refuse to sign it, as they and Mason had done in the previous session. Blount said he, too, opposed much of the document, but would underwrite it to demonstrate the unanimity of the states. After various other delegates gave their opinion on the subject, Franklin's motion passed by a vote of 10 states to none, with South Carolina divided. King moved to destroy the convention's papers or to deposit them with its president; the convention voted to turn them over to Washington for safekeeping until Congress ordered their disposition.

About this time, Shallus, who likely was waiting outside the room, engrossed the closing block, probably before the signing though it is possible he did so afterward. To the left of the block, he also inscribed an errata statement, which included reference to the change from 40,000 to 30,000 inhabitants and three minor changes or interlineations. One of the latter (an interlineated "the") referred to the wrong lines; and other interlineated "the," between lines 51 and 52 of the second page, was not incorporated in the errata statement.

Sometime during the afternoon the signing began. All present except Randolph, Mason, and Gerry, or a total of 38 men, affixed their signatures. Accounting for the 39th name, Read signed at the behest of fellow Delawarean Dickinson, who had left the convention early because of illness. Washington, as the president of the meeting and delegate from Virginia, penned his name first, at the bottom of the fourth page of text. He was followed by the other delegates in the standard congressional voting order, by state generally from north to south: New Hampshire, Massachusetts, Connecticut, Hamilton from New York, New Jersey, Pennsylvania, Delaware, Maryland, Virginia, North Carolina, South Carolina, and Georgia. The names were arranged in two columns, the right-hand one being filled out first.

The signature of Hamilton, who also wrote the state names to the left of the block of each delegation as it signed, was misleading for it tended to give the impression that 12 instead of 11 states had approved the document. He was the only delegate from New York present, in an unofficial capacity, and he did not represent a quorum of his delegation as convention procedures required.

September. 1787.

Thursday. 13th.

Attended Convention. Dined at the Vice President's, Chas. Biddles.—Drank Tea at Mr. Powels.

Friday 14th.

Attended Convention.—Dined at the City Tavern, at an entertainmt. given on my acct. by the City light Horse.—Spent the evening at Mr. Meridiths.—

Saturday 15th.

Concluded the business of Convention all to signing the proceedings; to effect which the House sat till 6 O'clock, and adjourned till Monday that the Constitution which it was proposed to offer to the People might be engrossed—and a number of printed copies struck off.—Dined at Mr. Morris's & spent the evening there.

Mr. Gardoqui set off for returned to New York this forenoon.—

Sunday—16th.

Wrote many letters in the forenoon—Dined with Mr. & Mrs. Morris at the Hills & returned to town in the Eveng.

Monday. 17th.

Met in Convention when the Consti.

George Washington's diary, September 13–18, 1787, in which he recorded his reactions during the final days of the convention.

tution received the unanimous assent of 11 States and Colo. Hamilton's
from New York (the only delegate
from thence in Convention) and
was subscribed to by every Member present except Govr. Randolph
and Colo. Mason from Virginia – &
Mr. Gerry from Massachusetts. –
The business being thus closed, the
Members adjourned to the City Tavern, dined together and took a
cordial leave of each other. –
after which I returned to my lod-
gings – did some business with, and
received the papers from the secretary of the Convention, and retired
to meditate on the momentous wk.
which had been executed, after
not less than five, for a large part
of the time Six, and sometimes 7
hours sitting every day, sundays
& the ten days adjournment to
give a Comee. opportunity & time to
arrange the business for more than
four Months. –

Tuesday 18th.

Finished what private business
I had to do in the City this forenoon
– took my leave of those families
in wch. I had been most intimate
50
dined

Near the end of the signing, Franklin observed to nearby colleagues that he had noticed a sun and its rays were represented on the back of the president's chair. Throughout the vicissitudes of the convention, he said he had been unable to tell whether it was a rising or setting sun. But now, with the signing of the Constitution, he declared "I have the happiness to know that it is a rising and not a setting Sun."

The signing completed, about 4 p.m. the convention adjourned *sine die,* or indefinitely. The delegates walked over to the City Tavern for a final dinner and farewells. The question of public response to their work now became the leading issue in the nation.

The Approved Document

The Constitution—which ultimately emerged from the crucible of debate and conflicting interests—was a bundle of compromises and an imperfect instrument. Of the 39 delegates who subscribed to it, few expressed complete satisfaction with their work. And some even doubted it would endure. The public was even less sanguine. The advocates of the instrument labored for nearly a year before enough states ratified it and made it the law of the land. Yet, once the document went into effect, it soon became the pride and bulwark of the republic.

In most respects, the Constitution sprang from the American colonial, Revolutionary, and Confederation experiences. For example, the idea that a nation was bound by a constitution that limited and defined the powers of government had long been part of the English political consciousness. But, beginning with the colonial charters, Americans preferred written constitutions, which both citizens and officials could refer to for guidance. Liberties were not to be trusted to the benevolence of rulers, and the discretion of magistrates and legislators was to be restricted to fixed principles. Government was regarded as a necessary evil that needed to be circumscribed.

In other words, the basic institutions of constitutionalism were being established long before the War for Independence and the drafting of the first state constitutions (1775–80), the Articles of Confederation (1778), and federal Constitution (1787). These institutions were reflected in the royal charters, concessions by the king and royal proprietors, and legislative acts initiated by the people's representatives. All these recognized the basic importance of personal liberties in written form.

The system of checks and balances, which the framers utilized to prevent the dominance of any one branch of the government over any other and to maintain stability between the states and the national

We have the heart-felt pleaſure to inform our fellow citizens that the Fœderal Convention adjourned yeſterday, having completed the object of their deliberations—And we hear that Major W. Jackſon, the ſecretary of that honorable body, leaves this city for New-York, this morning, in order to lay the great reſult of their proceedings before the United States in Congreſs.

A correſpondent expreſſes his concern, that any propoſition ſhould have been made in the general aſſembly, for opening and prolonging the time for officers and ſoldiers to draw their donation lands, beyond the time allowed by law; he fears it will make many delay their application, on account of the advance they muſt make for the ſurveying fees—and at laſt be ſhut out; for certainly the meaſure will never be adopted by the legiſlature, as the ſame principle would unqueſtionably go to open again the door to the accounts for depreciation, and other numerous claims upon the public, which are barred and excluded by this ſtate, and by the United States.

A Mezzotinto Print of His Excellency GENERAL WASHINGTON, done by CHARLES WILSON PEALE of Philadelphia, from a portrait which he has painted ſince the ſitting of the Convention, is now compleated: the likeneſs is eſteemed the beſt that has been executed in a print.——This is one of an intended ſeries of prints, to be taken from Mr. Peale's collection of portraits of illuſtrious perſons, diſtinguiſhed in the late revolution. Thoſe of His Excellency Doctor Franklin and the honorable the Marquis de la Fayette, have been already publiſhed.

The price of theſe prints, in a neat oval frame, (the inner frame gilt) is two dollars each, or one dollar for the print only: and a large allowance will be made to thoſe who purchaſe to ſell again.—Apply to Charles W. Peale, at the corner of Third and Lombard ſtreets, Philadelphia.

, The printers in the ſeveral ſtates, who are deſirous of encouraging the fine arts in America, are requeſted to publiſh this as an article of intelligence; which will oblige the numerous friends of the General.

The ſtates of Holland and Weſt Frieſland have, in anſwer to the baron de Thulemeyer, miniſter to the king of Pruſſia, declared, that they, as ſovereign of the province, always ſhould act for the good of their country, and make no alterations in any of their reſolutions, by paying regard to the threats or intreaties of any foreign power whatſoever.

By private letters from Holland, dated July 22, 1787, we are informed, "that propoſitions are preſented to different towns and provinces to re-eſtabliſh the old conſtitution ſo far that the ſovereigns in every province ſhall chuſe officers for the ſea and land ſervices and never to ſet an upper admiral or general over them, but ſtate deputies will be appointed with the ſecret orders of the ſovereign in the fleets and in the armies—and the government in the ſeveral towns to be choſen by the votes of the citizens and the Gildens, which are the ſocieties of tradeſmen of every denomination. At the ſame time there ſhall be a general congreſs to rectify the abuſes crept from time to time into the different parts of government, when without partiality the offſpring of ancient families will be choſen, if they by their abilities and good conduct deſerve it; and others for their capacities though of foreign extraction, provided they have had their reſidence in the country the time which the law requires, will with equal impartiality be elected. Thus the ſtates will without mediation of foreigners, ſettle their differences by their ſea and land forces, with their command of money, which is very properly called the nerves of a long war, and the ſucceſsful means of inducing every German to engage with ſpirit in the ſervice of thoſe patriots, who will ſet them the example in fighting in the glorious cauſe of liberty, as his Britannic majeſty and miniſters experienced in the late war when they were paid and hired to ſerve tyranny and oppreſſion, but afterwards ſhewed their fond love for liberty by their deſertion and flying at once from Engliſh ſervice and German ſlavery. Thus will the republic of Netherland (for their proſperity has always been envied by nations and kings) ſettle their own affairs, and eſtabliſh their liberty and independence on a ſolid foundation.

, The American Philoſophical Society will hold a ſpecial meeting This Evening, the 18th inſt about 7 o'clock, at the houſe of his excellency Dr Franklin. The buſineſs requires a general attendance of members.
Sept. 18. SAMUEL MAGAW, Secretary.

Univerſity of Pennſylvania,
Auguſt 20, 1787.
The Medical Lectures
will begin on the firſt Monday of November.

Robert Baſs,

HAS this day imported in the Harmony, Captain Willet, from London, a ſmall Caſe of pure, genuine

Red Peruvian Bark.

He will receive by the next veſſel from London, a full ſupply of freſh Drugs, Medicines, and Shop Furniture, to compleat his aſſortment till next ſpring.
Sept. 18 eotf

To be Seen near the new Chapel,

A young Kitten,

Of the brutal creation; the head and ſhoulders like a cat, the hind parts like a rabbet, and has two tails. Children one penny, almoſt grown children 2d. gentlemen and ladies what they pleaſe. *Sept 17* r

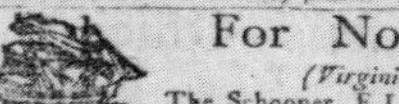

For Norfolk,
(Virginia)
The Schooner ELEANOR,
John Burke, Maſter;

TO ſail in five days. For freight or paſſage apply to the Maſter on board, at Fiſher's wharf, or to
Sept 18 5ſp DEAVES, BAKER & ABELL.

FIRST NOTICE.
In the Caſe of Joſeph Deane,
BANKRUPT.

WHEREAS a commiſſion of bankrupt is awarded and iſſued forth againſt *Joſeph Deane*, of the city of Philadelphia, merchant; and he being declared a bankrupt, is hereby required to ſurrender himſelf to the commiſſioners in the ſaid commiſſion named, or the major part of them, on *Tueſday* the 18th day of September inſt. on *Thurſday* the 11th day of October following, and on *Monday* the 29th day of the ſame month, at 10 o'clock in the forenoon of each of the ſaid days, at the State-houſe in the city of Philadelphia, and make a full diſcovery and diſcloſure of his eſtate and effects; when and where the creditors are to come prepared to prove their debts: at the ſecond meeting to chuſe aſſignees; and at the laſt meeting the ſaid bankrupt is required to finiſh his examination.

All perſons indebted to the ſaid bankrupt, or who have any of his effects, are not to pay or deliver the ſame but to whom the commiſſioners ſhall appoint, but give notice to the ſubſcriber.

By Order of the Commiſſioners,
JOHN JENNINGS, Clerk.
Office, in Watkins's alley, Sept. 17, 1787. 18 8.21

THOSE gentlemen who are appointed to receive ſubſcriptions for the encouragement of American manufactures, are requeſted to collect the money ſubſcribed, and to pay whatſoever monies they may have received, into the hands of John Nixon, eſquire, treaſurer, as ſoon as poſſible.
By direction of the Board.
GEO. FOX, Sec'ry.

For *LONDON*,
The Ship HARMONY,
John Willett, Maſter;

FOR freight or paſſage apply to the Commander on board at Meaſe's wharf, or to
Sept 15 d *MORDECAI LEWIS & CO.*

Iriſh Linens,

Juſt arrived in the Harmony and Pigou from London, and for SALE by

***Roſs* and *Vaughan*.**

September 15

This Day is PUBLISHED, by

Prichard & Hall,

And to be had at *Prichard*'s Book-Store and Circulating Library, in Market ſtreet,
(*Neatly bound and lettered—Price* 3/9)
THE
***ALGERINE* SPY**
In Pennſylvania:
Being the epiſtolary correſpondence between Mehemet, the *ſecret deputy* from the ſublime Porte, reſident in

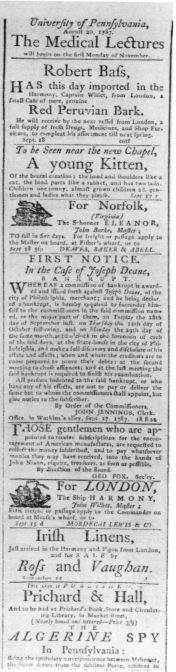

A Philadelphia newspaper's account of the adjournment of the convention.

We the People of the United States, in Order to form a more perfect Union, establish Justice, insure domestic Tranquility, provide for the common defence, promote the general Welfare, and secure the Blessings of Liberty to ourselves and our Posterity, do ordain and establish this Constitution for the United States of America.

Article I

Section 1. All legislative Powers herein granted shall be vested in a Congress of the United States, which shall consist of a Senate and House of Representatives.

Constitution of the United States

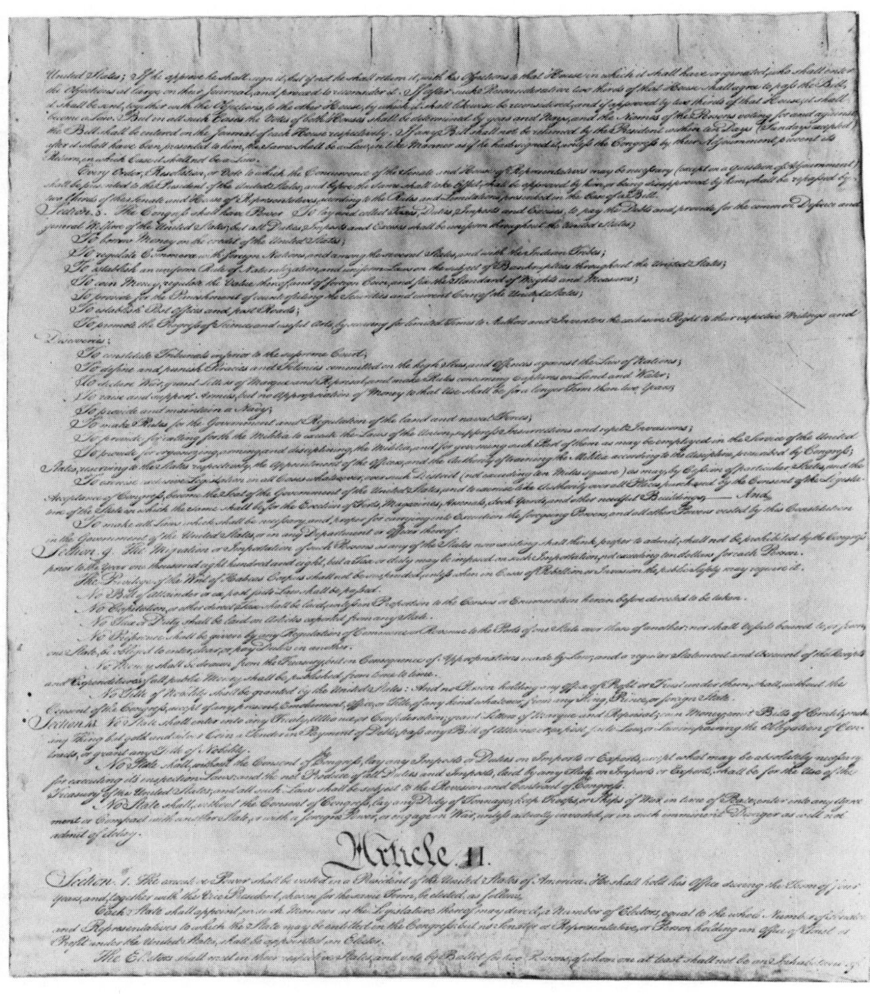

Constitution of the United States

the same State with themselves. And they shall make a List of all the Persons voted for, and of the Number of Votes for each; which List they shall sign and certify, and transmit sealed to the Seat of the Government of the United States, directed to the President of the Senate. The President of the Senate shall, in the Presence of the Senate and House of Representatives, open all the Certificates, and the Votes shall then be counted. The Person having the greatest Number of Votes shall be the President, if such Number be a Majority of the whole Number of Electors appointed; and if there be more than one who have such Majority, and have an equal Number of Votes, then the House of Representatives shall immediately chuse by Ballot one of them for President; and if no Person have a Majority, then from the five highest on the List the said House shall in like Manner chuse the President. But in chusing the President, the Votes shall be taken by States, the Representation from each State having one Vote; A quorum for this Purpose shall consist of a Member or Members from two thirds of the States, and a Majority of all the States shall be necessary to a Choice. In every Case, after the Choice of the President, the Person having the greatest Number of Votes of the Electors shall be the Vice President. But if there should remain two or more who have equal Votes, the Senate shall chuse from them by Ballot the Vice President.

The Congress may determine the Time of chusing the Electors, and the Day on which they shall give their Votes; which Day shall be the same throughout the United States.

No Person except a natural born Citizen, or a Citizen of the United States, at the time of the Adoption of this Constitution, shall be eligible to the Office of President; neither shall any Person be eligible to that Office who shall not have attained to the Age of thirty five Years, and been fourteen Years a Resident within the United States.

In Case of the Removal of the President from Office, or of his Death, Resignation, or Inability to discharge the Powers and Duties of the said Office, the Same shall devolve on the Vice President, and the Congress may by Law provide for the Case of Removal, Death, Resignation or Inability, both of the President and Vice President, declaring what Officer shall then act as President, and such Officer shall act accordingly, until the Disability be removed, or a President shall be elected.

The President shall, at stated Times, receive for his Services, a Compensation, which shall neither be encreased nor diminished during the Period for which he shall have been elected, and he shall not receive within that Period any other Emolument from the United States, or any of them.

Before he enter on the Execution of his Office, he shall take the following Oath or Affirmation:—"I do solemnly swear (or affirm) that I will faithfully execute the Office of President of the United States, and will to the best of my Ability, preserve, protect and defend the Constitution of the United States."

Section. 2. The President shall be Commander in Chief of the Army and Navy of the United States, and of the Militia of the several States, when called into the actual Service of the United States; he may require the Opinion, in writing, of the principal Officer in each of the executive Departments, upon any Subject relating to the Duties of their respective Offices, and he shall have Power to grant Reprieves and Pardons for Offences against the United States, except in Cases of Impeachment.

He shall have Power, by and with the Advice and Consent of the Senate, to make Treaties, provided two thirds of the Senators present concur; and he shall nominate, and by and with the Advice and Consent of the Senate, shall appoint Ambassadors, other public Ministers and Consuls, Judges of the supreme Court, and all other Officers of the United States, whose Appointments are not herein otherwise provided for, and which shall be established by Law: but the Congress may by Law vest the Appointment of such inferior Officers, as they think proper, in the President alone, in the Courts of Law, or in the Heads of Departments.

The President shall have Power to fill up all Vacancies that may happen during the Recess of the Senate, by granting Commissions which shall expire at the End of their next Session.

Section. 3. He shall from time to time give to the Congress Information of the State of the Union, and recommend to their Consideration such Measures as he shall judge necessary and expedient; he may, on extraordinary Occasions, convene both Houses, or either of them, and in Case of Disagreement between them, with Respect to the Time of Adjournment, he may adjourn them to such Time as he shall think proper; he shall receive Ambassadors and other public Ministers; he shall take Care that the Laws be faithfully executed, and shall Commission all the Officers of the United States.

Section. 4. The President, Vice President and all civil Officers of the United States, shall be removed from Office on Impeachment for, and Conviction of, Treason, Bribery, or other high Crimes and Misdemeanors.

Article III.

Section. 1. The judicial Power of the United States, shall be vested in one supreme Court, and in such inferior Courts as the Congress may from time to time ordain and establish. The Judges, both of the supreme and inferior Courts, shall hold their Offices during good Behaviour, and shall, at stated Times, receive for their Services, a Compensation, which shall not be diminished during their Continuance in Office.

Section. 2. The judicial Power shall extend to all Cases, in Law and Equity, arising under this Constitution, the Laws of the United States, and Treaties made, or which shall be made, under their Authority;—to all Cases affecting Ambassadors, other public Ministers and Consuls;—to all Cases of admiralty and maritime Jurisdiction;—to Controversies to which the United States shall be a Party;—to Controversies between two or more States;—between a State and Citizens of another State;—between Citizens of different States,—between Citizens of the same State claiming Lands under Grants of different States, and between a State, or the Citizens thereof, and foreign States, Citizens or Subjects.

In all Cases affecting Ambassadors, other public Ministers and Consuls, and those in which a State shall be Party, the supreme Court shall have original Jurisdiction. In all the other Cases before mentioned, the supreme Court shall have appellate Jurisdiction, both as to Law and Fact, with such Exceptions, and under such Regulations as the Congress shall make.

The Trial of all Crimes, except in Cases of Impeachment, shall be by Jury; and such Trial shall be held in the State where the said Crimes shall have been committed; but when not committed within any State, the Trial shall be at such Place or Places as the Congress may by Law have directed.

Section. 3. Treason against the United States, shall consist only in levying War against them, or in adhering to their Enemies, giving them Aid and Comfort. No Person shall be convicted of Treason unless on the Testimony of two Witnesses to the same overt Act, or on Confession in open Court.

The Congress shall have Power to declare the Punishment of Treason, but no Attainder of Treason shall work Corruption of Blood, or Forfeiture except during the Life of the Person attainted.

Article IV.

Section. 1. Full Faith and Credit shall be given in each State to the public Acts, Records, and judicial Proceedings of every other State. And the

Constitution of the United States

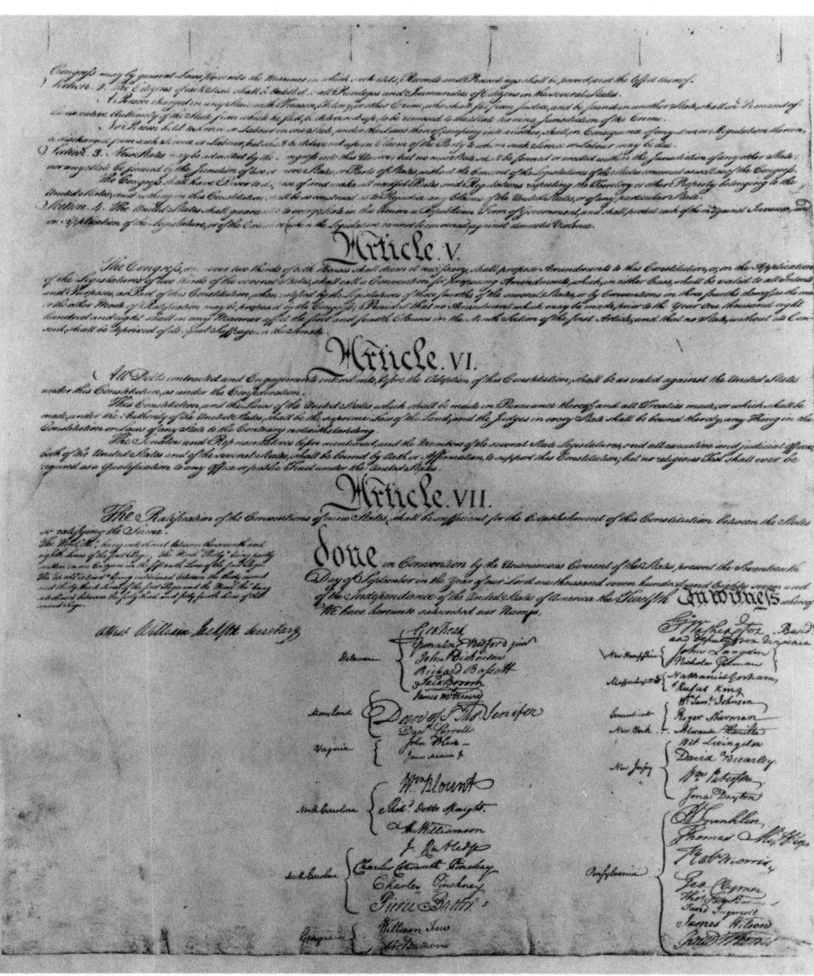

Article. V.

Article. VI.

Article. VII.

Constitution of the United States

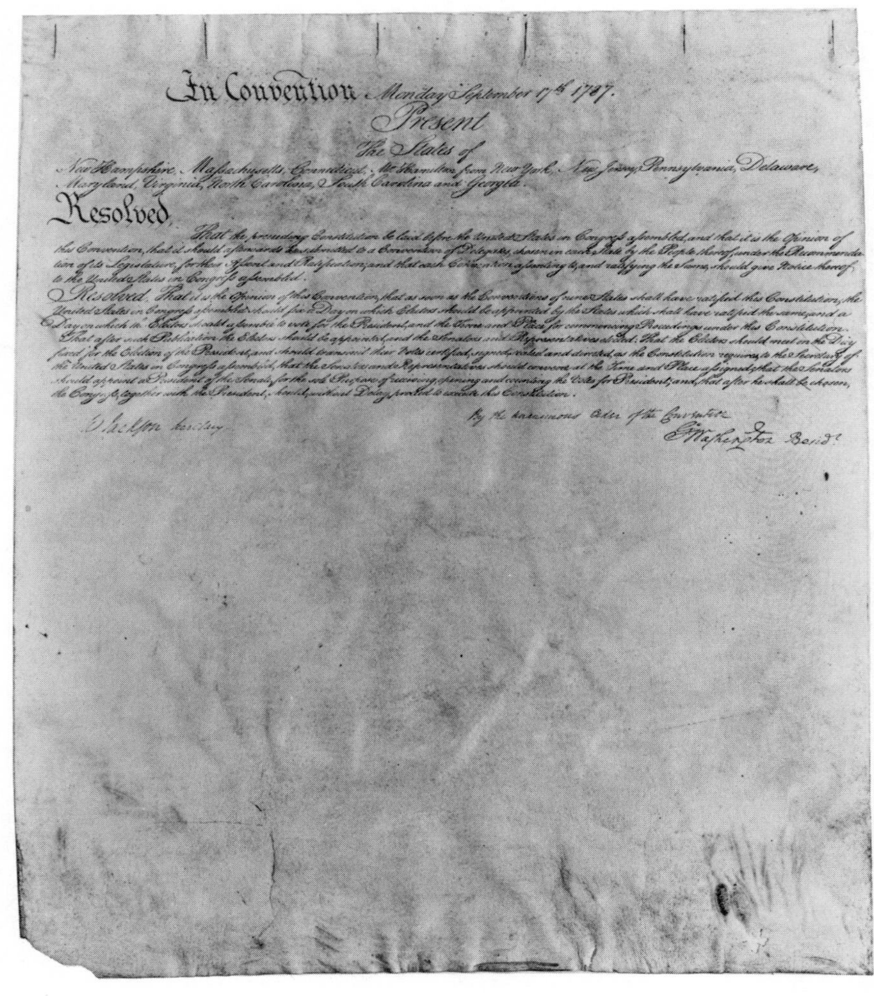

In Convention Monday September 17th 1787.

Present

The States of

New Hampshire, Massachusetts, Connecticut, Mr. Hamilton from New York, New Jersey, Pennsylvania, Delaware, Maryland, Virginia, North Carolina, South Carolina and Georgia.

Resolved,

That the preceding Constitution be laid before the United States in Congress assembled, and that it is the Opinion of this Convention, that it should afterwards be submitted to a Convention of Delegates, chosen in each State by the People thereof, under the Recommendation of its Legislature, for their Assent and Ratification; and that each Convention assenting to, and ratifying the Same, should give Notice thereof to the United States in Congress assembled.

Resolved, That it is the Opinion of this Convention, that as soon as the Conventions of nine States shall have ratified this Constitution, the United States in Congress assembled should fix a Day on which Electors should be appointed by the States which shall have ratified the same, and a Day on which the Electors should assemble to vote for the President, and the Time and Place for commencing Proceedings under this Constitution. That after such Publication the Electors should be appointed, and the Senators and Representatives elected: That the Electors should meet on the Day fixed for the Election of the President, and should transmit their Votes certified, signed, sealed and directed, as the Constitution requires, to the Secretary of the United States in Congress assembled, that the Senators and Representatives should convene at the Time and Place assigned; that the Senators should appoint a President of the Senate, for the sole Purpose of receiving, opening and counting the Votes for President; and, that after he shall be chosen, the Congress, together with the President, should, without Delay, proceed to execute this Constitution.

By the unanimous Order of the Convention

W. Jackson Secretary

G° Washington Presid^t

Constitution of the United States

government, was traceable to the ideas of the French political theorist Baron de Montesquieu and to the English conception that a balance of power among the king, the aristocracy, and the House of Commons prevented the undue ascendancy of any one group or majority. Also affecting the Constitution were other aspects of English law and thought, especially the ideas of John Locke. Included among those was the belief of apostles of the Enlightenment that natural laws governed man as well as the universe. Various additional European influences and Greek and Roman political concepts also made their mark on the Constitution.

Within that framework, however, the instrument was the product of a body of men who were experienced in self-government and were practical politicians. Confronting a definite and unique situation, for the most part they shunned abstract political speculation, though they drew on the lessons of history and political theroy. Principle, expedience, and compromise all played roles, and their interplay was incredibly complex. A new frame of government was created that in its totality embodied much that was unprecedented and that has served as a model for constitutions since established by various other countries.

Considering all the difficulties they encountered in fashioning the Constitution, its makers could not conceivably have covered all basic topics or treated those they did cover without ambiguity. In many cases, the ambiguity was deliberate to prevent further disagreement in the convention.

Above all, the framers could not be expected to be visionary enough to foresee and address all major matters that might be of future concern to the United States, especially subsequent political, economic, and social complexities. Many questions were left to be arbitrated and answered over the course of time. For example, the founders did not furnish mechanisms for the acquisition of new territory, establish specific terms for the admission of new states, specify the number of judges who would sit on the Supreme Court, or indicate what major departments should be created. While the framers extended the powers of Congress by specific grants to the maximum degree they felt was safe, by means of the elastic "general welfare" and "necessary and proper" clauses they made possible augmentation of the enumerated powers of Congress. The broad definition of presidential responsibilities has also allowed a similar amplification. To provide for reform, omissions, unforeseen factors, and changes, the Founding Fathers offered a system of amendments.

Other revisions or additions have been made by legislation or custom—in the "Unwritten Constitution." This includes such elements as the power of the Supreme Court to decide on the constitutionality of federal and state laws, a practice implied in the Constitution but originated by Chief Justice John Marshall, and the establishment of the presidential cabinet, a group of advisers made up of the heads

(55)

London. Nov. 10. 1787

My dear Sir

Mr Boylston is going to Paris, with a Cargo of Sperma Caeti oil, and will be obliged to you for any assistance or advice you can give him.

I forwarded a few days ago, from Mr Gerry, a Copy as I suppose of the Result of Convention. — It seems to be admirably calculated to preserve the Union, to increase affection, and to bring us all to the same mode of thinking. They have adopted the Idea of the Congress at Albany in 1754 of a President to nominate officers and a Council to Consent: but thank heaven they have adopted a third Branch, which that Congress did not. I think that Senates and assemblies should have nothing to do with executive Power. But still I hope the Constitution will be adopted, and Amendments be made at a more convenient opportunity.

5888

Writing to Thomas Jefferson from London, John Adams praised the results of the convention but acknowledged the need for amendments.

of executive departments. The 22d amendment, which prohibits the President from serving more than two terms, is an example of a custom once part of the unwritten Constitution that has been incorporated into the document.

This elasticity, or capacity for expansion, while making it certain that interpretation of the Constitution would generate disputation over the years, has at the same time allowed it to adjust to changing circumstances and endure throughout the decades.

During that time, the instrument, one of the oldest written charters of government, has won the laudation of the world. British Prime Minister William Gladstone effusively called it the "most wonderful work ever struck off at a given time by the brain and purpose of man." William Pitt, the younger, who had occupied the same office, said the document would be the "pattern for all future constitutions and the admiration of all future ages." But signer Robert Morris provided a more realistic appraisal: "While some have boasted [the Constitution] as a work from Heaven, others have given it a less righteous origin. I have many reasons to believe that it is the work of plain, honest men, and such, I think, it will appear."

WORKING late on the night of September 17 and possibly into the morning hours to make the final revisions in the type he had been holding since September 13, the printer had available for Secretary Jackson on the morning of the 18th a large quantity, apparently 500, of official 6-page copies of the Constitution. For about a day, this version, which contained one error (1708 instead of 1808 in Article V), was the only printed one.

Secretary Jackson departed on the morning of the 18th for New York, where he arrived the next afternoon. The following day, he transmitted to Secretary Charles Thomson of the Continental Congress the engrossed copy of the Constitution; the accompanying documents, including George Washington's letter of transmittal; and, undoubtedly, the official printed copies. That same day, the engrossed or one of the printed copies was read to Congress, but it took no action and set the 26th as the day on which the instrument would be considered.

Meantime, the Constitution had apparently been read to the public for the first time, and the Philadelphia newspapers had been busy. At the September 18 meeting of the Pennsylvania assembly, in the east room on the second floor of Independence Hall, Speaker Thomas Mifflin read it before the legislators and numerous spectators. Although no copies have survived, possibly the *Evening Chronicle* published the document on Tuesday evening, September 18. All other five newspapers in the city definitely did the next day. Only the version in Dunlap & Claypoole's *Pennsylvania Packet* contained a "pure" text, for it included the 1708 error. All the other four renditions corrected this mistake and by error or design made additional changes, including those in abbreviation, spelling, and punctuation.

From these have stemmed a proliferation of printings, both in the United States and abroad, that have continued right up to the present day—in newspapers, magazines, broadsides, pamphlets, handbills, leaflets, almanacs, and books.

Ratification: Federalists vs. Antifederalists

In Article VII and in the fifth-page "resolution of transmittal" to the Continental Congress, the convention provided a procedure for making the Constitution the law of the land. Each state would call a convention, whose delegates would be elected by the voters. After nine of these groups ratified, the new government could begin operation.

On September 26, 1787, the Continental Congress, including 10 or 12 men who had been in attendance at Philadelphia, began considering the document. A vociferous minority of members raised numerous objections during 2 days of debate. They charged that the instrument was too sweeping and clearly exceeded the amendment of the Articles of Confederation that had been authorized, criticized omission of a bill of rights, and attacked various details. It was even proposed that a series of amendments be attached to the Constitution before it was submitted to the states. But on September 28 supporters and critics of adoption compromised on a noncommittal forwarding of the new governmental framework without change to the state legislatures, which were to set up the conventions. The copies sent to the states were apparently from a new printing that John Dunlap had subcontracted to John McLean (M'Lean), a New York City newspaper publisher.

DURING the yearlong political struggle that ensued in the states before the establishment of the new government, two distinct factions emerged. The advocates of the Constitution adopted the name "Federalists" and cleverly pinned on their opponents the label "Antifederalists," which had formerly described those who had fought against formation of the Confederation. Realizing that the "Anti" prefix placed them in the role of obstructionists and that they had no positive plan of their own to offer, the Antifederalists not only used the name reluctantly but also often tried to reject it and to transfer it to the Federalists, whom they claimed better deserved it.

The Pennſylvania Packet, *and Daily Advertiſer.*

[Price Four-Pence.] WEDNESDAY, September 19, 1787. [No. 2690.]

WE, the People of the United States, in order to form a more perfect Union, eſtabliſh Juſtice, inſure domeſtic Tranquility, provide for the common Defence, promote the General Welfare, and ſecure the Bleſſings of Liberty to Ourſelves and our Poſterity, do ordain and eſtabliſh this Conſtitution for the United States of America.

ARTICLE I.

Sect. 1. ALL legiſlative powers herein granted ſhall be veſted in a Congreſs of the United States, which ſhall conſiſt of a Senate and Houſe of Repreſentatives.

Sect. 2. The Houſe of Repreſentatives ſhall be compoſed of members choſen every ſecond year by the people of the ſeveral ſtates, and the electors in each ſtate ſhall have the qualifications requiſite for electors of the moſt numerous branch of the ſtate legiſlature.

No perſon ſhall be a repreſentative who ſhall not have attained to the age of twenty-five years, and been ſeven years a citizen of the United States, and who ſhall not, when elected, be an inhabitant of that ſtate in which he ſhall be choſen.

Repreſentatives and direct taxes ſhall be apportioned among the ſeveral ſtates which may be included within this Union, according to their reſpective numbers, which ſhall be determined by adding to the whole number of free perſons, including thoſe bound to ſervice for a term of years, and excluding Indians not taxed, three-fifths of all other perſons. The actual enumeration ſhall be made within three years after the firſt meeting of the Congreſs of the United States, and within every ſubſequent term of ten years, in ſuch manner as they ſhall by law direct. The number of repreſentatives ſhall not exceed one for every thirty thouſand, but each ſtate ſhall have at leaſt one repreſentative; and until ſuch enumeration ſhall be made, the ſtate of New-Hampſhire ſhall be entitled to chuſe three, Maſſachuſetts eight, Rhode-Iſland and Providence Plantations one, Connecticut five, New-York ſix, New-Jerſey four, Pennſylvania eight, Delaware one, Maryland ſix, Virginia ten, North-Carolina five, South-Carolina five, and Georgia three.

When vacancies happen in the repreſentation from any ſtate, the Executive authority thereof ſhall iſſue writs of election to fill ſuch vacancies.

The Houſe of Repreſentatives ſhall chuſe their Speaker and other officers; and ſhall have the ſole power of impeachment.

Sect. 3. The Senate of the United States ſhall be compoſed of two ſenators from each ſtate, choſen by the legiſlature thereof, for ſix years; and each ſenator ſhall have one vote.

Immediately after they ſhall be aſſembled in conſequence of the firſt election, they ſhall be divided as equally as may be into three claſſes. The ſeats of the ſenators of the firſt claſs ſhall be vacated at the expiration of the ſecond year, of the ſecond claſs at the expiration of the fourth year, and of the third claſs at the expiration of the ſixth year, ſo that one-third may be choſen every ſecond year; and if vacancies happen by reſignation, or otherwiſe, during the receſs of the Legiſlature of any ſtate, the Executive thereof may make temporary appointments until the next meeting of the Legiſlature, which ſhall then fill ſuch vacancies.

No perſon ſhall be a ſenator who ſhall not have attained to the age of thirty years, and been nine years a citizen of the United States, and who ſhall not, when elected, be an inhabitant of that ſtate for which he ſhall be choſen.

The Vice-Preſident of the United States ſhall be Preſident of the ſenate, but ſhall have no vote, unleſs they be equally divided.

The Senate ſhall chuſe their other officers, and alſo a Preſident pro tempore, in the abſence of the Vice-Preſident, or when he ſhall exerciſe the office of Preſident of the United States.

The Senate ſhall have the ſole power to try all impeachments. When ſitting for that purpoſe, they ſhall be on oath or affirmation. When the Preſident of the United States is tried, the Chief Juſtice ſhall preſide: And no perſon ſhall be convicted without the concurrence of two-thirds of the members preſent.

Judgment in caſes of impeachment ſhall not extend further than to removal from office, and diſqualification to hold and enjoy any office of honor, truſt or profit under the United States; but the party convicted ſhall nevertheleſs be liable and ſubject to indictment, trial, judgment and puniſhment, according to law.

Sect. 4. The times, places and manner of holding elections for ſenators and repreſentatives, ſhall be preſcribed in each ſtate by the legiſlature thereof; but the Congreſs may at any time by law make or alter ſuch regulations, except as to the places of chuſing Senators.

The Congreſs ſhall aſſemble at leaſt once in every year, and ſuch meeting ſhall be on the firſt Monday in December, unleſs they ſhall by law appoint a different day.

Sect. 5. Each houſe ſhall be the judge of the elections, returns and qualifications of its own members, and a majority of each ſhall conſtitute a quorum to do buſineſs; but a ſmaller number may adjourn from day to day, and may be authoriſed to compel the attendance of abſent members, in ſuch manner, and under ſuch penalties as each houſe may provide.

Each houſe may determine the rules of its proceedings, puniſh its members for diſorderly behaviour, and, with the concurrence of two-thirds, expel a member.

Each houſe ſhall keep a journal of its proceedings, and from time to time publiſh the ſame, excepting ſuch parts as may in their judgment require ſecrecy; and the yeas and nays of the members of either houſe on any queſtion ſhall, at the deſire of one-fifth of thoſe preſent, be entered on the journal.

Neither houſe, during the ſeſſion of Congreſs, ſhall, without the conſent of the other, adjourn for more than three days, nor to any other place than that in which the two houſes ſhall be ſitting.

Sect. 6. The ſenators and repreſentatives ſhall receive a compenſation for their ſervices, to be aſcertained by law, and paid out of the treaſury of the United States. They ſhall in all caſes, except treaſon, felony and breach of the peace, be privileged from arreſt during their attendance at the ſeſſion of their reſpective houſes, and in going to and returning from the ſame; and for any ſpeech or debate in either houſe, they ſhall not be queſtioned in any other place.

No ſenator or repreſentative ſhall, during the time for which he was elected, be appointed to any civil office under the authority of the United States, which ſhall have been created, or the emoluments whereof ſhall have been encreaſed during ſuch time; and no perſon holding any office under the United States, ſhall be a member of either houſe during his continuance in office.

Sect. 7. All bills for raiſing revenue ſhall originate in the houſe of repreſentatives; but the ſenate may propoſe or concur with amendments as on other bills.

Every bill which ſhall have paſſed the houſe of repreſentatives and the ſenate, ſhall, before it become a law, be preſented to the preſident of the United States; if he approve he ſhall ſign it, but if not he ſhall return it, with his objections to that houſe in which it ſhall have originated, who ſhall enter the objections at large on their journal, and proceed to reconſider it. If after ſuch reconſideration two-thirds of that houſe ſhall agree to paſs the bill, it ſhall be ſent, together with the objections, to the other houſe, by which it ſhall likewiſe be reconſidered, and if approved by two-thirds of that houſe, it ſhall become a law. But in all ſuch caſes the votes of both houſes ſhall

One of the first newspaper printings of the Constitution. It appeared in the *Pennsylvania Packet,* published by Dunlap & Claypoole, who were also the official printers for the convention.

With good reason. The so-called Antifederalists were not really opposed to a federation; and many of them, especially those who advocated immediate amendment of the Constitution, believed they were the true defenders of the federal system. Most of them favored preservation of the Confederation. One of their strongest objections to the Constitution was that, in their minds, it established a national rather than a federal government. For these reasons, they made a vain attempt to claim the Federalist name, which they sometimes even employed in the titles of their tracts or in the pseudonyms they frequently attached to them.

Thus, the two terms are grossly misleading. The Federalists might more aptly have been called "Centralists" or "Nationalists" and the Antifederalists "Federalists" or "States righters." Furthermore, despite the bitterness of the ratification battles, the two designations imply a greater degree of basic antithesis than actually existed. Both sides sought an effective national government and safeguards against tyranny, but they differed on the efficacy of specific constitutional provisions in achieving those goals. Use of the two labels is also unfortunate in that it falsely indicates a compartmentalization that was lacking. Within each of the two camps, a wide range and strong shades of opinions were manifested and some people switched allegiance.

The composition of the two groups differed in practically every state. A host of geographical, economic, social, and political factors determined alignment. Although clear-cut divisions were blurred, the Federalists loosely encompassed those whose livelihoods were significantly linked to commerce, such as merchants, shippers, urban artisans, and farmers and planters residing near water transport, as well as members of the professions and creditors. All these groups were mainly concerned about the economic benefits and property safeguards against state actions a stronger central government would provide. Many of the leaders enjoyed national political experience and had served as officers during the War for Independence. Usually more worldly than their Antifederalist counterparts, many had been educated abroad and were more experienced in foreign affairs.

The Antifederalists tended to be more locally oriented. They included residents of isolated villages and towns, small farmers, frontiersmen, and debtors. These classes usually preferred maximum individual and local autonomy rather than the expansion of governmental power.

Exceptions to these generalizations, however, were numerous. All rich merchants and planters did not necessarily favor the Constitution, nor poor farmers and mechanics oppose it. Nor was the eastern seaboard totally Federalist and the West completely Antifederalist. Sometimes a healthy minority of divergent opinion existed among similar groups within a particular section of a state or region. Several Antifederalists were well-to-do creditors, and some Federalists were heavily in debt. Back-country farmers in Georgia, concerned about the Indian and Spanish threats, backed a powerful central government. Local circumstances also contributed to the Antifederalist stance of a number of large estate owners in the Hudson River area of New York State.

The Antifederalists were as a whole probably more democratic than the Federalists, but many of the leaders were members of the aristocracy and maintained reservations about democracy; ordinarily only the poorer and less sophisticated Antifederalists espoused it. But neither side used the word "democracy" very often. When the Federalists did so it was usually with scorn; and, when the Antifederalists did so, it was more likely with favor.

The Antifederalists were saddled with numerous disadvantages. They were not only less well organized and united than the opposition, but they were also on the defensive because they were objecting to a bold and comprehensive new plan of government. Many of them believed some changes in the Articles of Confederation were needed, especially in the field of commerce, but they could not effectively object to all those recommended in the Constitution.

The Antifederalists also had fewer leaders of national stature. They included only six men who had attended the Constitutional Convention: Luther Martin, John F. Mercer, Robert Yates, John Lansing, Jr., George Mason, and Elbridge Gerry. Only the latter two had stayed for its duration though they, too, had not signed the Constitution. Other members of the group were Richard Henry Lee and Benjamin Harrison of Virginia and Samuel Chase of Maryland, all signers of the Declaration of Independence; Gov. George Clinton of New York; and Patrick Henry and James Monroe of Virginia. Like Henry, Lee had been elected to but did not attend the convention. He chose not to do so because he felt it would be improper for members of the Continental Congress to take part. He was the author of a powerful statement of the Antifederalist case, *Letters From the Federal Farmer to the Republican.*

On the other hand, in the front rank of the Federalists were practically all the delegates to the convention, including every one of the signers of the Constitution, among them such preeminent men as Washington, Franklin, Madison, and Hamilton; Randolph, who switched over from the Antifederalist side; signer of the Declaration Benjamin Rush; and diplomat John Jay, Jr.

OBSERVATIONS

LEADING TO A FAIR EXAMINATION

OF THE

SYSTEM OF GOVERNMENT

PROPOSED BY THE LATE

CONVENTION;

AND TO SEVERAL ESSENTIAL AND NECESSARY ALTERATIONS IN IT.

IN A NUMBER OF

LETTERS

FROM THE

FEDERAL FARMER TO THE REPUBLICAN.

PRINTED IN THE YEAR M,DCCLXXVII.

Title page of the original edition (1787) of Richard Henry Lee's *Letters from the Federal Farmer to the Republican,* a leading Antifederalist tract.

The cohesive Federalists evolved a concrete program, conducted a vigorous and well-tuned campaign, and benefited from strong newspaper support. Skillfully presenting their case, they wisely chose to emphasize issues on which national consensus could easily be obtained and ignored those that would align section against section, rich against poor, or debtors against creditors. They also worked more quickly than their opponents and organized more effectively. They were more deft in parliamentary maneuvering at the ratifying conventions. The many compromises they had made in the creation of the Constitution made it more defensible and also more acceptable to various groups that might otherwise have opposed it.

But the Federalists, too, faced several problems. They needed to convince the country that a totally new frame of government was needed. And many of those they were trying to convince were not sufficiently aware of the nation's domestic and international problems and thus did not understand the need for and value of the remedies recommended. A large part of the populace, especially because of the recent clash with Britain, was opposed to any more change, to a strong central government, and to the imposition of too many controls on state and local governments. Then, too, these governments resented any augmentation of national power at their expense.

The Federalists also faced a significant handicap in that they needed to win the ratification contests in at least nine of the states, and particularly in the large and strategic states of Virginia and New York, as well as Massachusetts and Pennsylvania. The Antifederalists, on the other hand, could thwart the whole effort by winning any five states, and probably could accomplish the same if they won in either New York or Virginia.

The arguments of the Federalists and Antifederalists—voiced and written in speeches, letters to newspaper editors and others, tracts, pamphlets, and at the state conventions—ranged from the theoretical to the practical and from the low-keyed to the highly emotional. Regional, sectional, and individual differences were demonstrated.

The Antifederalists tended to defend the Articles of Confederation, though they felt they needed to be modified, or advocated a weak central government that would allow maximum participation of the people and ensure state sovereignty. Most Antifederalists insisted that conditions were not as desperate as the Federalists painted and questioned the need for a drastically new government. They felt the Constitution was too extreme a remedy for the problems of the Confederation. Thus, if they could not stop ratification of the document entirely, they committed themselves to its immediate revision by a second convention or by amendment.

Other fears were stressed: that many of the framers had ulterior motives, a charge that seemed plausible because of the secrecy of the convention and the rush to ratify the Constitution; that the proposed new government, especially with its strong executive and powerful Senate, would be more tyrannical than that of the British had been and would result in a monarchy or aristocratic rule; that, lacking a bill of rights, as the Constitution did, it would destroy personal liberties; that the checks and balances written into the document were insufficient to protect the rights of state and local governments; that power was being transferred from the many to the few to inhibit or prevent future political change and reform; and that the large states would overpower the small ones.

Patrick Henry, who had declined to serve in the convention because he "smelt a rat," began his objections with the first three words of the Constitution. Who, he wondered, were the delegates to say "We the People"? They should have said "We the States." Otherwise, the government would no longer be a compact among equal states but a "consolidated, national government of the people of all the states."

Another charge was that the convention had ignored or exceeded its instructions from Congress to amend the Articles of Confederation, had abandoned their federal basis, and violated procedures for their amendment with the nine-state ratification requirement. The Federalists were also accused of having ties with foreigners and with being sympathetic to a monarchy.

The Antifederalists rarely mentioned national security or foreign affairs. Even when they did, they did not deny Federalist arguments but contended that the good that might be gained in these fields by the Constitution would be offset by the disadvantages of such great central power and that amendments to the Articles of Confederation could bring about the necessary improvements. There would be enough time to provide an adequate defense once war broke out, and direct federal taxation could be resorted to if the old requisitioning system on the states failed to work.

Another point made by some Antifederalists was that a single government would be unable to rule a country as large and complex as the United States, which was far larger than any earlier federation, without becoming tyrannical. Regional confederations were considered to be more effective.

Some aversion to the Constitution was sectional in nature. For example, the southern states feared the commerce clause would allow the northeastern states, which owned and built most of the ships, to control their trade. The maritime states might obtain a monopoly by securing the passage of navigation laws restricting commerce to American ships or of tariffs unfavorable to the South. It was felt, too, that the Senate might use its treaty power to surrender free navigation of the Mississippi, which was critically important to the region, as well as to the West.

The Federalists, who asserted that the convention had followed the spirit of its congressional instructions, stressed the deficiencies in the Articles of Confederation. Viewing the Constitution as a workable compromise of divergent opinions and granting that it was not perfect, its advocates held that it was nevertheless vastly superior to the Articles and that subsequent amendments could purge its imperfections. Constitutional supporters, warning that delays in ratification would result in disastrous disunion and that a second convention would likely destroy the agreements already achieved, fought for quick and unconditional ratification.

Denying that the government they proposed would sweep aside states rights, the Federalists pointed out that all powers not specifically granted to it, like the protection of individual rights, were by implication state prerogatives; and that under any system of government large states could usually overpower small ones but that they would be less likely to do so within the framework of a friendly and voluntary union.

As a counter to Antifederalist charges that a federation would not work in such a huge country, the Federalists argued that the larger a federation was the less chance there would be that any of its members could dominate the others. Furthermore, the system devised at Philadelphia, they stated, was a balanced and federal structure in which no one institution or individual could gain undue dominance. It was, therefore, a judicious application of the principles of republicanism.

The Federalists wisely concentrated their fire on three practical issues with broad appeal. The first was national security, which most people agreed was weak under the Articles. Under that instrument, advocates of the Constitution said that, though the Continental Congress could declare war, it could not procure enough money and men to wage it. Direct taxation was required in wartime to obtain sufficient revenue. The standing army and navy the Constitution authorized could protect the country from invasion, enhance its prestige, discourage foreign intervention, and perhaps offer an opportunity to drive the British out of the posts in the Great Lakes area as well as to thwart Spanish designs in the Southwest. Some Federalists related the foreign-debt problem to national security. They held that the debt was a potential source of conflict and might result in attacks on U.S. commerce unless Congress was assured steady revenue, as it would be under the Constitution.

The second issue stressed by the Federalists was the bad economic situation, including the decline in shipbuilding and trade. They said this condition resulted primarily from the incapability of Congress to conclude favorable commercial treaties with other countries or to execute those it had negotiated. As a result, it was difficult to retaliate against foreign trade restrictions, especially those of the British, or to arrange for American instead of British ships to carry goods.

The Federalists related both the national security and commerce issues to congressional ineffectiveness in meeting its treaty commitments. Unless Congress could help British merchants collect the prewar debts owed to them by Americans, the British could use that excuse to continue occupying the Great Lakes posts. And Britain would likely not agree to a commercial treaty until Congress had the power to speak for all the states.

Third, the Federalists appealed to national pride. Referring to the insults inflicted on U.S. diplomats and appealing to the prevalent Anglophobia, they contended that the increased military power and governmental strength the Constitution afforded would enhance national prestige and elevate the United States in the eyes of other nations. If the document were not adopted, dissolution of the Union was likely and the states as independent entities would possess little power.

But perhaps the most simple and direct pleading of the Federalist cause was the letter Washington sent along with the Constitution when he submitted it to the Continental Congress. Its purpose, he wrote, was the "consolidation of our Union, in which is involved our prosperity, felicity, safety, perhaps our national existence."

ARGUMENTS were important, but the actual process of ratification involved practical politics. Some of the state battles were fierce. Reason sometimes yielded to passion and both sides on occasion resorted to mudslinging and rough-and-tumble tactics. Yet, for the most part, the conventions were democratically conducted.

Giving the Federalists an initial momentum, in December 1787 and January 1788 the conventions of five states promptly ratified the Constitution. In all these cases, opposition was either lacking or ratification action was quick enough to forestall it. The votes in Delaware (December 7), New Jersey (December 18), and Georgia (January 2) were unanimous. Before opposition could be organized, two-thirds of the Pennsylvania convention (December 12) balloted for ratification. The Constitution passed in Connecticut (January 9)

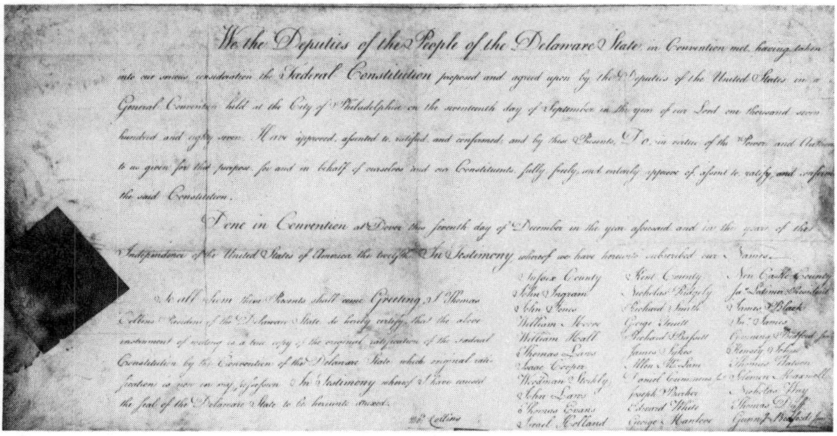

We the Deputies of the People of the Delaware State in Convention met having taken into our serious consideration the Federal Constitution proposed and agreed upon by the Deputies of the United States in a General Convention held at the City of Philadelphia on the seventeenth day of September in the year of our Lord one thousand seven hundred and eighty seven Have approved, assented to, ratified, and confirmed, and by these Presents, Do, in virtue of the Power and Authority to us given for that purpose, for and in behalf of ourselves and our Constituents, fully, freely, and entirely approve of, assent to, ratify, and confirm the said Constitution.

Done in Convention at Dover this seventh day of December in the year aforesaid and in the year of the Independence of the United States of America the twelfth. In Testimony whereof we have hereunto subscribed our Names.

Delaware, whose ratification notice is reproduced above, was the first state to approve the Constitution on December 7, 1787.

by a 3 to 1 margin. Except for Pennsylvania, where the vote may not have accurately indicated the opinion of the electorate because of the haste with which the convention was held, Federalist strength was overpowering in these states.

Between February 6 and June 21, 1788, four more conventions ratified the new instrument of government. The first major test came in Massachusetts. Although he was not a member of the convention, Elbridge Gerry, who had attended the Constitutional Convention for its duration but had refused to sign the document, led the Antifederalists. Federalist leaders included signers of the Constitution Rufus King and Nathaniel Gorham, as well as Caleb Strong. On February 6, after the popular John Hancock and Samuel Adams, both underwriters of the Declaration of Independence, converted to the Federalist cause, the convention narrowly (187–168) approved ratification, but it recommended nine amendments.

All the subsequent states except Maryland were also to propose amendments, many including recommendations for adoption of a bill of rights and a second convention. Exercise of the amendment technique, which obviously required compromise on the part of the Federalists, came at a time when in many places their opponents were suggesting the calling of another convention to consider amendments. Such action would probably have been chaotic, especially if certain states specified the adoption of particular amendments as a condition of ratification. Thus, for the Federalists, the Massachusetts action in merely proposing amendments provided a desirable precedent.

The New Hampshire convention convened in February 1788 but adjourned until June to allow time for further debate in the delegates' home districts. The tempo of ratification revived, however, when Maryland (April 28) and South Carolina (May 23) accepted the Constitution by substantial margins.

But people knew the real trials would come in the large states of Virginia and New York. Without their approval, the success of the new government would be jeopardized. Serious clashes occurred in both places and the votes were close. When the Virginia convention began on June 2, the pro-Federalist delegates believed that their state, the largest and most populous, would fittingly be the ninth to ratify and thus make possible inauguration of the new government.

Among those arguing the Antifederalist side were George Mason, Patrick Henry, and James Monroe. Their opponents included James Madison, John Marshall, George Wythe, and Edmund Pendleton, as well as Edmund J. Randolph after Madison won him over. One factor that apparently swung over some enemies of the Constitution was the belief that, if it were approved, Washington would likely be the first President. The vote in its favor, on June 26, was close, 89 to 79. But, meantime, 5 days earlier, New Hampshire, where the Federalists won another narrow victory, had become the ninth state to approve the Constitution. This was not known in Virginia until after the final vote there.

Another crucial race took place in New York, where the convention had been meeting since June 17. Hamilton was the chief strategist of the Federalists. Although he felt the Constitution granted insufficient power to the central government, he was convinced it was the best that could be obtained politically at that time. He did not publicly acknowledge the extent of his reservations and worked diligently and cleverly for adoption.

Hamilton conceived the idea of *The Federalist*. A series of 85 essays first published by the newspapers in 1787–88 and almost immediately reissued in book form, the papers presented one of the most effective statements of the Federalist position and carried considerable weight in the New York battle, as well as in Virginia. Although the essays were issued under a pseudonym, the actual authors were Hamilton, who probably wrote 51; Madison, 26; and John Jay, 5. Madison and Hamilton jointly wrote three.

Gov. George Clinton, who strongly urged a second federal convention, headed the New York Antifederalists. Other leaders were Robert

SUPPLEMENT
TO THE
Independent Journal,
New-York, July 2, 1788.

In our Independent Journal of this Morning, we announced the Ratification of the New Conſtitution by the Convention of Virginia: For the gratification of our Readers, we publiſh the following particulars, received by this day's poſt:—

Ratification of the New Conſtitution, by the Convention of Virginia, on Wedneſday laſt, by a Majority of 10:---88 for it, 78 againſt it.

WE the delegates of the people of Virginia, duly elected, in purſuance of a recommendation of the General Aſſembly, and now met in Convention, having fully and fairly inveſtigated and diſcuſſed the proceedings of the Federal Convention, and being prepared as well as the moſt mature deliberation will enable us to decide thereon, DO, in the name and on behalf of the people of Virginia, declare and make known, that the powers granted under the Conſtitution being derived from the people of the United States, may be reſumed by them whenſoever the ſame ſhall be perverted to their injury or oppreſſion, and that every power not granted thereby, remains with them, and at their will: That therefore no right, of any denomination, can be cancelled, abridged, reſtrained or modified by the Congreſs, by the Senate, or Houſe of Repreſentatives, acting in any capacity, by the Preſident, or any department or officer of the United States, except in thoſe inſtances where power is given by the Conſtitution for thoſe purpoſes: That among other eſſential rights, the liberty of conſcienee, and of the preſs, cannot be cancelled,, abridged, reſtrained or modified by any authority of the United States.

With theſe impreſſions, with a ſolemn appeal to the ſearcher of hearts for the purity of our intentions, and under the conviction, that whatſoever imperfections may exiſt in the Conſtitution, ought rather to be examined in the mode preſcribed therein, than to bring the UNION into danger by a delay, with a hope of obtaining amendments previous to the ratification:

We the ſaid delegates, in the name and in behalf of the people of Virginia, do by theſe preſents aſſent to and ratify the Conſtitution, recommended on the 17th day of September, 1787, by the Federal Convention, for the government of the United States; hereby announcing to all thoſe whom it may concern, that the ſaid Conſtitution is binding upon the ſaid people, according to an authentic copy hereto annexed, in the words following:—

[*Here followed a copy of the Conſtitution.*]

A letter from Richmond adviſes, "that a motion for previous amendments was rejected by a majority of EIGHT; but that ſome days would be paſſed in conſidering ſubſequent amendments, and theſe, it appeared, from the temper of the Convention, would be RECOMMENDED."

NEW-YORK: Printed by J. and A. M'LEAN, FRANKLIN'S HEAD, No. 41, Hanover-Square.

A New York City newspaper announces details of Virginia's ratification.

THE

FEDERALIST:

A COLLECTION

OF

ESSAYS,

WRITTEN IN FAVOUR OF THE

NEW CONSTITUTION,

AS AGREED UPON BY THE FEDERAL CONVENTION,
SEPTEMBER 17, 1787.

IN TWO VOLUMES.

VOL. I.

NEW-YORK:

PRINTED AND SOLD BY J. AND A. M'LEAN,
No. 41, HANOVER-SQUARE.
M,DCC,LXXXVIII.

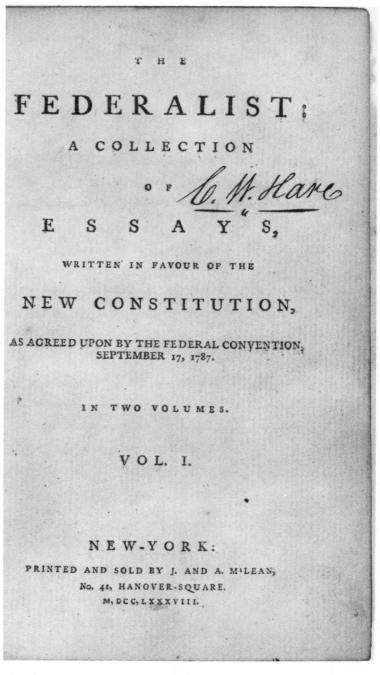

In a series of anonymous newspaper essays during 1787–88, soon published in book form (1788) as *The Federalist,* Alexander Hamilton, James Madison, and John Jay strongly advocated ratification of the Constitution.

Yates and John Lansing, Jr., who had left the Constitutional Convention early, at least partially because of objections to its nationalistic tenor.

Hamilton was forced to wage an uphill fight, characterized by threats and bargains. At the beginning of the convention, the Antifederalists were clearly in the majority, though New York City had sent a Federalist delegation. Hamilton, arguing that conditional ratification would endanger the state by keeping it out of the Union, fought a delaying action and managed to postpone a final vote until the anticipated news arrived that Virginia and New Hampshire had ratified. The balance of power then swung to the Federalists. On July 26, 1788, by a bare margin of 30–27 New York became the 11th state to ratify. But it appended the record number of 32 suggested amendments and sent along various other resolutions, including a vigorous recommendation for a second convention.

Two states that had printed large amounts of paper money and had been active in debtor relief, North Carolina and Rhode Island, did not ratify until after the new government was set up. On August 2, 1788, the former, unaware of the New York decision, overwhelmingly voted to defer action on the Constitution until a second federal convention considered a declaration of rights and other amendments. Influenced by the First Congress' proposal of the Bill of Rights and other factors, on November 21, 1789, a second North Carolina convention ratified the Constitution.

Rhode Island and Providence Plantations, which had been the lone absentee at the Philadelphia convention, stayed out of the Union until 1790. During that period, the legislature seven times defeated resolutions calling for a convention. Under threats of economic coercion by the federal government and the secession of Providence and other towns, on May 29, 1790, the state narrowly ratified. It was the last of the 13 original states to do so.

For all the passions generated by the ratification battles, most of the Antifederalists gracefully accepted defeat—though their efforts soon won the Bill of Rights. With that exception, they would give the Constitution an oppportunity to stand or fall on its own merits. With amendments, it has stood until this day.

The First Presidential Election

New Hampshire's ratification in June 1788 had fulfilled the nine-state requirement to establish the government. But, for various reasons, the Continental Congress did not take steps to do so until July 28, or 2 days after New York adopted the instrument. At that time, Congress, meeting in New York City, set dates for the selection and

8.

as they shall be declared, submitting it to the wisdom of this House to appoint one or more of its Members for the like purpose. And then he withdrew.

On motion, Resolved that Mr. Speaker attended by the House do now withdraw to the Senate chamber for the purpose expressed in the Message from the Senate, and that Mr. Parker and Mr. Heister be appointed on the part of this House to sit at the Clerks table with the Member of the Senate, and make a list of the Votes as the same shall be declared.

Mr. Speaker accordingly left the Chair, and attended by the House withdrew to the Senate chamber, and after some time returned into the House.

Mr. Speaker resumed the Chair.

Mr. Parker and Mr. Heister then delivered in at the Clerks table, a list of the votes of the Electors of the several States, in the choice of a President and Vice-President of the United States, as the same were declared by the President of the Senate in the presence of the Senate and this House, which was ordered to be entered on the Journal, and is as followeth;

	George Washington.	John Adams.	Samuel Huntington.	John Jay.	John Hancock.	Robert H. Harrison.	George Clinton.	John Rutledge.	John Milton.	James Armstrong.	Edward Telfair.	Benjamin Lincoln.
New Hampshire	5.	5										
Massachusetts	10.	10										
Connecticut	7.	5	2									
New Jersey	6.	1		5								
Pennsylvania	10.	8			2							
Delaware	3			3								
Maryland	6					6						
Virginia	10.	5		1	1		3					
South Carolina	7.				1			6				
Georgia	5								2	1	1	1
	69.	34.	2.	9.	4.	6.	3.	6.	2.	1.	1.	1.

The tally for the first Presidential election.

meeting of electors. In September it named New York City as the temporary capital.

Not restricted by specific constitutional requirements, the state legislatures chose the dates for the election of their representatives and senators and made arrangements for selecting electors. In accordance with the timetable fixed by the Continental Congress, on February 4, 1789, the presidential electors cast their ballots. The formal counting of the electoral votes was delayed pending the opening of the First Congress, which was scheduled to meet on March 4. But it was not until April 6 that Congress reached a quorum and began sitting at City (later Federal) Hall in New York City, where the Continental Congress had been meeting. That same day, the electoral votes were counted before a joint congressional session. George Washington was unanimously elected as President, and John Adams as Vice President. At Federal Hall on April 30 Washington was inaugurated. The new government, the creation of the Constitution, was underway.

All along the route, the populace paid tribute to George Washington as he traveled from Mount Vernon to his inauguration in New York City. Here is an artist's depiction of the salute he received in New York Harbor.

Washington's inauguration on the balcony of Federal Hall, New York City, April 30, 1789. This is the only known contemporary rendition of the event.

Amending the Constitution

Since 1787 the Constitution has been considerably modified to perfect, amplify, and keep it abreast of changing times. The main mechanisms have been amendments and judicial interpretation. The amending process is outlined in Article V of the Constitution. Amendments may be proposed to the states either by Congress, based on a two-thirds vote in both houses, or by a convention called by

Congress at the request of the legislatures of two-thirds of the states. Ratification requires the approval of three-fourths of the states, either by their legislatures or special conventions as Congress may direct. No national constitutional convention has ever been called, and the only amendment ratified by special state convention was the 21st.

The number of amendments to date totals 26, the first 10 of which (Bill of Rights) were enacted shortly after ratification of the original document. Those that have been accepted have survived a grueling process. Thousands of proposals for amendments of all sorts—praiseworthy and frivolous, realistic and impractical, even including suggestions for a virtually new Constitution—have been recommended over the years by congressmen, political scientists, and others. But these have either failed to win the favor of Congress or the states.

Of the successful amendments, some, reflecting changing national aspirations and mores as well as fundamental social transformations, have produced governmental reforms and social changes. Others have refined the constitutional structure for such purposes as democratizing the political system, improving its functioning, or relieving associated abuses. The first 10 amendments came into being because of fear of national governmental tyranny.

Except for the Bill of Rights, before World War I amendments were relatively rare. For 122 years after 1791, when the Bill of Rights was adopted, only five (two in the early years of the republic and three in the aftermath of the Civil War) were enacted—or an average of one about every 25 years. Since 1913, on the other hand, the nation has approved 11, or 1 every 5½ years or so. The increased frequency in recent times is doubtless to a considerable extent attributable to the rapidity of social and economic change.

The Bill of Rights

From the beginning regarded as virtually a part of the original Constitution, the Bill of Rights was mainly designed to prevent the federal government from infringing on the basic rights of citizens and the states. Essentially a reassertion of the traditional rights of Englishmen as modified and strengthened by the American experience, these measures had already been delineated in various forms—in the Northwest Ordinance of 1787; the declarations, or bills, of rights that had been adopted by most states, either separately or as part of their constitutions; the Declaration of Independence (1776); the Declaration of Rights that the First Continental Congress had issued in 1774; and early colonial manifestoes.

State of North-Carolina.

IN CONVENTION, AUGUST 1, 1788.

Reſolved, That a Declaration of Rights, aſſerting and ſecuring from incroachment the great Principles of civil and religious Liberty, and the unalienable Rights of the People, together with Amendments to the moſt ambiguous and exceptionable Parts of the ſaid Conſtitution of Government, ought to be laid before Congreſs, and the Convention of the States that ſhall or may be called for the Purpoſe of Amending the ſaid Conſtitution, for their conſideration, previous to the Ratification of the Conſtitution aforeſaid, on the part of the State of North Carolina.

DECLARATION OF RIGHTS.

1ſt That there are certain natural rights of which men, when they form a ſocial compact, cannot deprive or diveſt their poſterity, among which are the enjoyment of life, and liberty, with the means of acquiring, poſſeſſing and protecting property, and purſuing and obtaining happineſs and ſafety.

2d. That all power is naturally veſted in, and conſequently derived from the people; that magiſtrates therefore are their truſtees, and agents, and at all times amenable to them.

3d. That Government ought to be inſtituted for the common benefit, protection and ſecurity of the people; and that the doctrine of non-reſiſtance againſt arbitrary power and oppreſſion is abſurd, ſlaviſh, and deſtructive to the good and happineſs of mankind.

4th That no man or ſet of men are entitled to excluſive or ſeparate public emoluments or privileges from the community, but in conſideration of public ſervices; which not being deſcendible, neither ought the offices of magiſtrate, legiſlator or judge, or any other public office to be hereditary.

5th. That the legiſlative, executive and judiciary powers of government ſhould be ſeparate and diſtinct, and that the members of the two firſt may be reſtrained from oppreſſion by feeling and participating the public burthens, they ſhould at fixed periods be reduced to a private ſtation, return into the maſs of the people; and the vacancies be ſupplied by certain and regular elections; in which all or any part of the former members to be eligible or ineligible, as the rules of the Conſtitution of Government, and the laws ſhall direct.

6th. That elections of Repreſentatives in the legiſlature ought to be free and frequent, and all men having ſufficient evidence of permanent common intereſt with, and attachment to the community, ought to have the right of ſuffrage: and no aid, charge, tax or fee can be ſet, rated, or levied upon the people without their own conſent, or that of their repreſentatives, ſo elected, nor can they be bound by any law, to which they have not in like manner aſſented for the public good.

7th. That all power of ſuſpending laws, or the execution of laws by any authority without the conſent of the repreſentatives, of the people in the Legiſlature, is injurious to their rights, and ought not to be exerciſed.

8th. That in all capital and criminal proſecutions, a man hath a right to demand the cauſe and nature of his accuſation, to be confronted with the accuſers and witneſſes, to call for evidence and be allowed counſel in his favor, and to a fair and ſpeedy trial by an impartial jury of his vicinage, without whoſe unanimous conſent he cannot be found guilty (except in the government of the land and naval forces) nor can he be compelled to give evidence againſt himſelf.

9th. That no freeman ought to be taken, impriſoned, or diſſeized of his freehold, liberties, privileges or franchiſes, or outlawed or exiled, or in any manner deſtroyed or deprived of his life, liberty, or property but by the law of the land.

10th. That every freeman reſtrained of his liberty is entitled to a remedy to enquire into the lawfulneſs thereof, and to remove the ſame, if unlawful, and that ſuch remedy ought not to be denied nor delayed.

11th. That in controverſies reſpecting property, and in ſuits between man and man, the ancient trial by jury is one of the greateſt ſecurities to the rights of the people, and ought to remain ſacred and inviolable.

12th. That every freeman ought to find a certain remedy by recourſe to the laws for all injuries and wrongs he may receive in his perſon, property, or character. He ought to obtain right and juſtice freely without ſale, completely and without denial, promptly and without delay, and that all eſtabliſhments, or regulations contravening theſe rights, are oppreſſive and unjuſt.

13th. That exceſſive bail ought not to be required, nor exceſſive fines impoſed, nor cruel and unuſual puniſhments inflicted,

14 That every freeman has a right to be ſecure from all unreaſonable ſearches, and ſeizures of his perſon, his papers, and property: all warrants therefore to ſearch ſuſpected places, or ſeize any freeman, his papers or property, without information upon oath (or affirmation of a perſon religiouſly ſcrupulous of taking an oath) of legal and ſufficient cauſe, are grievous and oppreſſive, and all general warrants to ſearch ſuſpected places, or to apprehend any ſuſpected perſon without ſpecially naming or deſcribing the place or perſon, are dangerous and ought not to be granted.

15th. That the people have a right peaceably to aſſemble together to conſult for the common good, or to inſtruct their repreſentatives; and that every freeman has a right to petition or apply to the Legiſlature for redreſs of grievances.

16th. That the people have a right to freedom of ſpeech, and of writing and publiſhing their ſentiments; that the freedom of the preſs is one of the greateſt bulwarks of Liberty, and ought not to be violated.

17th. That the people have a right to keep and bear arms; that a well regulated militia compoſed of the body of the people, trained to arms, is the proper, natural and ſafe defence of a free ſtate. That ſtanding armies in time of peace are dangerous to Liberty, and therefore ought to be avoided, as far as the circumſtances and protection of the community will admit; and that in all caſes, the military ſhould be under ſtrict ſubordination to, and governed by the civil power.

18th. That no ſoldier in time of peace ought to be quartered in any houſe without the conſent of the owner, and in time of war in ſuch manner only as the Laws direct.

19th. That any perſon religiouſly ſcrupulous of bearing arms ought to be exempted upon payment of an equivalent to employ another to bears arms in his ſtead.

10. That religion, or the duty which we owe to our Creator, and the manner of diſcharging it, can be directed only by reaſon and conviction, not by force or violence, and therefore all men have an equal, natural and unalienable right to the free exerciſe of religion according to the dictates of conſcience, and that no particular religious ſect or ſociety ought to be favoured or eſtabliſhed by law in preference to others.

Amendments to the Conſtitution.

I. THAT each ſtate in the union ſhall, reſpectively, retain every power, juriſdiction and right, which is not by this conſtitution delegated to the Congreſs of the United States, or to the departments of the Federal Government.

North Carolina's first convention to consider the Constitution voted to defer action until a declaration of rights was adopted.

During the Constitutional Convention and the ratification struggle in the states, many objections had been made to the exclusion from the Constitution of similar guarantees. When ratifying, many states expressed reservations and suggested numerous amendments, especially a bill of rights. North Carolina, decrying the absence of a declaration of rights in the Constitution, even refused to ratify in 1788 and did not do so until the following year, after the new government had been established and by which time such provisions had been proposed for addition to the instrument.

Washington called attention to the lack of a bill of rights in his inaugural address, and the First Congress moved quickly to correct this fault. Madison, in a prodigious effort, synthesized most of the amendments the states had recommended into nine propositions. The House committee, on which he sat, expanded these to 17. The Senate, with House concurrence, later reduced the number to 12. Meantime, the decision had been made to append all amendments to the Constitution rather than to insert them in the text at appropriate spots, as Madison had originally desired.

By December 1791 the States had ratified the last 10 of the 12 amendments Congress had submitted to them in September 1789. The first of the two that were not sanctioned proposed a future change in the numerical constituency of representatives and in their number; the second would have deferred any changes in congressional salaries that might be made until the term of the succeeding Congress.

The first amendment, covering the free expression of opinion, prohibits congressional interference with the freedom of religion, speech, press, assembly, and petition. Amendments two through four guarantee the rights of citizens to bear arms for lawful purposes, disallow the quartering of troops in private homes without the consent of the owner, and bar unreasonable searches and seizures by the government.

Amendments five, six, and eight essentially provide protection against arbitrary arrest, trial, and punishment, principally in federal criminal cases though over the course of time the judiciary has held that many of the provisions also apply in state cases. Mainly to prevent harassment of the citizenry by governmental officials, these measures established the right of civilian defendants to grand jury indictments for major crimes; prohibit "double jeopardy," or duplicate trial, for the same offense, as well as self-incrimination; deny deprivation of "life, liberty, or property without due process of law"; ensure the right of the accused to have legal counsel, be informed of the nature and cause of the accusation, subpoena witnesses on his own behalf,

Congress of the United States,
begun and held at the City of New-York, on
Wednesday the fourth of March, one thousand seven hundred and eighty nine.

The Bill of Rights

confront the witnesses against him, and receive an expeditious and public jury trial; and ban excessive bails and fines, as well as "cruel and unusual punishments." The fifth amendment also prohibits the government seizure of private property under the doctrine of eminent domain without proper compensation.

The seventh amendment guarantees the right of a jury trial in virtually all civil cases.

Amendment nine states that the rights enumerated in the Constitution are not to be "construed to deny or disparage others retained by the people." The 10th amendment, somewhat different from the other nine because of its allusion to the states, reserves to them and the people all "powers not delegated to the United States by the Constitution, nor prohibited by it to the States."

Contrary to a popular misconception, the main body of the Constitution also contains various safeguards similar to those in the Bill of Rights that protect citizens and the states against unreasonable actions. Article I prohibits the government from suspending the writ of *habeas corpus,* which would otherwise allow arbitrary arrest, and both the national government and the states from enacting bills of attainder (legislative punishment of crimes) and *ex post facto* laws (retroactively making acts criminal). Article III requires a jury trial for federal crimes and limits the definition of treason and penalties for the offense.

Article IV guarantees that the acts, records, and judicial proceedings of one state are valid in all the others; grants to citizens of every state the privileges and immunities of the others as defined by law; warrants the representative government and territorial integrity of the states; and promises them the protection of the national government against foreign invasion and domestic insurrection. Article VI excludes religious tests for officeholding.

Nevertheless, it is the Bill of Rights that has become the main bulwark of the civil liberties of the American people. These measures, which make the Constitution a defender of liberty as well as an instrument of governmental power, represented another swing of the pendulum. The Articles of Confederation had created a weak league of semi-independent states. As a result, citizens looked primarily to the states for protection of their basic rights, which were defined in constitutions or separate declarations. Then the Constitution provided a strong central government. This was counterbalanced by the Bill of Rights, which allowed continuance of such a government with full regard for the rights of the people.

In recent decades, the Bill of Rights has acquired increased significance to all citizens because the Supreme Court has ruled that many parts of it are applicable to the states as well as to the federal government.

Subsequent Amendments

The 11th amendment, which was passed by Congress in 1794 and ratified the next year, was engendered by state objections to the power of the federal judiciary and represents the only occasion to date whereby an amendment has limited its authority. Curtailing federal power in actions brought against individual states, the

As early as 1788, the year this magazine drawing appeared, Americans revered the Constitution. The allegory depicts Cupid presenting a copy of the document to Concord as she approaches the 13-pillared Temple of Liberty, Justice, and Peace. Clio, the muse of history, kneels beside Concord and records the message Cupid is delivering.

measure denies the federal courts jurisdiction over private suits brought against one state by citizens of another or of a foreign country.

The 12th amendment, which won the approbation of Congress in 1803 and state approval the following year, is a constitutional accommodation to the formation of political parties. Many of the Founding Fathers, who had themselves not been immune to divisiveness, had feared their growth, which they believed would stimulate factional strife. But parties soon proved to be necessary vehicles for the nation's political life.

As they grew, the method of electing the President and Vice President as originally set forth at Philadelphia became cumbersome and controversial, if not practically unworkable. The election of 1796 produced a President and Vice President of different parties. In 1800 a tied electoral vote occurred between members of the same party, and the House of Representatives was forced to choose a President. These two experiences created the necessary sentiment to modify the electoral process. The principal provision of the 12th amendment required future electors to cast separate ballots for the two executives.

For more than six decades after the ratification of the 12th, no further amendments were enacted. Then the Civil War crisis created three, the so-called "national supremacy" amendments, which congressional Radical Reconstructionists proposed. The 13th, sent out to the states in 1864 and ratified in 1865, was the first attempt to use the amending process to institute national social reform. It followed upon Lincoln's limited and preliminary action in the Emancipation Proclamation (1863) to free the slaves. Although the amendment declared slavery and involuntary servitude (except as punishment for crimes) to be unconstitutional, it did not provide blacks with civil-rights guarantees equal to those of whites.

During the Reconstruction period, therefore, two more additions to the Constitution became the law of the land. Their main objectives were to insure the rights of black men to full citizenship. Ultimately, however, because of their broad phraseology, the two amendments have come to have significant repercussions for all citizens. The 14th, proposed in 1866 and ratified 2 years later, decrees that all persons born or naturalized in the United States are citizens of the nation and of the state in which they live. The legislation also forbids the states from making any laws that abridge the "privileges or immunities of citizens of the United States," deprive them of "life, liberty, or property, without due process of law," or deny them the "equal protection of the laws."

Thirty-Eighth Congress of the United States of America;

At the Second Session,

Begun and held at the City of Washington, on Monday, the fifth day of December, one thousand eight hundred and sixty-four.

A RESOLUTION

Submitting to the legislatures of the several States a proposition to amend the Constitution of the United States.

Resolved *by the Senate and House of Representatives of the United States of America in Congress assembled,* (two-thirds of both houses concurring), that the following article be proposed to the legislatures of the several States as an amendment to the Constitution of the United States, which, when ratified by three-fourths of said legislatures shall be valid to all intents and purposes, as a part of the said Constitution namely: Article XIII. Section 1. Neither slavery nor involuntary servitude, except as a punishment for crime whereof the party shall have been duly convicted, shall exist within the United States, or any place subject to their jurisdiction. Section 2. Congress shall have power to enforce this article by appropriate legislation.

Schuyler Colfax
Speaker of the House of Representatives.

H. Hamlin
Vice President of the United States and President of the Senate.

Approved February 1. 1865.

Abraham Lincoln

The resolution proposing the 13th amendment, which outlawed slavery and was the first attempt to use the amending process to institute national social reform.

The amendment also expanded representation in the House of Representatives from that contained in the original Constitution (the free, essentially white, population plus three-fifths of all slaves) to include all persons except untaxed Indians. Another provision stated that the representation of states arbitrarily denying the vote to adult men would be reduced. The measure also barred from federal officeholding those Confederates who had held federal or state offices before the Civil War, except when Congress chose to waive this disqualification, and ruled invalid all debts contracted to aid the Confederacy as well as claims for compensation covering the loss or emancipation of slaves.

The most important goal for which the amendment was added to the Constitution, the legal equality of blacks, was not fully realized until the 24th outlawed the poll tax in 1964. The attempt to limit the political participation of ex-Confederate leaders failed. In recent years, however, the Supreme Court has often used the amendment to achieve fuller state conformance with the Bill of Rights. Furthermore, judicial interpretations have broadened the meaning of such key phrases as "privileges or immunities," "due process," and "equal protection of the laws." Congress has also passed new enforcement legislation.

Despite the legislative efforts of the Radical Republicans, black men continued to be denied equal voting rights. In 1869, therefore, Congress passed and the next year the states ratified the 15th amendment. Attempting to protect the rights of ex-slaves it explicitly stated: "The right of citizens of the United States to vote shall not be denied or abridged by the United States or by any State on account of race, color, or previous condition of servitude."

Not until 1913 was the Constitution again changed. Before that time, Congress had only enjoyed the power to levy direct taxes in proportion to the populations of the states. During the late 19th century, the need for a federal income tax began to become apparent to many people in the country, but the Supreme Court on various occasions declared such a tax to be unconstitutional. By 1909 support for it was strong enough to warrant passage of the 16th amendment. Many Congressmen who voted affirmatively felt the states would never approve the action. Yet, 4 years later, they ratified it. The income tax quickly became a principal source of federal revenue and facilitated governmental expansion.

Later in 1913 the states approved another amendment, which Congress had sanctioned the previous year. The 17th authorized the direct election of senators by the voters rather than by state legislatures, as specified in the Constitution. The original method had long been a target of reformers. Numerous times between 1893 and 1911 the House of Representatives proposed amendments calling for popular selection of senators. The Senate, however, apparently concerned among other things about the tenure of its members and resenting the invasion of their prerogatives by the lower House, refused to give its stamp of approval to the legislation. But, by the latter year, pressure for change had become intense, particularly because the popular image of the Senate had become that of a millionaires' club divorced from the interests of the people. That same year, an Illinois election scandal helped turn the tide. Also, many states had by that time adopted senatorial preference primaries as an expression of popular sentiment to the legislators.

The highly controversial "prohibition" amendment, the 18th, cleared Congress in 1917 and was ratified 2 years later. It prohibited the manufacture, sale, or transportation of intoxicating liquors for beverage purposes" and their importation into or exportation from the United States. This legislation was the result of nearly a century of temperance efforts to eliminate or limit use of alcoholic beverages. But unsuccessful enforcement and opposition by large elements of the public, particularly in urban areas, soon doomed the "noble experiment." In the only instance when an amendment has been repealed by another, the 21st, which was both proposed and ratified in 1933, voided the 18th. It returned control of alcohol to states and local jurisdictions, which could choose to remain "dry" if they so preferred.

The persistence of reformers likewise produced the 19th amendment, passed in 1919 and ratified the next year. Equal voting rights in federal and state elections were granted to women. Especially after the Civil War, they had begun to improve their legal status, and some states in the West had granted them the right to vote. During the early years of the 20th century, more states extended the privilege. These and other factors, coupled with the efforts of suffragists, facilitated adoption of the amendment. It marked a major step toward fuller political equality for women.

Congress gave its imprimatur to the so-called "lame duck" amendment, the 20th, in 1932 and it became effective the next year. Designed mainly to hasten and smooth the post-election succession of the President and Congress, it specified that the terms of the President and Vice President would begin on January 20 following the fall elections instead of on March 4 and required Congress to convene on January 3, when the terms of all newly elected Congressmen were also to begin. Correcting another defect in the Constitution was the stipulation that the Vice President-elect would succeed to the highest office in the land in the event the President-elect died before his inauguration or no President-elect had qualified.

Proposed to the states by Congress in 1947, the 22d amendment was ratified in 1951. Aimed in large part at preventing the repetition of the unprecedented four terms to which Franklin D. Roosevelt had

Women's suffrage parades, such as this one in Washington, helped pave the way for the 19th amendment (1919).

been elected as President, it limited the service of chief executives to a maximum of the traditional two full terms. Vice Presidents succeeding to the office were to be restricted to one term if the unexpired portion of that to which they succeeded was longer than 2 years. The incumbent, Harry S. Truman, who was serving when this amendment was added to the Constitution, was exempted from it, though he did not choose to run for a second full term.

District of Columbia residents won the right to vote for presidential electors in the 23d amendment, which gained congressional approval in 1960 and was ratified the following year. It was part of the endeavor to obtain for D.C. residents political rights equal to those of citizens of the states. Although this step fell short of the "home rule" sought for the District, it was a major step toward more extensive political participation by its citizens.

The civil rights struggle of black people in the 1950s and early 1960s resulted in the 24th amendment, which was proposed in 1962 and ratified 2 years later. It outlawed poll taxes as a prerequisite for

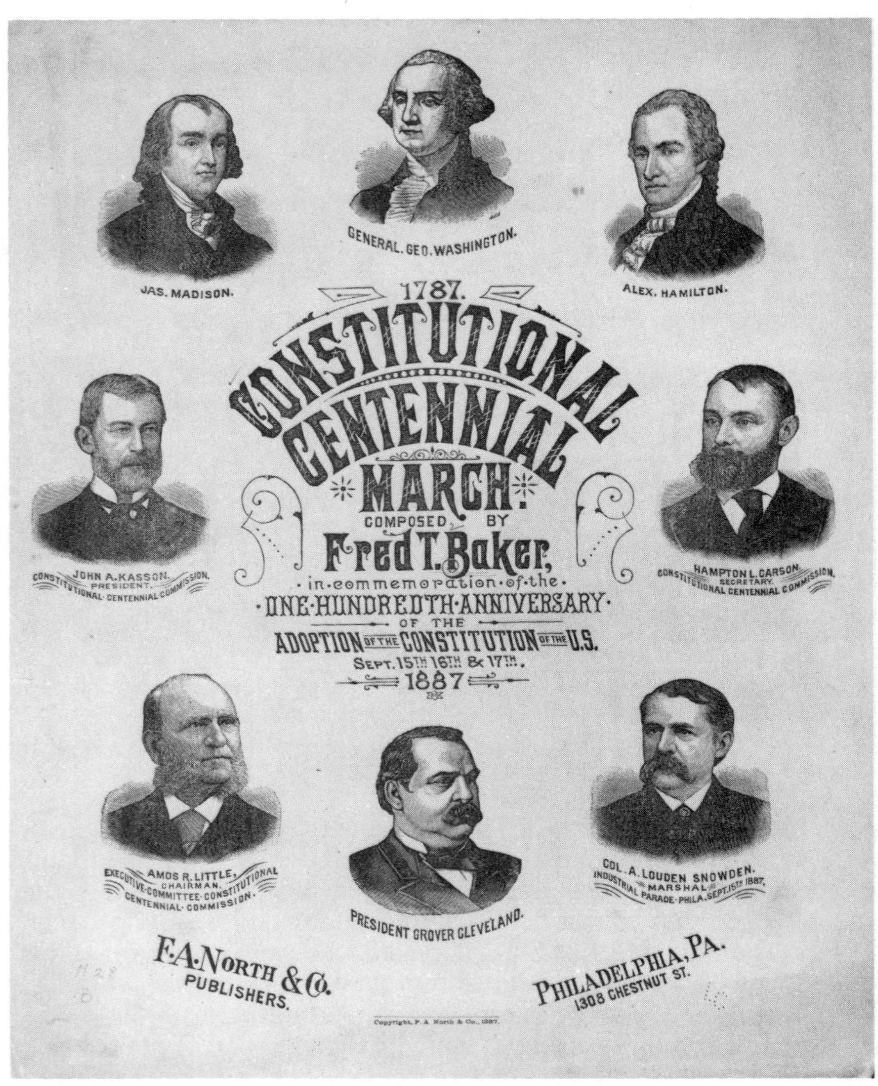

The 100th anniversary of the Constitution occasioned celebrations across the land and such special tributes as a "Centennial March."

voting in federal elections. This device had long been used in some places to limit political participation, especially by blacks.

The long illnesses of Presidents Woodrow Wilson and Dwight D. Eisenhower and the assassination of President John F. Kennedy, coupled with the enormous contemporary importance of the presidency, gave rise to the 25th amendment. It was passed by Congress in 1965 and ratified in 1967. Steps to be followed in the event of presidential disability were outlined, and a method was established for expeditiously filling vacancies in the office of Vice President. When there is no Vice President, the President will nominate a replacement, who needs only approval by a congressional majority. In the event of presidential disability, the Vice President will temporarily hold the office of Acting President.

The 26th amendment, proposed and ratified in 1971, provided another extension of the franchise. In recognition of the increasing contributions of youth to American society, the minimum voting age in all elections was lowered to 18 years. Although a few states, in accordance with their discretionary rights at the time, had earlier reduced the voting age from 21, this constitutional addition made the national franchise uniform in terms of minimum age.

DESPITE its numerous advantages, the amendment process has proven to be less than perfect as a vehicle of change. Although the rigorous procedure required to enact amendments has prevented hasty and ill-advised action, it has on occasion delayed the inauguration of badly needed reforms. The brief and sometimes imprecise wording of the amendments, as well as of the Constitution itself, has necessitated prolonged and complex interpretation by the Supreme Court. The public and various governmental organs have on occasion failed to heed or fully execute our highest national law.

Whatever the flaws in our constitutional system, it enunciates our democratic principles and provides a superlative formula and instrument of government, which has established its primacy among the efforts of men to govern themselves. Yet the true guardian of our sacred charter of liberties is the vigilance of the people.

PART TWO

Framers of the Constitution: BIOGRAPHICAL SKETCHES

The 55 delegates who attended the Constitutional Convention were a distinguished body of men who represented a cross section of 18th-century American leadership. Almost all of them were well-educated men of means who were dominant in their communities and states, and many were also prominent in national affairs. Virtually every one had taken part in the Revolution; at least 29 had served in the Continental forces, most of them in positions of command.

Political Experience

The practical political experience of the group was extensive. At the time of the convention, four-fifths, or 44 individuals, were or had been members of the Continental Congress. Mifflin and Gorham had served as president of the body. The only ones who lacked congressional experience were Bassett, Blair, Brearly, Broom, Davie, Houstoun, Mason, McClurg, Paterson, Charles Cotesworth Pinckney, Strong, and Yates. Eight men (Clymer, Franklin, Gerry, Robert Morris, Read, Sherman, Wilson, and Wythe) had signed the Declaration of Independence. Six (Carroll, Dickinson, Gerry, Gouverneur Morris, Robert Morris, and Sherman) had affixed their signatures to the Articles of Confederation. But only two, Sherman and Robert Morris, underwrote all three of the nation's basic documents. Practically all of the 55 delegates had experience in colonial and state government. Dickinson, Franklin, Langdon, Livingston, Alexander Martin, Randolph, Read, and Rutledge had been governors, and the majority had held county and local offices.

Occupations

Among the delegates, the range of occupations was wide, and many men simultaneously pursued more than one career. Thirty-five were lawyers or had benefited from legal training, though not all of them relied on the profession for a livelihood. Some had also become judges.

At the time of the convention, 13 individuals were businessmen, merchants, or shippers: Blount, Broom, Clymer, Dayton, Fitzsimons, Gerry, Gilman, Gorham, Langdon, Robert Morris, Pierce, Sherman, and Wilson. Six were major land speculators: Blount, Dayton, Fitzsimons, Gorham, Robert Morris, and Wilson. Eleven speculated in securities on a large scale: Bedford, Blair, Clymer, Dayton, Fitzsimons, Franklin, King, Langdon, Robert Morris, Charles Cotesworth Pinckney, and Sherman. Twelve owned or managed slave-operated plantations or large farms: Bassett, Blair, Blount, Butler, Carroll, Jenifer, Mason,

Charles Pinckney, Charles Cotesworth Pinckney, Rutledge, Spaight, and Washington. Madison also owned slaves. Broom and Few were small farmers.

Nine of the men received a substantial part of their income from public office: Baldwin, Blair, Brearly, Gilman, Jenifer, Livingston, Madison, and Rutledge. Three had retired from active economic endeavors: Franklin, McHenry, and Mifflin. Franklin and Williamson were scientists, among their other activities. McClurg, McHenry, and Williamson were physicians, and Johnson was a university president. Baldwin had been a minister, and Williamson, Madison, Ellsworth, and possibly others had studied in this field but had never been ordained.

A few of the delegates were rich. Washington and Robert Morris ranked among the nation's wealthiest men. Carroll, Houstoun, Jenifer, and Mifflin were also extremely well-to-do. The financial resources of the majority of the rest ranged from good to excellent. Among those with the most straitened circumstances were Baldwin, Brearly, Broom, Few, Madison, Paterson, and Sherman, though they all managed to live comfortably.

A considerable number of the men were born into leading families: Blair, Butler, Carroll, Houstoun, Ingersoll, Jenifer, Johnson, Livingston, Mifflin, Gouverneur Morris, both Pinckneys, Randolph, Rutledge, Washington, and Wythe. Others were self-made men who had risen from humble beginnings: Few, Franklin, Gorham, Hamilton, and Sherman.

Geographic and Educational Background

Most of the group were natives of the 13 colonies. Only eight were born elsewhere: four (Butler, Fitzsimons, McHenry, and Paterson) in Ireland, two (Davie and Robert Morris) in England, one (Wilson) in Scotland, and one (Hamilton) in the West Indies. But, if most of the signers were native-born, many of them had moved from one state to another. Reflecting the mobility that has always characterized American life, 16 individuals had already lived or worked in more than one state or colony: Baldwin, Bassett, Bedford, Dickinson, Few, Franklin, Ingersoll, Livingston, Alexander Martin, Luther Martin, Mercer, Gouverneur Morris, Robert Morris, Read, Sherman, and Williamson. Others had studied or traveled abroad.

The educational background of the Founding Fathers was diverse. Some, Franklin for example, were largely self-taught and had received scant formal training. Others had obtained instruction from private tutors or at academies. About half of the individuals had attended or graduated from college in the present United States or abroad. Some

Several delegates attended the College of New Jersey (present Princeton University), shown here about 1764. Nassau Hall, the main building, is on the left; the president's house, on the right.

men held advanced and honorary degrees. All in all, the delegates were a well-educated group.

Longevity and Family Life

For their era, the delegates to the convention, like the signers of the Declaration of Independence, were remarkably long-lived. The average age at death was almost 67. Johnson reached 92 years, and Few, Franklin, Madison, Williamson, and Wythe lived into their eighties. Passing away in their eighth decade were 15 or 16 (because Fitzsimons was either 69 or 70 at the time of his death), and 20 or 21 in their sixties. Eight lived into their fifties; five lived only into their forties, and two of them (Hamilton and Spaight) were killed in duels. The first to die, in 1788, was Houston; the last, Madison, in 1836.

Most of the delegates married and raised children. Sherman fathered the largest family, 15 children by 2 wives. At least nine (Bassett, Brearly, Johnson, Mason, Paterson, Charles Cotesworth Pinckney, Sherman, Wilson, and Wythe) married more than once. Four (Baldwin, Gilman, Jenifer, and Alexander Martin) were lifelong bachelors. In terms of religious affiliation, the men mirrored the overwhelmingly Protestant character of American religious life at the time and were members of various denominations. Only two, Carroll and Fitzsimons, were Roman Catholics.

Post-Convention Careers

The later careers of the delegates reflected their abilities as well as the vagaries of fate. Most were successful, though seven (Fitzsimons, Gorham, Luther Martin, Mifflin, Robert Morris, Pierce, and Wilson) suffered serious financial reverses that left them in or near bankruptcy. Two, Blount and Dayton, were involved in possibly treasonous activities. Yet, as they had done before the convention, most of the group continued to render outstanding public service, particularly to the new government they had helped to create.

Washington and Madison became President of the United States, and King and Charles Cotesworth Pinckney were nominated as candidates for the office. Gerry served as Madison's Vice President. Hamilton, McHenry, Madison, and Randolph attained cabinet posts. Nineteen men became U.S. senators: Baldwin, Bassett, Blount, Butler, Dayton, Ellsworth, Few, Gilman, Johnson, King, Langdon, Alexander Martin, Gouverneur Morris, Robert Morris, Paterson, Charles Pinckney, Read, Sherman, and Strong. Thirteen served in the House of Representatives: Baldwin, Carroll, Clymer, Dayton, Fitzsimons, Gerry, Gilman, Madison, Mercer, Charles Pinckney, Sherman, Spaight, and Williamson. Of these, Dayton served as Speaker. Four men (Bassett, Bedford, Brearly, and Few) served as federal judges, four more (Blair, Paterson, Rutledge, and Wilson) as associate justices of the Supreme Court. Rutledge and Ellsworth also held the position of Chief Justice. Seven others, Davie, Ellsworth, Gerry, King, Gouverneur Morris, Charles Pinckney, and Charles Cotesworth Pinckney, were named to diplomatic missions for the nation.

Many delegates held important state positions, including governor (Blount, Davie, Franklin, Gerry, Langdon, Livingston, Alexander Martin, Mifflin, Paterson, Charles Pinckney, Spaight, and Strong) and legislator. And most of the delegates contributed in many ways to the cultural life of their cities, communities, and states. Not surprisingly, many of their sons and other descendants were to occupy high positions in American political and intellectual life.

Abraham Baldwin

Georgia

Baldwin was born at Guilford, Conn., in 1754, the second son of a blacksmith who fathered 12 children by 2 wives. Besides Abraham, several of the family attained distinction. His sister Ruth married the poet and diplomat Joel Barlow, and his half-brother Henry attained the position of justice of the U.S. Supreme Court. Their ambitious father went heavily into debt to educate his children.

After attending a local village school, Abraham matriculated at Yale, in nearby New Haven. He graduated in 1772. Three years later, he became a minister and tutor at the college. He held that position until 1779, when he served as a chaplain in the Continental Army. Two years later, he declined an offer from his alma mater of a professorship of divinity. Instead of resuming his ministerial or educational duties after the war, he turned to the study of law and in 1783 gained admittance to the bar at Fairfield, Conn.

Within a year, Baldwin moved to Georgia, won legislative approval to practice his profession, and obtained a grant of land in Wilkes County. In 1785 he sat in the assembly and the Continental Congress. Two years later, his father died and Baldwin undertook to pay off his debts and educate, out of his own pocket, his half-brothers and half-sisters.

That same year, Baldwin attended the Constitutional Convention, from which he was absent for a few weeks. Although usually inconspicuous, he sat on the committee on postponed matters and helped resolve the large-small state representation crisis. At first, he favored representation in the Senate based upon property holdings, but possibly because of his close relationship with the Connecticut delegation he later came to fear alienation of the small states and changed his mind to representation by state.

After the convention, Baldwin returned to the Continental Congress (1787–89). He was then elected to the U.S. Congress, where he served for 18 years (House of Representatives, 1789–99; Senate, 1799–1807). During these years, he came to be a bitter opponent of Hamiltonian policies and, unlike most other native New Englanders, an ally of Madison and Jefferson and the Democratic-Republicans. In the Senate, he presided for a while as president *pro tem.*

By 1790 Baldwin had taken up residence in Augusta. Beginning in the preceding decade, he had begun efforts to advance the educational system in Georgia. Appointed with six others in 1784 to oversee the founding of a state college, he saw his dream come true in 1798 when Franklin College was founded. Modeled after Yale, it became the nucleus of the University of Georgia.

Baldwin, who never married, died after a short illness during his 53d year in 1807. Still serving in the Senate at the time, he was buried in Washington's Rock Creek Cemetery.

Richard Bassett

Delaware

Bassett (Basset) was born in Cecil County, Md., in April 1745. After his tavern-keeper father deserted his mother, he was reared by a relative, Peter Lawson, from whom he later inherited Bohemia Manor (Md.) estate. He read for the law at Philadelphia and in 1770 received a license to practice in Dover, Del. Prospering as a lawyer-planter, he eventually came to own not only Bohemia Manor, but also homes in Dover and Wilmington.

During the Revolution, Bassett captained a troop of Dover cavalry militia and served on the Delaware council of safety. Subsequently, he participated in Delaware's constitutional convention and sat in both the upper and lower houses of the legislature. In 1786, on behalf of his state, he took part in the Annapolis Convention.

At the U.S. Constitutional Convention the next year, Bassett attended diligently but made no speeches, served on no committees, and cast no critical votes. Like several other delegates of estimable reputation and talent, he allowed others to make the major steps.

Bassett subsequently went on to a bright career in the state and federal governments. In the Delaware ratifying convention, he joined in the 30–0 vote for the Constitution. Subsequently, in the years 1789–93, he served in the U.S. Senate. In that capacity, he voted in favor of the power of the President to remove governmental officers and against Hamilton's plan for the federal assumption of state debts.

From 1793 until 1799 he held the chief justiceship of the court of common pleas. Espousing the federalist cause in the 1790s, he served as a presidential elector, on behalf of John Adams, in 1797. Two years later, Bassett was elected Governor of Delaware and continued in that post until 1801. That year, he became one of President Adams' "midnight" appointments, as a judge of the U.S. Circuit Court. Subsequently, the Jeffersonian Republicans abolished his judgeship, and he spent the rest of his life in retirement.

Twice married, to Ann Ennals and a woman named Bruff, Bassett fathered several children. He was a devout Methodist, held religious meetings at Bohemia Manor, and financially supported the church. He died in 1815 at the age of 70 and is interred at the Wilmington and Brandywine Cemetery, Wilmington, Del.

Gunning Bedford, Jr.

Delaware

Born in 1747 at Philadelphia, Bedford was reared there. The fifth of seven children, he was descended from a distinguished family that originally settled in Jamestown, Va. Usually he referred to himself as Gunning Bedford, Jr., to avoid confusion with his cousin and contemporary Delaware statesman and soldier, Col. Gunning Bedford.

In 1771 signer Bedford graduated with honors from the College of New Jersey (later Princeton), where he was a classmate of James Madison. Apparently while still in school, Bedford wed Jane B. Parker, who was to bear at least one daughter. After reading law with Joseph Read in

Philadelphia, Bedford won admittance to the bar and set up a practice. Subsequently he moved to Dover and then to Wilmington. He apparently served in the Continental Army, possibly as an aide to General Washington.

Following the war, Bedford figured prominently in the politics of his state and nation. He sat in the legislature, on the state council, and in the Continental Congress (1783–85). In the latter year, he was chosen as a delegate to the Annapolis Convention but for some reason did not attend. From 1784 to 1789 he was attorney general of Delaware.

Bedford numbered among the more active members of the Constitutional Convention and he missed few sessions. A large and forceful man, he spoke on several occasions and was a member of the committee that drafted the Great Compromise. An ardent small-state advocate, he attacked the pretensions of the large states over the small and warned that the latter might be forced to seek foreign alliances unless their interests were accommodated. He attended the Delaware ratifying convention.

For another 2 years, Bedford continued as Delaware's attorney general. In 1789 Washington designated him as a federal district judge for his state, an office he was to occupy for the rest of his life. His only other ventures into national politics came in 1789 and 1793, as a Federalist presidential elector. In the main, however, he spent his later years in judicial pursuits, in aiding Wilmington Academy, in fostering abolitionism, and in enjoying his Lombardy Hall farm.

Bedford died at the age of 65 in 1812 and was buried in the First Presbyterian Churchyard in Wilmington. Later, when the cemetery was abandoned, his body was transferred to the Masonic Home, on the Lancaster Turnpike in Christiana Hundred, Del.

John Blair

Virginia

Scion of a prominent Virginia family, Blair was born at Williamsburg in 1732. He was the son of John Blair, a colonial official and nephew of James Blair, founder and first president of the College of William and Mary. Signer Blair graduated from that institution and studied law at London's Middle Temple. Thereafter, he practiced at Williamsburg. In the years 1766–70 he sat in the Virginia House of Burgesses as the representative of William and Mary. From 1770 to 1775 he held the position of clerk of the colony's council.

An active patriot, Blair signed the Virginia Association of June 22, 1770, which pledged to abandon importation of British goods until the Townshend Duties were repealed. He also underwrote the Association of May 27, 1774, calling for a meeting of the colonies in a Continental Congress and supporting the Bostonians. He took part in the Virginia constitutional convention (1776), at which he sat on the committee that framed a declaration of rights as well as the plan for a new government. He next served on the Privy Council (1776–78). In the latter year, the legislature elected him as a judge of the General Court, and he soon took over the chief justiceship. In 1780 he won election to Virginia's high chancery court, where his colleague was George Wythe.

Blair attended the Constitutional Convention religiously but never spoke or served on a committee. He usually sided with the position of the Virginia delegation. And, in the commonwealth ratifying convention, Blair helped win backing for the new framework of government.

In 1789 Washington named Blair as an associate justice of the U.S. Supreme Court, where he helped decide many important cases. Resigning that post in 1796, he spent his remaining years in Williamsburg. A widower, his wife (born Jean Balfour) having died in 1792, he lived quietly until he succumbed in 1800. He was 68 years old. His tomb is in the graveyard of Bruton Parish Church.

William Blount

North Carolina

William Blount was the great-grandson of Thomas Blount, who came from England to Virginia soon after 1660 and settled on a North Carolina plantation. William, the eldest in a large family, was born in 1749 while his mother was visiting his grandfather's Rosefield estate, on the site of present Windsor near Pamlico Sound. The youth apparently received a good education.

Shortly after the War for Independence began, in 1776, Blount enlisted as a paymaster in the North Carolina forces. Two years later, he wed Mary Grainger (Granger); of their six children who reached adulthood, one son also became prominent in Tennessee politics.

Blount spent most of the remainder of his life in public office. He sat in the lower house of the North Carolina legislature (1780–84), including service as speaker, as well as in the upper (1788–90). In addition, he took part in national politics, serving in the Continental Congress in 1782–83 and 1786–87.

Appointed as a delegate to the Constitutional Convention at the age of 38, Blount was absent for more than a month because he chose to attend the Continental Congress on behalf of his state. He said almost nothing in the debates and signed the Constitution reluctantly—only, he said, to make it "the unanimous act of the States in Convention." Nonetheless, he favored his state's ratification of the completed document.

Blount hoped to be elected to the first U.S. Senate. When he failed to achieve that end, in 1790 he pushed westward beyond the Appalachians, where he held speculative land interests and had represented North Carolina in dealings with the Indians. He settled in what became Tennessee, to which he devoted the rest of his life. He resided first at Rocky Mount, a cabin near present Johnson City and in 1792 built a mansion in Knoxville.

Two years earlier, Washington had appointed Blount as Governor for the Territory South of the River Ohio (which included

Tennessee) and also as Superintendent of Indian Affairs for the Southern Department, in which positions he increased his popularity with the frontiersmen. In 1796 he presided over the constitutional convention that transformed part of the territory into the State of Tennessee. He was elected as one of its first U.S. senators (1796–97).

During this period, Blount's affairs took a sharp turn for the worse. In 1797 his speculations in western lands led him into serious financial difficulties. That same year, he also apparently concocted a plan involving use of Indians, frontiersmen, and British naval forces to conquer for Britain the Spanish provinces of Florida and Louisiana. A letter he wrote alluding to the plan fell into the hands of President Adams, who turned it over to the Senate on July 3, 1797. Five days later, that body voted 25 to 1 to expel Blount. The House impeached him, but the Senate dropped the charges in 1799 on the grounds that no further action could be taken beyond his dismissal.

The episode did not hamper Blount's career in Tennessee. In 1798 he was elected to the senate and rose to the speakership. He died 2 years later at Knoxville in his early fifties. He is buried there in the cemetery of the First Presbyterian Church.

David Brearly

New Jersey

Brearly (Brearley) was descended from a Yorkshire, England, family, one of whose members migrated to New Jersey around 1680. Signer Brearly was born in 1745 at Spring Grove near Trenton, was reared in the area, and attended but did not graduate from the nearby College of New Jersey (later Princeton). He chose law as a career and originally practiced at Allentown, N.J. About 1767 he married Elizabeth Mullen.

Brearly avidly backed the Revolutionary cause. The British arrested him for high treason, but a group of patriots freed him. In 1776 he took part in the convention that drew up the state constitution. During the War for Independence, he rose from a captain to a colonel in the militia.

In 1779 Brearly was elected as chief justice of the New Jersey supreme court, a position he held until 1789. He presided over the precedent-setting case of *Holmes* v. *Walton.* His decision, rendered in 1780, represented an early expression of the principle of judicial review. The next year, the College of New Jersey bestowed an honorary M.A. degree on him.

Brearly was 42 years of age when he participated in the Constitutional Convention. Although he did not rank among the leaders, he attended the sessions regularly. A follower of Paterson, who introduced the New Jersey Plan, Brearly opposed proportional representation of the states and favored one vote for each of them in Congress. He also chaired the committee on postponed matters.

Brearly's subsequent career was short, for he had only 3 years to live. He presided at the New Jersey convention that ratified the Constitution in 1788, and served as a presidential elector in 1789. That same year, President Washington appointed him as a federal district judge, and he served in that capacity until his death.

When free from his judicial duties, Brearly devoted much energy to lodge and church affairs. He was one of the leading members of the Masonic Order in New Jersey, as well as state vice president of the Society of the Cincinnati, an organization of former officers of the Revolutionary War. In addition, he served as a delegate to the Episcopal General Conference (1786) and helped write the church's prayer book. In 1783, following the death of his first wife, he had married Elizabeth Higbee.

Brearly died in Trenton at the age of 45 in 1790. He was buried there at St. Michael's Episcopal Church.

Jacob Broom

Delaware *(No Portrait Available)*

Broom was born in 1752 at Wilmington, Del., the eldest son of a blacksmith who prospered in farming. The youth was educated at home and probably at the local Old Academy. Although he followed his father into farming and also studied surveying, he was to make his career primarily in mercantile pursuits, including shipping and the import trade, and in real estate. In 1773 he married Rachel Pierce, who bore eight children.

Broom was not a distinguished patriot. His only recorded service was the preparation of maps for George Washington before the Battle of Brandywine, Pa. In 1776, at 24 years of age, Broom became assistant burgess of Wilmington. Over the next several decades, he held that office six times and that of chief burgess four times, as well as those of borough assessor, president of the city "street regulators," and justice of the peace for New Castle County.

Broom sat in the state legislature in the years 1784–86 and 1788, during which time he was chosen as a delegate to the Annapolis Convention, but he did not attend. At the Constitutional Convention, he never missed a session and spoke on several occasions, but his role was only a minor one.

After the convention, Broom returned to Wilmington, where in 1795 he erected a home near the Brandywine River on the outskirts of the city. He was its first postmaster (1790–92) and continued to hold various local offices and to participate in a variety of economic endeavors. For many years, he chaired the board of directors of Wilmington's Delaware Bank. He also operated a cotton mill, as well as a machine shop that produced and repaired mill machinery. He was involved, too, in an unsuccessful scheme to mine bog iron ore. A further interest was internal improvements: toll roads, canals, and bridges.

Broom also found time for philanthropic and religious activities. He served on the board of trustees of the College of Wilmington and as a lay leader at Old Swedes Church. He died at the age of 58 in 1810 while in Philadelphia on business and was buried there at Christ Church Burial Ground.

Pierce Butler

South Carolina

One of the most aristocratic delegates at the convention, Butler was born in 1744 in County Carlow, Ireland. His father was Sir Richard Butler, member of Parliament and a baronet.

Like so many younger sons of the British aristocracy who could not inherit their fathers' estates because of primogeniture, Butler pursued a military career. He became a major in His Majesty's 29th Regiment and during the colonial unrest was posted to Boston in 1768 to quell disturbances there. In 1771 he married Mary Middleton, daughter of a wealthy South Carolinian, and before long resigned his commission to take up a planter's life in the Charleston area. The couple was to have at least one daughter.

When the Revolution broke out, Butler took up the Whig cause. He was elected to the assembly in 1778, and the next year he served as adjutant general in the South Carolina militia. While in the legislature through most of the 1780s, for some reason he took over leadership of the democratic upcountry faction in the state and refused to support his own planter group. The War for Independence cost him much of his property, and his finances were so precarious for a time that he was forced to travel to Amsterdam to seek a personal loan. In 1786 the assembly appointed him to a commission charged with settling a state boundary dispute.

The next year, Butler won election to both the Continental Congress (1787–88) and the Constitutional Convention. In the latter assembly, he was an outspoken nationalist who attended practically every session and was a key spokesman for the Madison-Wilson caucus. Butler also supported the interests of southern slaveholders. He served on the committee on postponed matters.

On Butler's return to South Carolina he defended the Constitution but did not participate in the ratifying convention. Service in the U.S. Senate (1789–96) followed. Although nominally a Federalist, he often crossed party lines. He supported Hamilton's fiscal program but opposed Jay's Treaty and Federalist judiciary and tariff measures.

Out of the Senate and back in South Carolina from 1797 to 1802, Butler was considered for but did not attain the governorship. He sat briefly in the Senate again in 1803–4 to fill out an unexpired term, and he once again demonstrated party independence. But, for the most part, his later career was spent as a wealthy planter. In his last years, he moved to Philadelphia, apparently to be near a daughter who had married a local physician. Butler died there in 1822 at the age of 77 and was buried in the yard of Christ Church.

Daniel Carroll

Maryland

Daniel Carroll was a member of a prominent Maryland family of Irish descent. A collateral branch was led by Charles Carroll of Carrollton, signer of the Declaration of Independence. Daniel's older brother was John Carroll, the first Roman Catholic bishop in the United States.

Daniel was born in 1730 at Upper Marlboro, Md. Befitting the son of a wealthy Roman Catholic family, he studied for 6 years (1742–48) under the Jesuits at St. Omer's in Flanders. Then, after a tour of Europe, he sailed home and soon married Eleanor Carroll, apparently a first cousin of Charles Carroll of Carrollton. Not much is known about the next two decades of his life except that he only reluctantly backed the War for Independence and remained out of the public eye. No doubt he lived the life of a gentleman planter.

In 1781 Carroll entered the political arena. Elected to the Continental Congress that year, he carried to Philadelphia the news that Maryland was at last ready to accede to the Articles of Confederation, to which he soon penned his name. During the decade, he also began a tour in the Maryland senate that was to span his lifetime and helped George Washington promote the Patowmack Company, a scheme to canalize the Potomac River so as to provide a transportation link between the East and the trans-Appalachian West.

Carroll did not arrive at the Constitutional Convention until July 9, but thereafter he attended quite regularly. He spoke about 20 times during the debates and served on the committee on postponed matters. Returning to Maryland after the convention, he campaigned for ratification of the Constitution but was not a delegate to the state convention.

In 1789 Carroll won a seat in the U.S. House of Representatives, where he voted for locating the Nation's Capital on the banks of the Potomac and for Hamilton's program for the federal assumption of state debts. In 1791 George Washington named his friend Carroll as one of three commissioners to survey and define the District of Columbia, where Carroll owned much land. Ill health caused him to resign this post 4 years later, and the next year at the age of 65 he died at his home near Rock Creek in Forest Glen, Md. He was buried there in St. John's Catholic Cemetery.

George Clymer

Pennsylvania

Clymer was orphaned in 1740, only a year after his birth in Philadelphia. A wealthy uncle reared and informally educated him and advanced him from clerk to full-fledged partner in his mercantile firm, which on his death he bequeathed to his ward. Later Clymer merged operations with the Merediths, a prominent business family, and cemented the relationship by marrying his senior partner's daughter, Elizabeth, in 1765.

Motivated at least partly by the impact of British economic restrictions on his business, Clymer early adopted the Revolutionary cause and was one of the first to recommend independence. He attended patriotic meetings, served on the Pennsylvania council of safety, and in 1773 headed a committee that forced the resignation of Philadelphia tea consignees appointed by Britain under the Tea Act. Inevitably, in light of his economic background, he channeled his energies into financial matters. In 1775–76 he acted as one of the first two Continental treasurers, even personally underwriting the war by exchanging all his own specie for Continental currency.

In the Continental Congress (1776–77 and 1780–82) the quiet and unassuming Clymer rarely spoke in debate but made his mark in committee efforts, especially those pertaining to commerce, finance, and military affairs. During the War for Independence, he also served on a series of commissions that conducted important field investigations. In December 1776, when Congress fled from Philadelphia to Baltimore, he and George Walton and Robert Morris remained behind to carry on congressional business. Within a year, after their victory at the Battle of Brandywine, Pa. (September 11, 1777), British troops advancing on Philadelphia detoured for the purpose of vandalizing Clymer's home in Chester County about 25 miles outside the city. His wife and children hid nearby in the woods.

After a brief retirement following his last term in the Continental Congress, Clymer was reelected for the years 1784–88 to the Pennsylvania legislature, where he had also served part time in 1780–82 while still in Congress. As a state legislator, he advocated a bicameral legislature and reform of the penal code and opposed capital punishment. At the Constitutional Convention, where he rarely missed a meeting, he spoke seldom but effectively and played a modest role in shaping the final document.

The next phase of Clymer's career consisted of service in the U.S. House of Representatives in the First Congress (1789–91), followed by appointment as collector of excise taxes on alcoholic beverages in Pennsylvania (1791–94). In 1795–96 he sat on a presidential commission that negotiated a treaty with the Cherokee and Creek Indians in Georgia.

During his retirement, Clymer advanced various community projects, including the Philadelphia Society for Promoting Agriculture and the Pennsylvania Academy of the Fine Arts, and served as the first president of the Philadelphia Bank. At the age of 73, in 1813, he died at Summerseat, an estate a few miles outside Philadelphia at Morrisville that he had purchased and moved to in 1806. His grave is in the Friends Meeting House Cemetery at Trenton, N.J.

William Richardson Davie
North Carolina

One of the eight delegates born outside of the Thirteen Colonies, Davie was born in Egremont, Cumberlandshire, England, on June 20, 1756. In 1763 Archibald Davie brought his son William to Waxhaw, S.C., where the boy's maternal uncle, William Richardson, a Presbyterian clergyman, adopted him. Davie attended Queen's Museum College in Charlotte, North Carolina, and graduated from the College of New Jersey (later Princeton) in 1776.

Davie's law studies in Salisbury, N.C., were interrupted by military service, but he won his license to practice before county courts in 1779 and in the superior courts in 1780. When the War for Independence broke out, he helped raise a troop of cavalry near Salisbury and eventually achieved the rank of colonel. While attached to Pulaski's division, Davie was wounded leading a charge at Stono, near Charleston, on June 20, 1779. Early in 1780 he raised another troop and operated mainly in western North Carolina. In January 1781 Davie was appointed commissary-general for the Carolina campaign. In this capacity he oversaw the collection of arms and supplies to Gen. Nathanael Greene's army and the state militia.

After the war, Davie embarked on his career as a lawyer, traveling the circuit in North Carolina. In 1782 he married Sarah Jones, the daughter of his former commander, Gen. Allen Jones, and settled in Halifax. His legal knowledge and ability won him great respect, and his presentation of arguments was admired. Between 1786 and 1798 Davie represented Halifax in the North Carolina legislature. There he was the principal agent behind that body's actions to revise and codify state laws, send representatives to the Annapolis and Philadelphia conventions, cede Tennessee to the Union, and fix disputed state boundaries.

During the Constitutional Convention Davie favored plans for a strong central government. He was a member of the committee that considered the question of representation in Congress and swung the North Carolina delegation's vote in favor of the Great Compromise. He favored election of senators and presidential electors by the legislature and insisted on counting slaves in determining representation. Though he left the convention on August 13, before its adjournment, Davie fought hard for the Constitution's ratification and took a prominent part in the North Carolina convention.

The political and military realms were not the only ones in which Davie left his mark. The University of North Carolina, of which he was the chief founder, stands as an enduring reminder of Davie's interest in education. Davie selected the location, instructors, and a curriculum that included the literary and social sciences as well as mathematics and classics. In 1810 the trustees conferred upon him the title of "Father of the University" and in the next year granted him the degree of Doctor of Laws.

Davie became Governor of North Carolina in 1798. His career also turned back briefly to the military when President John Adams appointed him a brigadier general in the U.S. Army that same year. Davie later served as a peace commissioner to France in 1799.

Davie stood as a candidate for Congress in 1803 but met defeat. In 1805, after the death of his wife, Davie retired from politics to his plantation, "Tivoli," in Chester County, South Carolina. In 1813 he declined an appointment as major-general from President Madison. Davie was 64 years old when he died on November 29, 1820, at "Tivoli," and he was buried in the Old Waxhaw Presbyterian Churchyard in northern Lancaster County.

Jonathan Dayton

New Jersey

Dayton was born at Elizabethtown (present Elizabeth), N.J., in 1760. His father was a storekeeper who was also active in local and state politics. The youth obtained a good education, graduating from the College of New Jersey (later Princeton) in 1776. He immediately entered the Continental Army and saw extensive action. Achieving the rank of captain by the age of 19 and serving under his father, Gen. Elias Dayton, and the Marquis de Lafayette, he was a prisoner of the British for a time and participated in the Battle of Yorktown, Va.

After the war, Dayton returned home, studied law, and established a practice. During the 1780s, he divided his time between land speculation, legal practice, and politics. He sat in the assembly in 1786–87. In the latter year, he was chosen as a delegate to the Constitutional Convention after the leaders of his political faction, his father and his patron, Abraham Clark, declined to attend. Dayton did not arrive at Philadelphia until June 21 but thereafter faithfully took part in the proceedings. He spoke with moderate frequency during the debates and, though objecting to some provisions of the Constitution, signed it.

After sitting in the Continental Congress in 1788, Dayton became a foremost Federalist legislator in the new government. Although elected as a representative, he did not serve in the First Congress in 1789, preferring instead to become a member of the New Jersey council and speaker of the state assembly. In 1791, however, he entered the U.S. House of Representatives (1791–99), becoming Speaker in the Fourth and Fifth Congresses. During this period, he backed Hamilton's fiscal program, suppression of the Whisky Rebellion, Jay's Treaty, and a host of other Federalist measures.

On the personal side, in 1795 Dayton purchased Boxwood Hall as his home in Elizabethtown and resided there until his death. He was elevated to the U.S. Senate (1799–1805). He supported the Louisiana Purchase (1803) and, in conformance with his Federalist views, opposed the repeal of the Judiciary Act of 1801.

In 1806 illness prevented Dayton from accompanying Aaron Burr's abortive expedition to the Southwest, where the latter apparently intended to conquer Spanish lands and create an empire. Subsequently indicted for treason, Dayton was not prosecuted but could not salvage his national political career. He remained popular in New Jersey, however, continuing to hold local offices and sitting in the assembly (1814–15).

In 1824 the 63-year-old Dayton played host to Lafayette during his triumphal tour of the United States, and his death at Elizabeth later that year may have been hastened by the exertion and excitement. He was laid to rest at St. John's Episcopal Church in his hometown. Because he owned 250,000 acres of Ohio land between the Big and Little Miami Rivers, the city of Dayton, was named after him—his major monument. He had married Susan Williamson, but the date of their wedding is unknown. They had two daughters.

John Dickinson

Delaware

J Dickinson, "Penman of the Revolution," was born in 1732 at Crosiadore estate, near the village of Trappe in Talbot County, Md. He was the second son of prosperous farmer Samuel and Mary (Cadwalader) Dickinson, his second wife. In 1740 the family moved to Kent County near Dover, Del., where private tutors educated the youth. In 1750 he began to study law with John Moland in Philadelphia. In 1753 Dickinson went to England to continue his studies at London's Middle Temple. Four years later, he returned to Philadelphia and became a prominent lawyer there. In 1770 he married Mary Norris, daughter of a wealthy merchant. The couple was to have at least one daughter.

By that time, Dickinson's superior education and talents had propelled him into politics. In 1760 he had served in the assembly of the Three Lower Counties (Delaware), where he held the speakership. Combining his Pennsylvania and Delaware careers in 1762, he won a seat as a Philadelphia member in the Pennsylvania assembly and sat there again in 1764. He became the leader of the conservative side in the colony's political battles. His defense of the proprietary governor against the faction led by Benjamin Franklin hurt his popularity but earned him respect for his integrity. Nevertheless, as an immediate consequence, he lost his legislative seat in 1764.

Meantime, the struggle between the colonies and the mother country had waxed strong and Dickinson had emerged in the forefront of Revolutionary thinkers. In the debates over the Stamp Act (1765), he played a key part. That year, he wrote *The Late Regulations Respecting the British Colonies . . . Considered,* an influential pamphlet that urged Americans to seek repeal of the act by pressuring British merchants. Accordingly, the Pennsylvania legislature appointed him as a delegate to the Stamp Act Congress, whose resolutions he drafted.

In 1767–68 Dickinson wrote a series of newspaper articles in the *Pennsylvania Chronicle* that came to be known collectively as *Letters from a Farmer in Pennsylvania.* They attacked British taxation policy and urged resistance to unjust laws, but also emphasized the possibility of a peaceful resolution. So popular were the *Letters* in the colonies that Dickinson received an honorary LL.D. from the College of New Jersey (later Princeton) and public thanks from a meeting in Boston. In 1768, responding to the Townshend Duties, he championed rigorous colonial resistance in the form of nonimportation and nonexportation agreements.

In 1771, back in the Pennsylvania legislature, Dickinson drafted a petition to the king that was unanimously approved. Because of his continued opposition to the use of force, however, by 1774 he had lost much of his popularity. Particularly resenting the tactics of New England leaders, that year he refused to support aid requested by Boston in the wake of the Intolerable Acts, though he sympathized with the city's plight. Reluctantly, Dickinson was drawn into the Revolutionary fray. In 1774 he chaired the Philadelphia committee of correspondence and briefly sat in the First Continental Congress, representing Pennsylvania.

Throughout 1775, though supporting the Whig cause, Dickinson continued to work for peace. He drew up petitions asking the king for redress of grievances. At the same time, he chaired a Philadelphia committee of safety and defense and held a colonelcy in the first battalion recruited in Philadelphia to defend the city.

After Lexington and Concord, Dickinson continued to hope for a peaceful solution. In the Second Continental Congress (1775–76), still a representative of Pennsylvania, he drew up the *Declaration of the Causes of Taking Up Arms.* In the Pennsylvania assembly, he drafted an authorization to send delegates to Congress in 1776. It directed them to seek redress of grievances but ordered them to oppose separation of the colonies from Britain.

By that time, Dickinson's moderate position had left him in the minority. In Congress he voted against the Declaration of Independence (1776) and refused to sign it. Nevertheless, he then became one of only two congressional members (with Thomas McKean) at the time who entered the military, but when he was not reelected he resigned his brigadier general's commission and withdrew to his estate in Delaware. Later in 1776, though reelected to Congress by his new constituency, he declined to serve and also resigned from the Pennsylvania assembly. He may have taken part in the Battle of Brandywine, Pa. (September 11, 1777), as a private in a special Delaware force but otherwise saw no further military action.

Dickinson came out of retirement to take a seat in the Continental Congress (1779–80), where he signed the Articles of Confederation; earlier he had headed the committee that had drafted them. In 1781 he became president of Delaware's Supreme Executive Council. Shortly thereafter, he moved back to Philadelphia. There, he became president of Pennsylvania (1782–85). In 1786, representing Delaware, he attended and chaired the Annapolis Convention.

The next year, Delaware sent Dickinson to the Constitutional Convention. He missed a number of sessions and left early because of illness, but he made worthwhile contributions, including service on the committee on postponed matters. Although he resented the forcefulness of Madison and the other nationalists, he helped engineer the Great Compromise and wrote public letters supporting constitutional ratification. Because of his premature departure from the convention, he did not actually sign the Constitution but authorized his friend and fellow-delegate George Read to do so for him.

Dickinson lived for two decades more but held no public offices. Instead, he devoted himself to writing on politics and in 1801 published two volumes of his collected works. He died at Wilmington in 1808 at the age of 75 and was entombed in the Friends Burial Ground.

Oliver Ellsworth

Connecticut

Oliver Ellsworth was born on April 29, 1745, in Windsor, Conn., to Capt. David and Jemima Ellsworth. He entered Yale in 1762 but transferred to the College of New Jersey (later Princeton) at the end of his second year. He continued to study theology and received his A.B. degree after 2 years. Soon afterward, however, Ellsworth turned to the law. After 4 years of study, he was admitted to the bar in 1771. The next year Ellsworth married Abigail Wolcott.

From a slow start Ellsworth built up a prosperous law practice. His reputation as an able and industrious jurist grew, and in 1777 Ellsworth became Connecticut's state attorney for Hartford County. That same year he was chosen as one of Connecticut's representatives in the Continental Congress. He served on various committees during six annual terms until 1783. Ellsworth was also active in his state's efforts during the Revolution. As a member of the Committee of the Pay Table, Oliver Ellsworth was one of the five men who supervised Connecticut's war expenditures. In 1779 he assumed greater duties as a member of the council of safety, which, with the governor, controlled all military measures for the state.

When the Constitutional Convention met in Philadelphia in 1787, Ellsworth once again represented Connecticut and took an active part in the proceedings. During debate on the Great Compromise, Ellsworth proposed that the basis of representation in the legislative branch remain by state, as under the Articles of Confederation. He also left his mark through an amendment to change the word "national" to "United States" in a resolution. Thereafter, "United States" was the title used in the convention to designate the government.

Ellsworth also served on the committee of five that prepared the first draft of the Constitution. Ellsworth favored the three-fifths compromise on the enumeration of slaves but opposed the abolition of the foreign slave trade. Though he left the convention near the end of August and did not sign the final document, he urged its adoption back in Connecticut and wrote the *Letters of a Landholder* to promote its ratification.

Ellsworth served as one of Connecticut's first two senators in the new federal government between 1789 and 1796. In the Senate he chaired the committee that framed the bill organizing the federal judiciary and helped to work out the organization and practical details necessary to run a new government. Among Ellsworth's other achievements in Congress were framing the measure that admitted North Carolina to the Union, devising the non-intercourse act that forced Rhode Island to join, drawing up the bill to regulate the consular service, and serving on the committee that considered Alexander Hamilton's plan for funding the national debt and for incorporating the Bank of the United States.

In the spring of 1796 he was appointed Chief Justice of the Supreme Court and also served as commissioner to France in 1799 and 1800. Upon his return to America in early 1801, Ellsworth retired from public life and lived in Windsor, Conn. There he died, on November 26, 1807, and he was buried in the cemetery of the First Church of Windsor.

William Few

Georgia

Few was born in 1748. His father's family had emigrated from England to Pennsylvania in the 1680s, but the father had subsequently moved to Maryland, where he married and settled on a farm near Baltimore. William was born there. He encountered much hardship and received minimal schooling. When he was 10 years of age, his father, seeking better opportunity, moved his family to North Carolina.

In 1771 Few, his father, and a brother associated themselves with the "Regulators," a group of frontiersmen who opposed the royal governor. As a result, the brother was hanged, the Few family farm was destroyed, and the father was forced to move once again, this time to Georgia. William remained behind, helping to settle his father's affairs, until 1776 when he joined his family near Wrightsboro, Ga. About this time, he won admittance to the bar, based on earlier informal study, and set up practice in Augusta.

When the War for Independence began, Few enthusiastically aligned himself with the Whig cause. Although largely self-educated, he soon proved his capacity for leadership and won a lieutenant-colonelcy in the dragoons. In addition, he entered politics. He was elected to the Georgia provincial congress of 1776 and during the war twice served in the assembly, in 1777 and 1779. During the same period, he also sat on the state executive council besides holding the positions of surveyor-general and Indian commissioner. He also served in the Continental Congress (1780–88), during which time he was reelected to the Georgia assembly (1783).

Four years later, Few was appointed as one of six state delegates to the Constitutional Convention, two of whom never attended and two others of whom did not stay for the duration. Few himself missed large segments of the proceedings, being absent during all of July and part of August because of congressional service, and never made a speech. Nonetheless, he contributed nationalist votes at critical times. Furthermore, as a delegate to the last sessions of the Continental Congress, he helped steer the Constitution past its first obstacle, approval by Congress. And he attended the state ratifying convention.

Few became one of his state's first U.S. senators (1789-93). When his term ended, he headed back home and served again in the assembly. In 1796 he received an appointment as a federal judge for the Georgia circuit. At 52 years of age in 1799, for some reason he resigned his judgeship and moved to New York City.

Few's career continued to blossom. He served 4 years in the legislature (1802–5) and then as inspector of prisons (1802–10), alderman (1813–14), and U.S. commissioner of loans (1804). From 1804 to 1814 he held a directorship at the Manhattan Bank and later the presidency of City Bank. A devout Methodist, he also donated generously to philanthropic causes.

When Few died in 1828 at the age of 80 in Fishkill-on-the-Hudson (present Beacon), he was survived by his wife (born Catherine Nicholson) and three daughters. Originally buried in the yard of the local Reformed Dutch Church, his body was later reinterred at St. Paul's Church, Augusta, Ga.

Thomas Fitzsimons

Pennsylvania *(No Portrait Available)*

Fitzsimons (FitzSimons; Fitzsimmons) was born in Ireland in 1741. Coming to America about 1760, he pursued a mercantile career in Philadelphia. The next year, he married Catherine Meade, the daughter of a prominent local merchant, Robert Meade, and not long afterward went into business with one of his brothers-in-law. The firm of George Meade and Company soon became one of the leading commercial houses in the city and specialized in the West India trade.

When the Revolution erupted, Fitzsimons enthusiastically endorsed the Whig position. During the war, he commanded a company of militia (1776–77). He also sat on the Philadelphia committee of correspondence, council of safety, and navy board. His firm provided supplies and "fire" ships to the military forces and, toward the end of the war, donated £5,000 to the Continental Army.

In 1782–83 Fitzsimons entered politics as a delegate to the Continental Congress. In the latter year, he became a member of the Pennsylvania council of censors and served as a legislator (1786–89). His attendance at the Constitutional Convention was regular, but he did not make any outstanding contributions to the proceedings. He was, however, a strong nationalist.

After the convention, Fitzsimons continued to demonstrate his nationalistic proclivities as a three-term U.S. representative (1789–95). He allied himself closely with the program of Hamilton and the emerging Federalist Party. Once again demonstrating his commercial orientation, he advocated a protective tariff and retirement of the national debt.

Fitzsimons spent most of the remainder of his life in private business, though he retained an interest in public affairs. His views remained essentially Federalist. During the maritime difficulties in the late 1790s, he urged retaliation against British and French interference with American shipping. In the first decade of the 19th century, he vigorously opposed Jefferson's embargo of 1807–9. In 1810, again clashing with the Jeffersonians, he championed the recharter of the First United States Bank.

But Fitzsimons' prominence stemmed from his business leadership. In 1781 he had been one of the founders of the Bank of North America. He also helped organize and held a directorship in the Insurance Company of North America and several times acted as president of the Philadelphia Chamber of Commerce. His financial affairs, like those somewhat earlier of his associate and fellow-signer Robert Morris, took a disastrous turn in 1805. He later regained some of his affluence, but his reputation suffered.

Despite these troubles, Fitzsimons never ceased his philanthropy. He was an outstanding supporter of Philadelphia's St. Augustine's Roman Catholic Church. He also strived to improve public education in the commonwealth and served as trustee of the University of Pennsylvania.

Fitzsimons died at Philadelphia in 1811 after seven decades of life. His tomb is there in the graveyard at St. Mary's Roman Catholic Church, which is in present Independence National Historical Park.

Benjamin Franklin

Pennsylvania

Franklin was born in 1706 at Boston. He was the tenth son of a soap- and candle-maker. He received some formal education but was principally self-taught. After serving an apprenticeship to his father between the ages of 10 and 12, he went to work for his half-brother James, a printer. In 1721 the latter founded the *New England Courant,* the fourth newspaper in the colonies. Benjamin secretly contributed to it 14 essays, his first published writings.

In 1723, because of dissension with his half-brother, Franklin moved to Philadelphia, where he obtained employment as a printer. He spent only a year there and then sailed to London for 2 more years. Back in Philadelphia, he rose rapidly in the printing industry. He published *The Pennsylvania Gazette* (1730–48), which had been founded by another man in 1728, but his most successful literary venture was the annual *Poor Richard's Almanac* (1733–58). It won a popularity in the colonies second only to the Bible, and its fame eventually spread to Europe.

Meantime, in 1730 Franklin had taken a common-law wife, Deborah Read, who was to bear him a son and daughter, and he also apparently had children with another nameless woman out of wedlock. By 1748 he had achieved financial independence and gained recognition for his philanthropy and the stimulus he provided to such civic causes as libraries, educational institutions, and hospitals. Energetic and tireless, he also found time to pursue his interest in science, as well as to enter politics.

Franklin served as clerk (1736–51) and member (1751–64) of the colonial legislature and as deputy postmaster of Philadelphia (1737–53) and deputy postmaster general of the colonies (1753–74). In addition, he represented Pennsylvania at the Albany Congress (1754), called to unite the colonies during the French and Indian War. The congress adopted his "Plan of Union," but the colonial assemblies rejected it because it encroached on their powers.

During the years 1757–62 and 1764–75, Franklin resided in England, originally in the capacity of agent for Pennsylvania and later for Georgia, New Jersey, and Massachusetts. During the latter period, which coincided with the growth of colonial unrest, he underwent a political metamorphosis. Until then a contented Englishman in outlook, primarily concerned with Pennsylvania provincial politics, he distrusted popular movements and saw little purpose to be served in carrying principle to extremes. Until the issue of parliamentary taxation undermined the old alliances, he led the Quaker party attack on the Anglican proprietary party and its Presbyterian frontier allies. His purpose throughout the years at London in fact had been displacement of the Penn family administration by royal authority—the conversion of the province from a proprietary to a royal colony.

It was during the Stamp Act crisis that Franklin evolved from leader of a shattered provincial party's faction to celebrated spokesman at London for American rights. Although as agent for Pennsylvania he opposed by every conceivable means the enactment of the bill in 1765, he did not at first realize the depth of colonial hostility. He regarded passage as unavoidable and preferred to submit to it while actually working for its repeal.

Franklin's nomination of a friend and political ally as stamp distributor for Pennsylvania, coupled with his apparent acceptance of the legislation, armed his proprietary opponents with explosive issues. Their energetic exploitation of them endangered his reputation at home until reliable information was published demonstrating his unabated opposition to the act. For a time, mob resentment threatened his family and new home in Philadelphia until his tradesmen supporters rallied. Subsequently, Franklin's defense of the American position in the House of Commons during the debates over the Stamp Act's repeal restored his prestige at home.

Franklin returned to Philadelphia in May 1775, and immediately became a distinguished member of the Continental Congress. Thirteen months later, he served on the committee that drafted the Declaration of Independence. He subsequently contributed to the government in other important ways, including service as postmaster general, and took over the duties of president of the Pennsylvania constitutional convention.

But, within less than a year and a half after his return, the aged statesman set sail once again for Europe, beginning a career as diplomat that would occupy him for most of the rest of his life. In the years 1776–79, as one of three commissioners, he directed the negotiations that led to treaties of commerce and alliance with France, where the people adulated him, but he and the other commissioners squabbled constantly. While he was sole commissioner to France (1779–85), he and John Jay and John Adams negotiated the Treaty of Paris (1783), which ended the War for Independence.

Back in the United States, in 1785 Franklin became president of the Supreme Executive Council of Pennsylvania. At the Constitutional Convention, though he did not approve of many aspects of the finished document and was hampered by his age and ill-health, he missed few if any sessions, lent his prestige, soothed passions, and compromised disputes.

In his twilight years, working on his *Autobiography,* Franklin could look back on a fruitful life as the toast of two continents. Energetic nearly to the last, in 1787 he was elected as first president of the Pennsylvania Society for Promoting the Abolition of Slavery—a cause to which he had committed himself as early as the 1730s. His final public act was signing a memorial to Congress recommending dissolution of the slavery system. Shortly thereafter, in 1790 at the age of 84, Franklin passed away in Philadelphia and was laid to rest in Christ Church Burial Ground.

Elbridge Gerry

Massachusetts

Gerry was born in 1744 at Marblehead, Mass., the third of 12 children. His mother was the daughter of a Boston merchant; his father, a wealthy and politically active merchant-shipper who had once been a sea captain. Upon graduating from Harvard in 1762, Gerry joined his father and two brothers in the family business, exporting dried codfish to Barbados and Spain. He entered the colonial legislature (1772–74), where he came under the influence of Samuel Adams, and took part in the Marblehead and Massachusetts committees of correspondence. When Parliament closed Boston harbor in June 1774, Marblehead became a major port of entry for supplies donated by patriots throughout the colonies to relieve Bostonians, and Gerry helped transport the goods.

Between 1774 and 1776 Gerry attended the first and second provincial congresses; served with Samuel Adams and John Hancock on the council of safety; and, as chairman of the committee of supply, a job for which his merchant background ideally suited him, raised troops and dealt with military logistics. On the night of April 18, 1775, Gerry attended a meeting of the council of safety at an inn in Menotomy (Arlington), between Cambridge and Lexington, and barely escaped the British troops marching on Lexington and Concord.

In 1776 Gerry entered the Continental Congress, where his congressional specialities were military and financial matters. In Congress and throughout his career his actions often appeared contradictory. He earned the nickname "soldiers' friend" for his advocacy of better pay and equipment, yet he vacillated on the issue of pensions; despite his disapproval of standing armies, he recommended long-term enlistments.

Until 1779 Gerry sat on and sometimes presided over the congressional board that regulated Continental finances. After a quarrel over the price schedule for suppliers, Gerry, himself a supplier, walked out of Congress. Although nominally a member, he did not reappear for 3 years. During the interim, he engaged in trade and privateering and served in the lower house of the Massachusetts legislature.

Back in Congress in the years 1783–85, Gerry numbered among those representatives who had possessed talent as Revolutionary agitators and wartime leaders but who could not effectually cope with the painstaking task of stabilizing the national government. He was experienced and conscientious but created many enemies with his lack of humor, suspicion of the motives of others, and obsessive fear of political and military tyranny. In 1786, the year after leaving Congress, he retired from business, married Ann Thompson, and took a seat in the state legislature.

Gerry was one of the most vocal delegates at the Constitutional Convention of 1787. He presided as chairman of the committee that produced the Great Compromise but disliked the compromise itself. He antagonized nearly everyone by his inconsistency and, according to a colleague, "objected to everything he did not propose." At first an advocate of a strong central government, Gerry ultimately rejected and refused to sign the Constitution because it lacked a bill of rights and because he deemed it a threat to republicanism. He led the drive against ratification in Massachusetts and denounced the document as "full of vices." Among the vices he listed inadequate representation of the people, dangerously ambiguous legislative powers, the blending of the executive and the legislative, and the danger of an oppressive judiciary. Gerry did see some merit in the Constitution, though, and believed that its flaws could be remedied through amendments. In 1789, after he announced his intention to support the Constitution, he was elected to the First Congress where, to the chagrin of the Antifederalists, he championed Federalist policies.

Gerry left Congress for the last time in 1793 and retired for 4 years. During this period he came to mistrust the aims of the Federalists, particularly their attempts to nurture an alliance with Britain, and sided with the pro-French Democratic-Republicans. In 1797 President John Adams appointed him as the only non-Federalist member of a three-man commission charged with negotiating a reconciliation with France, which was on the brink of war with the United States. During the ensuing XYZ affair (1797–98), Gerry tarnished his reputation. Talleyrand, the French foreign minister, led him to believe that his presence in France would prevent war, and Gerry lingered on long after the departure of John Marshall and Charles Cotesworth Pinckney, the two other commissioners. Finally, the embarrassed Adams recalled him, and Gerry met severe censure from the Federalists upon his return.

In 1800–1803 Gerry, never very popular among the Massachusetts electorate because of his aristocratic haughtiness, met defeat in four bids for the Massachusetts governorship but finally triumphed in 1810. Near the end of his two terms, scarred by partisan controversy, the Democratic-Republicans passed a redistricting measure to ensure their domination of the state senate. In response, the Federalists heaped ridicule on Gerry and coined the pun "gerrymander" to describe the salamander-like shape of one of the redistricted areas.

Despite his advanced age, frail health, and the threat of poverty brought on by neglect of personal affairs, Gerry served as James Madison's Vice President in 1813. In the fall of 1814, the 70-year old politician collapsed on his way to the Senate and died. He left his wife, who was to live until 1849, the last surviving widow of a signer of the Declaration of Independence, as well as three sons and four daughters. Gerry is buried in Congressional Cemetery at Washington, D.C.

Nicholas Gilman

New Hampshire

Member of a distinguished New Hampshire family and second son in a family of eight, Nicholas Gilman was born at Exeter in 1755. He received his education in local schools and worked at his father's general store. When the War for Independence began, he enlisted in the New Hampshire element of the Continental Army, soon won a captaincy, and served throughout the war.

Gilman returned home, again helped his father in the store, and immersed himself in politics. In the period 1786–88 he sat in the Continental Congress, though his attendance record was poor. In 1787 he represented New Hampshire at the Constitutional Convention. He did not arrive at Philadelphia until July 21, by which time much major business had already occurred. Never much of a debater, he made no speeches and played only a minor part in the deliberations. He did, however, serve on the committee on postponed matters. He was also active in obtaining New Hampshire's acceptance of the Constitution and in shepherding it through the Continental Congress.

Gilman later became a prominent Federalist politician. He served in the U.S. House of Representatives from 1789 until 1797; and in 1793 and 1797 was a presidential elector. He also sat in the New Hampshire legislature in 1795, 1802, and 1804, and in the years 1805–8 and 1811–14 he held the office of state treasurer.

Meantime, Gilman's political philosophy had begun to drift toward the Democratic-Republicans. In 1802, when he was defeated for the U.S. Senate, President Jefferson appointed him as a bankruptcy commissioner, and 2 years later as a Democratic-Republican he won election to the U.S. Senate. He was still serving there when he passed away at Philadelphia, while on his way home from the Nation's Capital, in 1814 at the age of 58. He is interred at the Winter Street Cemetery at Exeter.

Nathaniel Gorham

Massachusetts

Gorham, an eldest child, was born in 1738 at Charlestown, Mass., into an old Bay Colony family of modest means. His father operated a packet boat. The youth's education was minimal. When he was about 15 years of age, he was apprenticed to a New London, Conn., merchant. Quitting in 1759, he returned to his hometown and established a business, which quickly succeeded. In 1763 he wed Rebecca Call, who was to bear nine children.

Gorham began his political career as a public notary but soon won election to the colonial legislature (1771–75). During the Revolution, he unswervingly backed the Whigs. He was a delegate to the provincial congress (1774–75), member of the Massachusetts Board of War (1778–81), delegate to the constitutional convention (1779–80), and representative in both the upper (1780) and lower (1781–87) houses of the legislature, including speaker of the latter in 1781, 1782, and 1785. In the last year, though he apparently lacked formal legal training, he began a judicial career as judge of the Middlesex County court of common pleas (1785–96). During this same period, he sat on the Governor's Council (1788–89).

During the war, British troops had ravaged much of Gorham's property, though by privateering and speculation he managed to recoup most of his fortune. Despite these pressing business concerns and his state political and judicial activities, he also served the nation. He was a member of the Continental Congress (1782–83 and 1785–87), from June 1786 until January 1787 holding the office of president.

The next year, at age 49, Gorham attended the Constitutional Convention. A moderate nationalist, he played an influential part in the sessions, all of which he attended. He spoke often, acted as chairman of the committee of the whole, and sat on the committee of detail. As a delegate to the Massachusetts ratifying convention, he stood behind the Constitution.

Some unhappy years followed. Gorham did not serve in the new government he had helped to create. In 1788 he and Oliver Phelps of Windsor, Conn., and possibly others, contracted to purchase from the Commonwealth of Massachusetts 6 million acres of unimproved land in western New York. The price was $1 million in devalued Massachusetts scrip. Gorham and Phelps quickly succeeded in clearing Indian title to 2,600,000 acres in the eastern section of the grant and sold much of it to settlers. Problems soon arose, however. Massachusetts scrip rose dramatically in value, enormously swelling the purchase price of the vast tract. By 1790 the two men were unable to meet their payments. The result was a financial crisis that led to Gorham's insolvency—and a fall from the heights of Boston society and political esteem.

Gorham died in 1796 at the age of 58 and is buried at the Phipps Street Cemetery in Charlestown, Mass.

Alexander Hamilton

New York

Hamilton was born in 1757 on the island of Nevis, in the Leeward group, British West Indies. He was the illegitimate son of a common-law marriage between a poor itinerant Scottish merchant of aristocratic descent and an English-French Huguenot mother who was a planter's daughter. In 1766, after the father had moved his family elsewhere in the Leewards to St. Croix in the Danish (now United States) Virgin Islands, he returned to St. Kitts while his wife and two sons remained on St. Croix.

The mother, who opened a small store to make ends meet, and a Presbyterian clergyman provided Hamilton with a basic education, and he learned to speak fluent French. About the time of his mother's death in 1768, he became an apprentice clerk at Christiansted in a mercantile establishment, whose proprietor became one of his benefactors. Recognizing his ambition and superior intelligence, they raised a fund for his education.

In 1772, bearing letters of introduction, Hamilton traveled to New York City. Patrons he met there arranged for him to attend Barber's Academy at Elizabethtown (present Elizabeth), N.J. During this time, he met and stayed for a while at the home of William Livingston, who would one day be a fellow signer of the Constitution. Late the next year, 1773, Hamilton entered King's College (later Columbia College and University) in New York City, but the Revolution interrupted his studies.

Although not yet 20 years of age, in 1774–75 Hamilton wrote several widely read pro-Whig pamphlets. Right after the war broke out, he accepted an artillery captaincy and fought in the principal campaigns of 1776–77. In the latter year, winning the rank of lieutenant colonel, he joined the staff of General Washington as secretary and aide-de-camp and soon became his close confidant as well.

In 1780 Hamilton wed New Yorker Elizabeth Schuyler, whose family was rich and politically powerful; they were to have eight children. In 1781, after some disagreements with Washington, he took a command position under Lafayette in the Yorktown, Va., campaign (1781). He resigned his commission that November.

Hamilton then read law at Albany and quickly entered practice, but public service soon attracted him. He was elected to the Continental Congress in 1782–83. In the latter year, he established a law office in New York City. Because of his interest in strengthening the central government, he represented his state at the Annapolis Convention in 1786, where he urged the calling of the Constitutional Convention.

In 1787 Hamilton served in the legislature, which appointed him as a delegate to the convention. He played a surprisingly small part in the debates, apparently because he was frequently absent on legal business, his extreme nationalism put him at odds with most of the delegates, and he was frustrated by the conservative views of his two fellow delegates from New York. He did, however, sit on the committee of style, and he was the only one of the three delegates from his state who signed the finished document. Hamilton's part in New York's ratification the next year was substantial, though he felt the Constitution was deficient in many respects. Against determined opposition, he waged a strenuous and successful campaign, including collaboration with John Jay and James Madison in writing *The Federalist*. In 1787 Hamilton was again elected to the Continental Congress.

When the new government got underway in 1789, Hamilton won the position of Secretary of the Treasury. He began at once to place the nation's disorganized finances on a sound footing. In a series of reports (1790–91), he presented a program not only to stabilize national finances but also to shape the future of the country as a powerful, industrial nation. He proposed establishment of a national bank, funding of the national debt, assumption of state war debts, and the encouragement of manufacturing.

Hamilton's policies soon brought him into conflict with Jefferson and Madison. Their disputes with him over his pro-business economic program, sympathies for Great Britain, disdain for the common man, and opposition to the principles and excesses of the French revolution contributed to the formation of the first U.S. party system. It pitted Hamilton and the Federalists against Jefferson and Madison and the Democratic-Republicans.

During most of the Washington administration, Hamilton's views usually prevailed with the President, especially after 1793 when Jefferson left the government. In 1795 family and financial needs forced Hamilton to resign from the Treasury Department and resume his law practice in New York City. Except for a stint as inspector-general of the army (1798–1800) during the undeclared war with France, he never again held public office.

While gaining stature in the law, Hamilton continued to exert a powerful impact on New York and national politics. Always an opponent of fellow-Federalist John Adams, he sought to prevent his election to the presidency in 1796. When that failed, he continued to use his influence secretly within Adams' cabinet. The bitterness between the two men became public knowledge in 1800 when Hamilton denounced Adams in a letter that was published through the efforts of the Democratic-Republicans.

In 1802 Hamilton and his family moved into The Grange, a country home he had built in a rural part of Manhattan not far north of New York City. But the expenses involved and investments in northern land speculations seriously strained his finances.

Meanwhile, when Jefferson and Aaron Burr tied in presidential electoral votes in 1800, Hamilton threw valuable support to Jefferson. In 1804, when Burr sought the governorship of New York, Hamilton again managed to defeat him. That same year, Burr, taking offense at remarks he believed to have originated with Hamilton, challenged him to a duel, which took place at present Weehawken, N.J., on July 11. Mortally wounded, Hamilton died the next day. He was in his late forties at death. He was buried in Trinity Churchyard in New York City.

William C. Houston

New Jersey *(No Portrait Available)*

William Houston was born about 1746 to Margaret and Archibald Houston. He attended the College of New Jersey (later Princeton) and graduated in 1768 and became master of the college grammar school and then its tutor. In 1771 he was appointed professor of mathematics and natural philosophy.

From 1775 to 1776 Houston was deputy secretary of the Continental Congress. He also saw active military service in 1776 and 1777 when, as captain of the foot militia of Somerset County, he engaged in action around Princeton. During the Revolution, Houston also served in the New Jersey Assembly (1777) and the New Jersey Council of Safety (1778). In 1779 he was once again elected to the Continental Congress, where he worked mainly in the areas of supply and finance. In addition to serving in Congress, Houston remained active in the affairs of the College of New Jersey and also found time to study law. He was admitted to the bar in 1781 and won the appointment of clerk of the New Jersey Supreme Court in the same year. Houston resigned from the college in 1783 and concentrated on his Trenton law practice. He represented New Jersey in Congress once again in 1784 and 1785.

Houston represented New Jersey at both the Annapolis and Philadelphia conventions. Though illness forced him to leave after 1 week, he did serve on a committee to consider the distribution of seats in the lower house. Houston did not sign the Constitution, but he signed the report to the New Jersey legislature.

On August 12, 1788, William Houston succumbed to tuberculosis and died in Frankford, Pa., leaving his wife Jane, two daughters, and two sons. His body was laid to rest in the Second Presbyterian Churchyard in Philadelphia.

William Houstoun

Georgia

William Houstoun was the son of Sir Patrick Houstoun, a member of the council under the royal government of Georgia. He was born in 1755 in Savannah, Ga. Houstoun received a liberal education, which included legal training at Inner Temple in London. The War for Independence cut short his training, and Houstoun returned home to Georgia. For many years members of Houstoun's family had been high officials in the colony. With the onset of war, many remained loyal to the crown, but William, a zealous advocate of colonists' rights, was among the first to counsel resistance to British aggression.

Houstoun represented Georgia in the Continental Congress from 1783 through 1786. He was chosen as one of Georgia's agents to settle a boundary dispute with South Carolina in 1785 and was one of the original trustees of the University of Georgia at Athens.

When the Constitutional Convention convened in 1787, Houstoun presented his credentials as one of Georgia's delegates. He stayed for only a short time, from June 1 until about July 23, but he was present during the debate on the representation question. Houstoun split Georgia's vote on equal representation in the Senate, voting "nay" against Abraham Baldwin's "aye."

Houstoun died in Savannah on March 17, 1813, and is interred in St. Paul's Chapel, New York City.

Jared Ingersoll

Pennsylvania

The son of Jared Ingersoll, Sr., a British colonial official and later prominent Loyalist, Ingersoll was born at New Haven, Conn., in 1749. He received an excellent education and graduated from Yale in 1766. He then oversaw the financial affairs of his father, who had relocated from New Haven to Philadelphia. Later, the youth joined him, took up the study of law, and won admittance to the Pennsylvania bar.

In the midst of the Revolutionary fervor, which neither father nor son shared, in 1773, on the advice of the elder Ingersoll, Jared, Jr., sailed to London and studied law at the Middle Temple. Completing his work in 1776, he made a 2-year tour of the Continent, during which time for some reason he shed his Loyalist sympathies.

Returning to Philadelphia and entering the legal profession, Ingersoll attended to the clients of one of the city's leading lawyers and a family friend, Joseph Reed, who was then occupied with the affairs of the Supreme Executive Council of Pennsylvania. In 1781 Ingersoll married Elizabeth Pettit (Petit). The year before, he had entered politics by winning election to the Continental Congress (1780–81).

Although Ingersoll missed no sessions at the Constitutional Convention, had long favored revision of the Articles of Confederation, and as a lawyer was used to debate, he seldom spoke during the proceedings.

Subsequently, Ingersoll held a variety of public positions: member of the Philadelphia common council (1789); attorney general of Pennsylvania (1790–99 and 1811–17); Philadelphia city solicitor (1798–1801); U.S. District Attorney for Pennsylvania (1800–01); and presiding judge of the Philadelphia District Cout (1821–22). Meantime, in 1812, he had been the Federalist vice-presidential candidate, but failed to win election.

While pursuing his public activities, Ingersoll attained distinction in his legal practice. For many years, he handled the affairs of Stephen

Girard, one of the nation's leading businessmen. In 1791 Ingersoll began to practice before the U.S. Supreme Court and took part in some memorable cases. Although in both *Chisholm* v. *Georgia* (1792) and *Hylton* v. *United States* (1796) he represented the losing side, his arguments helped to clarify difficult constitutional issues. He also represented fellow-signer William Blount, a senator, when he was threatened with impeachment in the late 1790s.

Ingersoll's long career ended in 1822, when he died less than a week after his 73d birthday. Survived by three children, he was buried in the cemetery of Philadelphia's First Presbyterian Church.

Daniel of St. Thomas Jenifer

Maryland

Of Swedish and English descent, Jenifer was born in 1723 at Coates Retirement (now Ellerslie) estate, near Port Tobacco in Charles County, Md. Little is known about his childhood or education, but as an adult he came into possession of a large estate near Annapolis, called Stepney, where he lived most of his life. He never married. The web of his far-reaching friendships included such illustrious personages as George Washington.

As a young man, Jenifer served as agent and receiver-general for the last two proprietors of Maryland. He also filled the post of justice of the peace in Charles County and later for the western circuit of Maryland. In 1760 he sat on a boundary commission that settled disputes between Pennsylvania and Delaware. Six years later, he became a member of the provincial court and from 1773 to 1776 sat on the Maryland royal governor's council.

Despite his association with conservative proprietary politics, Jenifer supported the Revolutionary movement, albeit at first reluctantly. He served as president of the Maryland council of safety (1775–77), then as president of the first state senate (1777–80). He sat in the Continental Congress (1778–82) and held the position of state revenue and financial manager (1782–85).

A conservative nationalist, Jenifer favored a strong and permanent union of the states and a Congress with taxation power. In 1785 he represented Maryland at the Mount Vernon Conference. Although he was one of 29 delegates who attended nearly every session of the Constitutional Convention, he did not speak often but backed Madison and the nationalist element.

Jenifer lived only 3 more years and never again held public office. He died at the age of 66 or 67 at Annapolis in 1790. The exact location of his grave, apparently at Ellerslie estate, is unknown.

William Samuel Johnson

Connecticut

The son of Samuel Johnson, the first president of King's College (later Columbia College and University), William was born at Stratford, Conn., in 1727. His father, who was a well-known Anglican clergyman-philosopher, prepared him for college and he graduated from Yale in 1744. About 3 years later, he won a master of arts degree from the same institution and an honorary master's from Harvard.

Resisting his father's wish that he become a minister, Johnson embraced law instead—largely by educating himself and without benefit of formal training. After admittance to the bar, he launched a practice in Stratford, representing clients from nearby New York State as well as Connecticut, and before long he established business connections with various mercantile houses in New York City. In 1749, adding to his already substantial wealth, he married Anne Beach, daughter of a local businessman. The couple was to have five daughters and six sons, but many of them died at an early age.

Johnson did not shirk the civic responsibilities of one of his station. In the 1750s he began his public career as a Connecticut militia officer. In 1761 and 1765 he served in the lower house of the colonial assembly. In 1766 and 1771 he was elected to the upper house.

At the time of the Revolution, conflicting loyalties disturbed Johnson. Although he attended the Stamp Act Congress (1765), moderately opposed the Townshend Duties of 1767, and believed that most British policy was unwise, he retained strong transatlantic ties and found it difficult to choose sides. Many of his friends resided in Britain; in 1765 and 1766 Oxford University conferred honorary master's and doctor's degrees upon him; he had a strong association with the Anglican Church; he acted as Connecticut's agent in Britain during the years 1767–71; and he was friendly with men such as Jared Ingersoll, Sr., who were affiliated with the British administration.

Johnson finally decided to work for peace between Britain and the colonies and to oppose the extremist Whig faction. On this basis, he refused to participate in the First Continental Congress, to which he was elected in 1774, following service as a judge of the Connecticut colonial supreme court (1772–74). When hostilities broke out, he confined his activities to peacemaking efforts. In April 1775 Connecticut sent him and another emissary to speak to British Gen. Thomas Gage about ending the bloodshed. But the time was not ripe for negotiations and they failed. As radical patriot elements gained the ascendancy in Connecticut, Johnson fell out of favor with the government and no longer was called on to serve it. Although he was arrested in 1779 on charges of communicating with the enemy, he cleared himself and was released.

Once the passions of war had ebbed, Johnson resumed his political career. In the Continental Congress (1785–87), he was one of the most influential and popular delegates. Playing a major role in the Constitutional Convention, he missed no sessions after arriving on June 2; espoused the Connecticut Compromise; and chaired the committee of style, which shaped the final document. He also worked for ratification in Connecticut.

Johnson took part in the new government, in the U.S. Senate where he contributed to passage of the Judiciary Act of 1789. In 1791, the year after the government moved from New York to Philadelphia, he resigned mainly because he preferred to devote all his energies to the presidency of Columbia College (1787–1800), in New York City. During these years, he established the school on a firm basis and recruited a fine faculty.

Johnson retired from the college in 1800, a few years after his wife died, and the same year wed Mary Brewster Beach, a relative of his first bride. They resided at his birthplace, Stratford. He died there in 1819 at the age of 92 and was buried at Old Episcopal Cemetery.

Rufus King

Massachusetts

King was born at Scarboro (Scarborough), Mass. (present Maine), in 1755. He was the eldest son of a prosperous farmer-merchant. At age 12, after receiving an elementary education at local schools, he matriculated at Dummer Academy in South Byfield, Mass., and in 1777 graduated from Harvard. He served briefly as a general's aide during the War for Independence. Choosing a legal career, he read for the law at Newburyport, Mass., and entered practice there in 1780.

King's knowledge, bearing, and oratorical gifts soon launched him on a political career. From 1783 to 1785 he was a member of the Massachusetts legislature, after which that body sent him to the Continental Congress (1784–86). There, he gained a reputation as a brilliant speaker and an early opponent of slavery. Toward the end of his tour, in 1786, he married Mary Alsop, daughter of a rich New York City merchant. He performed his final duties for Massachusetts by representing her at the Constitutional Convention and by serving in the commonwealth ratifying convention.

At age 32, King was not only one of the most youthful of the delegates at Philadelphia, but was also one of the most important. He numbered among the most capable orators. Furthermore, he attended every session. Although he came to the convention unconvinced that major changes should be made in the Articles of Confederation, during the debates his views underwent a startling transformation. With Madison, he became a leading figure in the nationalist caucus. He served with distinction on the committee on postponed matters and the committee of style. He also took notes on the proceedings, which have been valuable to historians.

About 1788 King abandoned his law practice, moved from the Bay State to Gotham, and entered the New York political forum. He was elected to the legislature (1789–90), and in the former year was picked as one of the state's first U.S. senators. As political divisions grew in the new government, King's sympathies came to be ardently Federalist. In Congress, he supported Hamilton's fiscal program and stood among the leading proponents of the unpopular Jay's Treaty (1794).

Meantime, in 1791, King had become one of the directors of the First Bank of the United States. Reelected to the U.S. Senate in 1795, he served only a year before he was appointed as Minister to Great Britain (1796–1803).

King's years in this post were difficult ones in Anglo-American relations. The wars of the French Revolution trapped U.S. commerce between the French and the British. The latter in particular violated American rights on the high seas, especially by the impressment of sailors. Although King was unable to bring about a change in this policy, he smoothed relations between the two nations.

In 1803 King sailed back to the United States and to a career in politics. In 1804 and 1808 fellow-signer Charles Cotesworth Pinckney and he were the Federalist candidates for President and Vice President, respectively, but were decisively defeated. Otherwise, King largely contented himself with agricultural pursuits at King Manor, a Long Island estate he had purchased in 1805. During the War of 1812, he was again elected to the U.S. Senate (1813–25) and ranked as a leading critic of the war. Only after the British attacked Washington in 1814 did he come to believe that the United States was fighting a defensive action and to lend his support to the war effort.

In 1816 the Federalists chose King as their candidate for the presidency, but James Monroe handily beat him. Still in the Senate, that same year King led the opposition to the establishment of the Second Bank of the United States. Four years later, believing that the issue of slavery could not be compromised but must be settled once and for all by the immediate establishment of a system of compensated emancipation and colonization, he denounced the Missouri Compromise.

In 1825, suffering from ill health, King retired from the Senate. President John Quincy Adams, however, persuaded him to accept another assignment as Minister to Great Britain. He arrived in England that same year, but soon fell ill and was forced to return home the following year. Within a year, at the age of 72, in 1827, he died. Surviving him were several offspring, some of whom also gained distinction. He was laid to rest near King Manor in the cemetery of Grace Episcopal Church, Jamaica, Long Island, N.Y.

John Langdon

New Hampshire

Langdon was born in 1741 at or near Portsmouth, N.H. His father, whose family had emigrated to America before 1660, was a prosperous farmer who sired a large family. The youth's education was intermittent. He attended a local grammar school, worked as an apprentice clerk, and spent some time at sea. Eventually he went into the mercantile business for himself and prospered.

Langdon, a vigorous supporter of the Revolution, sat on the New Hampshire committee of correspondence and a nonimportation committee. He also attended various patriot assemblies. In 1774 he participated in the seizure and confiscation of British munitions from the Portsmouth fort.

The next year, Langdon served as speaker of the New Hampshire assembly and also sat in the Continental Congress (1775–76). During the latter year, he accepted a colonelcy in the militia of his state and became its agent for British prizes on behalf of the Continental Congress, a post he held throughout the war. In addition, he built privateers for operations against the British—a lucrative occupation.

Langdon also actively took part in the land war. In 1777 he organized and paid for Gen. John Stark's expedition from New Hampshire against British Gen. John Burgoyne and was present in command of a militia unit at Saratoga, N.Y., when the latter surrendered. Langdon later led a detachment of troops during the Rhode Island campaign, but found his major outlet in politics. He was speaker of the New Hampshire legislature from 1777 to 1781. In 1777, meantime, he had married Elizabeth Sherburne, who was to give birth to one daughter.

In 1783 Langdon was elected to the Continental Congress; the next year, to the state senate; and the following year, as president, or chief executive, of New Hampshire. In 1784 he built a home at Portsmouth. In 1786–87 he was back again as speaker of the legislature and during the latter year for the third time in the Continental Congress.

Langdon was forced to pay his own expenses and those of Nicholas Gilman to the Constitutional Convention because New Hampshire was unable or unwilling to pay them. The pair did not arrive at Philadelphia until late July, by which time much business had already been consummated. Thereafter, Langdon made a significant mark. He spoke more than 20 times during the debates and was a member of the committee that struck a compromise on the issue of slavery. For the most part, his sympathies lay on the side of strengthening the national government. In 1788, once again as state president (1788–89), he took part in the ratifying convention.

From 1789 to 1801 Langdon sat in the U.S. Senate, including service as the first President *pro tem* for several sessions. During these years, his political affiliations changed. As a supporter of a strong central government, he had been a member of the Federalist Party, but by the time of Jay's Treaty (1794) he was opposing its policies. By 1801 he was firmly backing the Democratic-Republicans.

That year, Langdon declined Jefferson's offer of the secretaryship of the navy. Between then and 1812, he kept active in New Hampshire politics. He sat again in the legislature (1801–5), twice holding the position of speaker. After several unsuccessful attempts, in 1805 he was elected as governor and continued in that post until 1811 except for a year's hiatus in 1809. Meanwhile, in 1805, Dartmouth College had awarded him an honorary doctor of laws degree.

In 1812 Langdon refused the Democratic-Republican vice-presidential nomination on the grounds of age and health. He enjoyed retirement for another 7 years before he died at the age of 78. His grave is at Old North Cemetery in Portsmouth.

John Lansing, Jr.

New York *(No Portrait Available)*

On January 30, 1754, John Lansing was born in Albany, N.Y., to Gerrit Jacob and Jannetje Lansing. At age 21 Lansing had completed his study of the law and was admitted to practice. In 1781 he married Cornelia Ray. They had 10 children, 5 of whom died in infancy. Lansing was quite wealthy; he owned a large estate at Lansingburg and had a lucrative law practice.

From 1776 to 1777 Lansing acted as military secretary to Gen. Philip Schuyler. From the military world Lansing turned to the political and served six terms in the New York Assembly—1780–84, 1786, and 1788. During the last two terms he was speaker of the assembly. In the 2-year gap between his first four terms in the assembly and the fifth, Lansing sat in the Confederation Congress. He rounded out his public service by serving as Albany's mayor between 1786 and 1790.

Lansing went to Philadelphia as part of the New York delegation to the Constitutional Convention. As the convention progressed, Lansing became disillusioned because he believed it was exceeding its instructions. Lansing believed the delegates had gathered together simply to amend the Articles of Confederation and was dismayed at the movement to write an entirely new constitution. After 6 weeks, John Lansing and fellow New York delegate Robert Yates left the convention and explained their departure in a joint letter to New York Governor George Clinton. They stated that they opposed any system that would consolidate the United States into one government, and they had understood that the convention would not consider any such consolidation. Furthermore, warned Lansing and Yates, the kind of government recommended by the convention could not "afford that security to equal and permanent liberty which we wished to make an invariable object of our pursuit." In 1788, as a member of the New York ratifying convention, Lansing again vigorously opposed the Constitution.

Under the new federal government Lansing pursued a long judicial career. In 1790 he began an 11-year term on the supreme court of New York; from 1798 until 1801 he served as its chief justice. Between 1801 and 1814 Lansing was chancellor of the state. Retirement from that post did not slow him down; in 1817 he accepted an appointment as a regent of the University of the State of New York.

Lansing's death was the most mysterious of all the delegates to the Constitutional Convention. While on a visit to New York City in 1829, he left his hotel to post some letters. No trace of him was ever found, and it was supposed that he had been murdered.

William Livingston

New Jersey

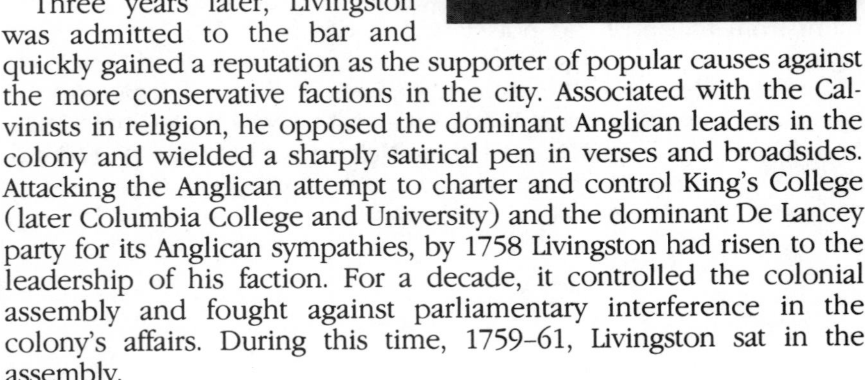

Livingston was born in 1723 at Albany, N.Y. His maternal grandmother reared him until he was 14, and he then spent a year with a missionary among the Mohawk Indians. He attended Yale and graduated in 1741.

Rejecting his family's hope that he would enter the fur trade at Albany or mercantile pursuits in New York City, young Livingston chose to pursue a career in law at the latter place. Before he completed his legal studies, in 1745 he married Susanna French, daughter of a well-to-do New Jersey landowner. She was to bear 13 children.

Three years later, Livingston was admitted to the bar and quickly gained a reputation as the supporter of popular causes against the more conservative factions in the city. Associated with the Calvinists in religion, he opposed the dominant Anglican leaders in the colony and wielded a sharply satirical pen in verses and broadsides. Attacking the Anglican attempt to charter and control King's College (later Columbia College and University) and the dominant De Lancey party for its Anglican sympathies, by 1758 Livingston had risen to the leadership of his faction. For a decade, it controlled the colonial assembly and fought against parliamentary interference in the colony's affairs. During this time, 1759–61, Livingston sat in the assembly.

In 1769 Livingston's supporters, split by the growing debate as to how to respond to British taxation of the colonies, lost control of the assembly. Not long thereafter, Livingston, who had also grown tired of legal practice, moved to the Elizabethtown (present Elizabeth), N.J., area, where he had purchased land in 1760. There, in 1772–73, he built the estate, Liberty Hall, continued to write verse, and planned to live the life of a gentleman farmer.

The Revolutionary upsurge, however, brought Livingston out of retirement. He soon became a member of the Essex County, N.J., committee of correspondence; in 1774 a representative in the First

Continental Congress; and in 1775-76 a delegate to the Second Continental Congress. In June 1776 he left Congress to command the New Jersey militia as a brigadier general and held this post until he was elected later in the year as the first governor of the state.

Livingston held the position throughout and beyond the war—in fact, for 14 consecutive years until his death in 1790. During his administration, the government was organized, the war won, and New Jersey launched on her path as a sovereign state. Although the pressure of affairs often prevented it, he enjoyed his estate whenever possible, conducted agricultural experiments, and became a member of the Philadelphia Society for Promoting Agriculture. He was also active in the antislavery movement.

In 1787 Livingston was selected as a delegate to the Constitutional Convention, though his gubernatorial duties prevented him from attending every session. He did not arrive until June 5 and missed several weeks in July, but he performed vital committee work, particularly as chairman of the one that reached a compromise on the issue of slavery. He also supported the New Jersey Plan. In addition, he spurred New Jersey's rapid ratification of the Constitution (1787). The next year, Yale awarded him an honorary doctor of laws degree.

Livingston died at Liberty Hall in his 67th year in 1790. He was originally buried at the local Presbyterian Churchyard, but a year later his remains were moved to a vault his son owned at Trinity Churchyard in Manhattan and in 1844 were again relocated, to Brooklyn's Greenwood Cemetery.

James McClurg

Virginia

James McClurg was born near Hampton, Va., in 1746. He attended the College of William and Mary and graduated in 1762. McClurg then studied medicine at the University of Edinburgh and received his degree in 1770. He pursued postgraduate medical studies in Paris and London and published *Experiments upon the Human Bile and Reflections on the Biliary Secretions* (1772) in London. His work and writings were well-received and respected by the medical community, and his article was translated into several languages. In 1773 McClurg returned to Virginia and served as a surgeon in the state militia during the Revolution.

Before the end of the war the College of William and Mary appointed McClurg its professor of anatomy and medicine. The same year, 1779, he married Elizabeth Seldon. James McClurg's reputation continued to grow, and he was regarded as one of the most eminent physicians in Virginia. In 1820 and 1821 he was president of the state medical society.

In addition to his medical practice, McClurg pursued politics. In 1782 James Madison advocated McClurg's appointment as secretary of foreign affairs for the United States but was unsuccessful. When Richard Henry Lee and Patrick Henry declined to serve as representatives to the Constitutional Convention in 1787, McClurg was asked to join Virginia's delegation. In Philadelphia McClurg advocated a life tenure for the President and argued for the ability of the federal government to override state laws. Even as some at the convention expressed apprehension of the powers allotted to the presidency, McClurg championed greater independence of the executive from the legislative branch. He left the convention in early August, however, and did not sign the Constitution.

James McClurg's political service did not end with the convention. During George Washington's administration McClurg served on Virginia's executive council. He died in Richmond, Va., on July 9, 1823.

James McHenry

Maryland

McHenry was born at Ballymena, County Antrim, Ireland, in 1753. He enjoyed a classical education at Dublin and in 1771 emigrated to Philadelphia. The following year, the rest of his family came to the colonies, and his brother and father established an import business at Baltimore. During that year, James continued schooling at Newark Academy in Delaware and then studied medicine for 2 years under the well-known Dr. Benjamin Rush in Philadelphia.

During the War for Independence, McHenry served as a military surgeon. Late in 1776, while he was on the staff of the 5th Pennsylvania Battalion, the British captured him at Fort Washington, N.Y. He was paroled early the next year and exchanged in March 1778. Returning immediately to duty, he was assigned to Valley Forge, Pa., and in May became secretary to George Washington. About this time, McHenry apparently quit the practice of medicine to devote himself to politics and administration; he apparently never needed to return to it after the war because of his excellent financial circumstances.

McHenry stayed on Washington's staff until 1780, when he joined that of the Marquis de Lafayette, and he remained in that assignment until he entered the Maryland senate (1781–86). During part of this period, he served concurrently in the Continental Congress (1783–86). In 1784 he married Margaret Allison Caldwell.

McHenry missed many of the proceedings at the Philadelphia convention, in part because of the illness of his brother, and played an insubstantial part in the debates when he was present. He did, however, maintain a private journal that has been useful to posterity. He campaigned strenuously for the Constitution in Maryland and attended the state ratifying convention.

From 1789 to 1791, McHenry sat in the state assembly and in the years 1791–96 again in the senate. A staunch Federalist, he then accepted Washington's offer of the post of Secretary of War and held it into the administration of John Adams. McHenry looked to Hamilton rather than to Adams for leadership. As time passed, the latter became increasingly dissatisfied with McHenry's performance and distrustful of his political motives and in 1800 forced him to resign. Subsequently, the Democratic-Republicans accused him of maladministration, but a congressional committee vindicated him.

McHenry returned to his estate near Baltimore and to semiretirement. He remained a loyal Federalist and opposed the War of 1812. He also held the office of president of a Bible society. He died in 1816 at the age of 62, survived by two of his three children. His grave is in Baltimore's Westminster Presbyterian Cemetery.

James Madison

Virginia

The oldest of 10 children and a scion of the planter aristocracy, Madison was born in 1751 at Port Conway, King George County, Va., while his mother was visiting her parents. With her newborn son, in a few weeks she journeyed back to Montpelier estate, in Orange County, which became his lifelong home. He received his early education from his mother, from tutors, and at a private school. An excellent scholar though frail and sickly in his youth, in 1771 he graduated from the College of New Jersey (later Princeton), where he demonstrated special interest in government and the law. But, considering the ministry for a career, he stayed on for a year of postgraduate study in theology.

Back at Montpelier, still undecided on a profession, Madison soon embraced the patriot cause, and state and local politics absorbed much of his time. In 1775 he served on the Orange County committee of safety; the next year at the Virginia convention, which, besides advocating various Revolutionary steps, framed the Virginia constitution; in 1776–77 in the House of Delegates; and in 1778–80 in the Council of State. His ill health precluded any military service.

In 1780 Madison was chosen to represent Virginia in the Continental Congress (1780–83 and 1786–88). Although originally the youngest delegate, he played a major role in the deliberations of that body.

Meantime, in the years 1784–86, he had again sat in the Virginia House of Delegates. He was a guiding force behind the Mount Vernon Conference (1785), attended the Annapolis Convention (1786), and was otherwise highly instrumental in the convening of the Constitutional Convention in 1787. He had also written extensively about deficiencies in the Articles of Confederation.

Madison was clearly the preeminent figure at the convention. Some of the delegates favored an authoritarian central Government; others, retention of state sovereignty; and most occupied positions in the middle of the two extremes. Madison, who was rarely absent and whose Virginia Plan was in large part the basis of the Constitution, tirelessly advocated a strong government, though many of his proposals were rejected. Despite his lack of special capability as a speaker, he took the floor more than 150 times, third only after Gouverneur Morris and James Wilson. Madison was also a member of numerous committees, the most important of which were those on postponed matters and style. His journal of the convention is the best single record of the event. He also played a key part in guiding the Constitution through the Continental Congress.

Playing a lead in the ratification process in Virginia, too, Madison defended the document against such powerful opponents as Patrick Henry, George Mason, and Richard Henry Lee. In New York, where Madison was serving in the Continental Congress, he collaborated with Alexander Hamilton and John Jay in a series of essays that in 1787–88 appeared in the newspapers and were soon published in book form as *The Federalist* (1788). This set of essays is a classic of political theory and a lucid exposition of the republican principles that dominated the framing of the Constitution.

In the U.S. House of Representatives (1789–97), Madison helped frame and ensure passage of the Bill of Rights. He also assisted in organizing the executive department and creating a system of federal taxation. As leaders of the opposition to Hamilton's policies, he and Jefferson founded the Democratic-Republican Party.

In 1794 Madison married a vivacious widow who was 16 years his junior, Dolley Payne Todd, who had a son; they were to raise no children of their own. Madison spent the period 1797–1801 in semiretirement, but in 1798 he wrote the Virginia Resolutions, which attacked the Alien and Sedition Acts. While he served as Secretary of State (1801–9), his wife often served as President Jefferson's hostess.

In 1809 Madison succeeded Jefferson. Like the first three Presidents, Madison was enmeshed in the ramifications of European wars. Diplomacy had failed to prevent the seizure of U.S. ships, goods, and men on the high seas, and a depression wracked the country. Madison continued to apply diplomatic techniques and economic sanctions, eventually effective to some degree against France. But continued British interference with shipping, as well as other grievances, led to the War of 1812.

The war, for which the young nation was ill prepared, ended in stalemate in December 1814 when the inconclusive Treaty of Ghent, which nearly restored prewar conditions, was signed. But, thanks mainly to Andrew Jackson's spectacular victory at the Battle of New Orleans (Chalmette) in January 1815, most Americans believed they had won. Twice tested, independence had survived, and an ebullient nationalism marked Madison's last years in office, during which period the Democratic-Republicans held virtually uncontested sway.

In retirement after his second term, Madison managed Montpelier but continued to be active in public affairs. He devoted long hours to editing his journal of the Constitutional Convention, which the government was to publish 4 years after his death. He served as cochairman of the Virginia constitutional convention of 1829–30 and as rector of the University of Virginia during the period 1826–36. Writing newspaper articles defending the administration of Monroe, he also acted as his foreign policy adviser.

Madison spoke out, too, against the emerging sectional controversy that threatened the existence of the Union. Although a slaveholder all his life, he was active during his later years in the American Colonization Society, whose mission was the resettlement of slaves in Africa.

Madison died at the age of 85 in 1836, survived by his wife and stepson.

Alexander Martin

North Carolina

Though he represented North Carolina at the Constitutional Convention, Alexander Martin was born in Hunterdon County, N.J., in 1740. His parents, Hugh and Jane Martin, moved first to Virginia, then to Guilford County, N.C., when Alexander was very young. Martin attended the College of New Jersey (later Princeton), received his degree in 1756, and moved to Salisbury. There he started his career as a merchant but turned to public service as he became justice of the peace, deputy king's attorney, and, in 1774 and 1775, judge of Salisbury district.

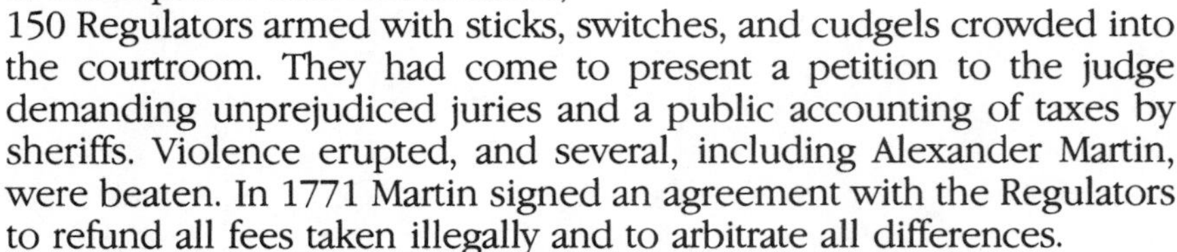

At the September 1770 session of the superior court at Hillsboro, 150 Regulators armed with sticks, switches, and cudgels crowded into the courtroom. They had come to present a petition to the judge demanding unprejudiced juries and a public accounting of taxes by sheriffs. Violence erupted, and several, including Alexander Martin, were beaten. In 1771 Martin signed an agreement with the Regulators to refund all fees taken illegally and to arbitrate all differences.

From 1773 to 1774 Martin served in the North Carolina House of Commons and in the second and third provincial congresses in 1775. In September 1775 he was appointed a lieutenant-colonel in the 2d North Carolina Continental Regiment. Martin saw military action in South Carolina and won promotion to a colonelcy. He joined Washington's army in 1777, but after the Battle of Germantown he was arrested for cowardice. A court-martial tried and acquitted Martin, but he resigned his commission on November 22, 1777.

Martin's misfortune in the army did not impede his political career. The year after his court-martial he entered the North Carolina Senate, where he served for 8 years (1778–82, 1785, and 1787–88). For every session except those of 1778–79, Martin served as speaker. From 1780 to 1781 he also sat on the Board of War and its successor, the Council Extraordinary. In 1781 Martin became acting governor of the state, and in 1782 through 1785 he was elected in his own right.

After his 1785 term in the North Carolina Senate, Martin represented his state in the Continental Congress, but he resigned in 1787. Of the five North Carolina delegates to the Constitutional Convention, Martin was the least strongly Federalist. He did not take an active part in the proceedings, and he left Philadelphia in late August 1787, before the Constitution was signed. Martin was considered a good politician but not suited to public debate. A colleague, Hugh Williamson, remarked that Martin needed time to recuperate after his great exertions as governor "to enable him again to exert his abilities to the advantage of the nation."

Under the new national government, Martin again served as Governor of North Carolina, from 1789 until 1792. After 1790 he moved away from the Federalists to the Republicans. In 1792 Martin, elected by the Republican legislature, entered the U.S. Senate. His vote in favor of the Alien and Sedition Acts cost him reelection. Back in North Carolina, Martin returned to the state senate in 1804 and 1805 to represent Rockingham County. In 1805 he once again served as speaker. From 1790 until 1807 he was a trustee of the University of North Carolina. Martin never married, and he died on November 2, 1807 at the age of 67 at his plantation, "Danbury," in Rockingham County and was buried on the estate.

Luther Martin
Maryland

Like many of the delegates to the Constitutional Convention, Luther Martin attended the College of New Jersey (later Princeton), from which he graduated with honors in 1766. Though born in Brunswick, N.J., in 1748, Martin moved to Maryland after receiving his degree and taught there for 3 years. He then began to study the law and was admitted to the Virginia bar in 1771.

Martin was an early advocate of American independence from Great Britain. In the fall of 1774 he served on the patriot committee of Somerset County, and in December he attended a convention of the Province of Maryland in Annapolis, which had been called to consider the recommendations of the Continental Congress. Maryland appointed Luther Martin its attorney general in early 1778. In this capacity, Martin vigorously prosecuted Loyalists, whose numbers were strong in many areas. Tensions had even led to insurrection and open warfare in some counties. While still attorney general, Martin joined the Baltimore Light Dragoons. In July 1781 his unit joined Lafayette's forces near Fredericksburg, Va., but Martin was recalled by the governor to prosecute a treason trial.

Martin married Maria Cresap on Christmas 1783. Of their five children, three daughters lived to adulthood. His postwar law practice grew to become one of the largest and most successful in the country. In 1785 Martin was elected to the Continental Congress, but this appointment was purely honorary. His numerous public and private duties prevented him from traveling to Philadelphia.

At the Constitutional Convention Martin opposed the idea of a strong central government. When he arrived on June 9, 1787, he expressed suspicion of the secrecy rule imposed on the proceedings. He consistently sided with the small states and voted against the Virginia Plan. On June 27 Martin spoke for more than 3 hours in opposition to the Virginia Plan's proposal for porportionate representation in both houses of the legislature. Martin was appointed to the committee formed to seek a compromise on representation, where he supported the case for equal numbers of delegates in at least one house. Before the convention closed, he and another Maryland delegate, John Francis Mercer, walked out.

In an address to the Maryland House of Delegates in 1787 and in numerous newspaper articles, Martin attacked the proposed new form of government and continued to fight ratification of the Constitution through 1788. He lamented the ascension of the national government over the states and condemned what he saw as unequal representation in Congress. Martin opposed including slaves in determining representation and believed that the absence of a jury in the Supreme Court gravely endangered freedom. At the convention, Martin complained, the aggrandizement of particular states and individuals often had been pursued more avidly than the welfare of the country. The assumption of the term "federal" by those who favored a national government also irritated Martin. Around 1791, however, Martin turned to the Federalist party because of his animosity toward Thomas Jefferson.

The first years of the 1800s saw Martin as defense counsel in two controversial national cases. In the first Martin won an acquittal for his close friend, Supreme Court Justice Samuel Chase, in his impeachment trial in 1805. Two years later Martin was one of Aaron Burr's defense lawyers when Burr stood trial for treason in 1807.

After a record 28 consecutive years as state attorney general, Luther Martin resigned in December 1805. In 1813 Martin became chief judge of the court of oyer and terminer for the City and County of Baltimore. He was re-appointed attorney general of Maryland in 1818, and in 1819 he argued Maryland's position in the landmark Supreme Court case *McCulloch* v. *Maryland*. The plaintiff, represented by Daniel Webster, William Pinckney, and William Wirt, won the decision, which determined that states could not tax federal institutions.

Martin's fortunes declined dramatically in his last years. Heavy drinking, illness, and poverty all took their toll. Paralysis, which had struck in 1819, forced him to retire as Maryland's attorney general in 1822. In 1826, at the age of 78, Luther Martin died in Aaron Burr's home in New York City and was buried in an unmarked grave in St. John's churchyard.

George Mason

Virginia

In 1725 George Mason was born to George and Ann Thomson Mason. When the boy was 10 years old his father died, and young George's upbringing was left in the care of his uncle, John Mercer. The future jurist's education was profoundly shaped by the contents of his uncle's 1500-volume library, one-third of which concerned the law.

Mason established himself as an important figure in his community. As owner of Gunston Hall he was one of the richest planters in Virginia. In 1750 he married Anne Eilbeck, and in 23 years of marriage they had five sons and four daughters. In 1752 he acquired an interest in the Ohio Company, an organization that speculated in western lands. When the crown revoked the company's rights in 1773, Mason, the company's treasurer, wrote his first major state paper, *Extracts from the Virginia Charters, with Some Remarks upon Them.*

During these years Mason also pursued his political interests. He was a justice of the Fairfax County court, and between 1754 and 1779 Mason was a trustee of the city of Alexandria. In 1759 he was elected to the Virginia House of Burgesses. When the Stamp Act of 1765 aroused outrage in the colonies, George Mason wrote an open letter explaining the colonists' position to a committee of London merchants to enlist their support.

In 1774 Mason again was in the forefront of political events when he assisted in drawing up the Fairfax Resolves, a document that outlined the colonists' constitutional grounds for their objections to the Boston Port Act. Virginia's Declaration of Rights, framed by Mason in 1776, was widely copied in other colonies, served as a model for Jefferson in the first part of the Declaration of Independence, and was the basis for the federal Constitution's Bill of Rights.

The years between 1776 and 1780 were filled with great legislative activity. The establishment of a government independent of Great Britain required the abilities of persons such as George Mason. He supported the disestablishment of the church and was active in the organization of military affairs, especially in the West. The influence of his early work, *Extracts from the Virginia Charters,* is seen in the 1783 peace treaty with Great Britain, which fixed the Anglo-American boundary at the Great Lakes instead of the Ohio River. After independence, Mason drew up the plan for Virginia's cession of its western lands to the United States.

By the early 1780s, however, Mason grew disgusted with the conduct of public affairs and retired. He married his second wife, Sarah Brent, in 1780. In 1785 he attended the Mount Vernon meeting that was a prelude to the Annapolis convention of 1786, but, though appointed, he did not go to Annapolis.

At Philadelphia in 1787 Mason was one of the five most frequent speakers at the Constitutional Convention. He exerted great influence, but during the last 2 weeks of the convention he decided not to sign the document.

Mason's refusal prompts some surprise, especially since his name is so closely linked with constitutionalism. He explained his reasons at length, citing the absence of a declaration of rights as his primary concern. He then discussed the provisions of the Constitution point by point, beginning with the House of Representatives. The House he criticized as not truly representative of the nation, the Senate as too powerful. He also claimed that the power of the federal judiciary would destroy the state judiciaries, render justice unattainable, and enable the rich to oppress and ruin the poor. These fears led Mason to conclude that the new government was destined to either become a monarchy or fall into the hands of a corrupt, oppressive aristocracy.

Two of Mason's greatest concerns were incorporated into the Constitution. The Bill of Rights answered his primary objection, and the 11th amendment addressed his call for strictures on the judiciary.

Throughout his career Mason was guided by his belief in the rule of reason and in the centrality of the natural rights of man. He approached problems coolly, rationally, and impersonally. In recognition of his accomplishments and dedication to the principles of the Age of Reason, Mason has been called the American manifestation of the Enlightenment. Mason died on October 7, 1792, and was buried on the grounds of Gunston Hall.

John Francis Mercer

Maryland

John Francis Mercer, born on May 17, 1759, was the fifth of nine children born to John and Ann Mercer of Stafford County, Va. He attended the College of William and Mary, and in early 1776 he joined the 3d Virginia Regiment. Mercer became Gen. Charles Lee's aide-de-camp in 1778, but after General Lee's court-martial in October 1779, Mercer resigned his commission. He spent the next year studying law at the College of William and Mary and then rejoined the army, where he served briefly under Lafayette.

In 1782 Mercer was elected to the Virginia House of Delegates. That December he became one of Virginia's representatives to the Continental Congress. He later returned to the House of Delegates in 1785 and 1786.

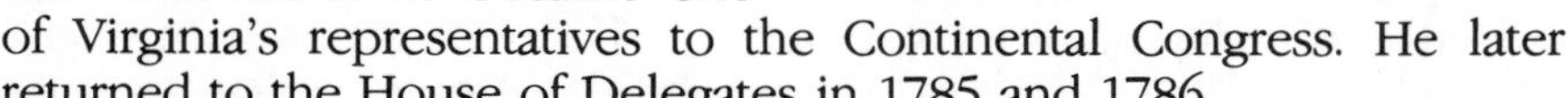

Mercer married Sophia Sprigg in 1785 and soon after moved to Anne Arundel County, Md. He attended the Constitutional Convention as part of Maryland's delegation when he was only 28 years old, the second youngest delegate in Philadelphia. Mercer was strongly opposed to centralization and both spoke and voted against the Constitution. He and fellow Marylander Luther Martin left the proceedings before they ended.

After the convention, Mercer continued in public service. He allied himself with the Republicans and served in the Maryland House of Delegates in 1778–89, 1791–92, 1800–1801, and 1803–6. Between 1791 and 1794 he also sat in the U.S. House of Representatives for Maryland and was chosen governor of the state for two terms, 1801–3. During Thomas Jefferson's term as President, Mercer broke with the Republicans and joined the Federalist camp.

Illness plagued him during his last years. In 1821 Mercer traveled to Philadelphia to seek medical attention, and he died there on August 30. His remains lay temporarily in a vault in St. Peter's Church in Philadelphia and were reinterred on his estate, "Cedar Park" in Maryland.

Thomas Mifflin

Pennsylvania

A member of the fourth generation of a Pennsylvania Quaker family who had emigrated from England, Mifflin was born at Philadelphia in 1744, the son of a rich merchant and local politician. He studied at a Quaker school and then at the College of Philadelphia (later part of the University of Pennsylvania), from which he won a diploma at the age of 16 and whose interests he advanced for the rest of his life.

Mifflin then worked for 4 years in a Philadelphia counting-house. In 1764 he visited Europe, and the next year entered the mercantile business in Philadelphia with his brother. In 1767 he wed Sarah Morris. Although he prospered in business, politics enticed him.

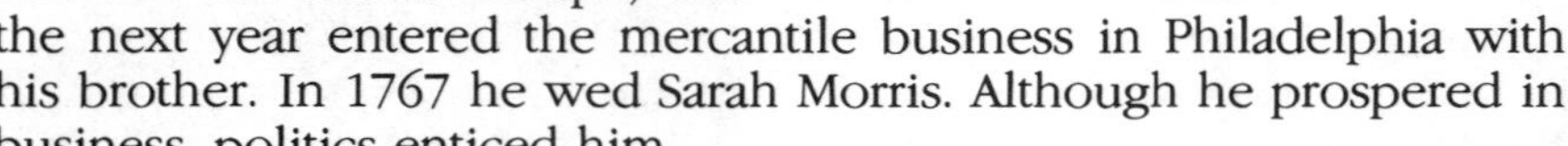

In the Pennsylvania legislature (1772–76), Mifflin championed the colonial position against the crown. In 1774 he attended the Continental Congress (1774–76). Meanwhile, he had helped to raise troops and in May 1775 won appointment as a major in the Continental Army, which caused him to be expelled from his Quaker faith. In the summer of 1775 he first became an aide-de-camp to Washington and then Quartermaster General of the Continental Army. Late in 1775 he became a colonel and in May 1776 a brigadier general. Preferring action to administration, after a time he began to perform his quartermaster duties perfunctorily. Nevertheless, he participated directly in the war effort. He took part in the Battles of Long Island, N.Y., Trenton, N.J., and Princeton, N.J. Furthermore, through his persuasive oratory, he apparently convinced many men not to leave the military service.

In 1777 Mifflin attained the rank of major general but, restive at criticism of his quartermaster activities, he resigned. About the same time, though he later became a friend of Washington, he became involved in the cabal that advanced Gen. Horatio Gates to replace him in command of the Continental Army. In 1777–78 Mifflin sat on the Congressional Board of War. In the latter year, he briefly reentered the military, but continuing attacks on his earlier conduct of the quartermastership soon led him to resign once more.

Mifflin returned immediately to politics. He sat in the state assembly (1778–79) and again in the Continental Congress (1782–84), from December 1783 to the following June as its president. In 1787 he was chosen to take part in the Constitutional Convention. He attended regularly, but made no speeches and did not play a substantial role.

Mifflin continued in the legislature (1785–88 and 1799–1800); succeeded Franklin as president of the Supreme Executive Council (1788–90); chaired the constitutional convention (1789–90); and held the governorship (1790–99), during which time he affiliated himself with the emerging Democratic-Republican Party.

Although wealthy most of his life, Mifflin was a lavish spender. Pressure from his creditors forced him to leave Philadelphia in 1799, and he died at Lancaster the next year, aged 56. The Commonwealth of Pennsylvania paid his burial expenses at the local Trinity Lutheran Church.

Gouverneur Morris

Pennsylvania

Of French and English descent, Morris was born at Morrisania estate, in Westchester (present Bronx) County, N.Y., in 1752. His family was wealthy and enjoyed a long record of public service. His elder half-brother, Lewis, signed the Declaration of Independence.

Gouverneur was educated by private tutors and at a Huguenot school in New Rochelle. In early life, he lost a leg in a carriage accident. He attended King's College (later Columbia College and University) in New York City, graduating in 1768 at the age of 16. Three years later, after reading law in the city, he gained admission to the bar.

When the Revolution loomed on the horizon, Morris became interested in political affairs. Because of his conservatism, however, he at first feared the movement, which he believed would bring mob rule. Furthermore, some of his family and many of his friends were Loyalists. But, beginning in 1775, for some reason he sided with the

Whigs. That same year, representing Westchester County, he took a seat in New York's Revolutionary provincial congress (1775–77). In 1776, when he also served in the militia, along with John Jay and Robert R. Livingston he drafted the first constitution of the state. Subsequently he joined its council of safety (1777).

In 1777–78 Morris sat in the legislature and in 1778–79 in the Continental Congress, where he numbered among the youngest and most brilliant members. During this period, he signed the Articles of Confederation and drafted instructions for Benjamin Franklin, in Paris, as well as those that provided a partial basis for the treaty ending the War for Independence. Morris was also a close friend of Washington and one of his strongest congressional supporters.

Defeated in his bid for reelection to Congress in 1779 because of the opposition of Gov. George Clinton's faction, Morris relocated to Philadelphia and resumed the practice of law. This temporarily removed him from the political scene, but in 1781 he resumed his public career when he became the principal assistant to Robert Morris, Superintendent of Finance for the United States, to whom he was unrelated. Gouverneur held this position for 4 years.

Morris emerged as one of the leading figures at the Constitutional Convention. His speeches, more frequent than those by anyone else, numbered 173. Although sometimes presented in a light vein, they were usually substantive. A strong advocate of nationalism and aristocratic rule, he served on many committees, including those on postponed matters and style, and stood in the thick of the decision-making process. Above all, it was apparently he who actually drafted the Constitution.

Morris subsequently left public life for a time to devote his attention to business. Having purchased the family home from his half-brother, Lewis, he moved back to New York, but soon, in 1789, on a venture in association with Robert Morris, traveled to France, where he witnessed the beginnings of the French Revolution.

Morris was to remain in Europe for about a decade. In 1790–91 he undertook a diplomatic mission to London to try to negotiate some of the outstanding problems between the United States and Great Britain. The mission failed, but in 1792 Washington appointed him as Minister to France, to replace Thomas Jefferson. Morris was recalled 2 years later but did not come home. Instead, he traveled extensively in Europe for more than 4 years, during which time he handled his complicated business affairs and contemplated the complex political situation.

Morris returned to the United States in 1799. The next year, he was elected to finish an unexpired term in the U.S. Senate. An ardent

Federalist, he was defeated in his bid for reelection in 1802 and left office the following year.

Morris retired to a glittering life at Morrisania, where he had built a new residence. In 1809 he married Anne Cary (Carey) Randolph of Virginia, and they had one son. During his last years, he continued to speak out against the Democratic-Republicans and violently opposed the War of 1812. In the years 1810–13, he served as chairman of the Erie Canal Commission.

Morris died at Morrisania in 1816 at the age of 64 and was buried at St. Anne's Episcopal Churchyard, in the Bronx, New York City.

Robert Morris

Pennsylvania

Morris was born at or near Liverpool, England, in 1734. When he reached 13 years of age, he emigrated to Maryland to join his father, a tobacco exporter at Oxford, Md. After brief schooling at Philadelphia, the youth obtained employment with Thomas and Charles Willing's well-known shipping-banking firm. In 1754 he became a partner and for almost four decades was one of the company's directors as well as an influential Philadelphia citizen. Wedding Mary White at the age of 35, he fathered five sons and two daughters.

During the Stamp Act turmoil in 1765, Morris had joined other merchants in protest, but not until the outbreak of hostilities a decade later did he fully commit himself to the Revolution. In 1775 the Continental Congress contracted with his firm to import arms and ammunition, and he was elected to the Pennsylvania council of safety (1775–76), the committee of correspondence, the provincial assembly (1775–76), the legislature (1776–78), and the Continental Congress (1775–78). In the last body, on July 1, 1776, he voted against independence, which he personally considered premature, but the next day he purposely absented himself to facilitate an affirmative ballot by his delegation.

Morris, a key congressman, specialized in financial affairs and military procurement. Although he and his firm profited handsomely, had it not been for his assiduous labors the Continental Army would probably have needed to demobilize. He worked closely with General Washington, wheedled money and supplies from the states, borrowed money in the face of overwhelming difficulties, and on occasion even obtained personal loans to further the war cause.

Immediately following his congressional service, Morris sat for two more terms in the Pennsylvania legislature (1778–81). During this time, Thomas Paine and others attacked him for profiteering in Congress, which investigated his accounts and vindicated him. Nevertheless, his reputation suffered.

Morris embarked on the most dramatic phase of his career by accepting the office of Superintendent of Finance (1781–84) under the Articles of Confederation. Congress, recognizing the perilous state of the nation's finances and its impotence to provide remedies, granted him dictatorial powers and acquiesced to his condition that he be allowed to continue his private commercial enterprises. He slashed all governmental and military expenditures, personally purchased army and navy supplies, tightened accounting procedures, prodded the states to fulfill quotas of money and supplies, and when necessary strained his personal credit by issuing notes over his own signature or borrowing from friends.

To finance Washington's Yorktown campaign in 1781, in addition to the above techniques, Morris obtained a sizable loan from France. He used part of it, along with some of his own fortune, to organize the Bank of North America, chartered that December. The first government-incorporated bank in the United States, it aided war financing.

Although Morris was reelected to the Pennsylvania legislature for 1785–86, his private ventures consumed most of his time. In the latter year, he attended the Annapolis Convention, and the following year the Constitutional Convention, where he sympathized with the Federalists but was, for a man of his eminence, strangely silent. Although in attendance at practically every meeting, he spoke only twice in debates and did not serve on any committees. In 1789, declining Washington's offer of appointment as the first Secretary of the Treasury, he took instead a U.S. Senate seat (1789–95).

During the later years of his public life, Morris speculated wildly, often on overextended credit, in lands in the West and at the site of Washington, D.C. To compound his difficulties, in 1794 he began constructing on Philadelphia's Chestnut Street a mansion designed by Maj. Pierre Charles L'Enfant. Not long thereafter, Morris attempted to escape creditors by retreating to The Hills, the country estate along the Schuylkill River on the edge of Philadelphia that he had acquired in 1770.

Arrested at the behest of creditors in 1798 and forced to abandon completion of the mansion, thereafter known in its unfinished state as "Morris' Folly," Morris was thrown into the Philadelphia debtors' prison, where he was nevertheless well treated. By the time he was released in 1801, under a federal bankruptcy law, however, his property and fortune had vanished, his health had deteriorated, and his spirit had been broken. He lingered on in poverty and obscurity, living in a simple Philadelphia home on an annuity obtained for his wife by fellow-signer Gouverneur Morris.

Robert Morris died in 1806 in his 73d year and was buried in the yard of Christ Church.

William Paterson

New Jersey

William Paterson (Patterson) was born in County Antrim, Ireland, in 1745. When he was almost 2 years of age, his family emigrated to America, disembarking at New Castle, Del. While the father traveled about the country, apparently selling tinware, the family lived in New London, other places in Connecticut, and in Trenton, N.J. In 1750 he settled in Princeton, N.J. There, he became a merchant and manufacturer of tin goods. His prosperity enabled William to attend local private schools and the College of New Jersey (later Princeton). He took a B.A. in 1763 and an M.A. 3 years later.

Meantime, Paterson had studied law in the city of Princeton under Richard Stockton, who later was to sign the Declaration of Independence, and near the end of the decade began practicing at New Bromley, in Hunterdon County. Before long, he moved to South Branch, in Somerset County, and then in 1779 relocated near New Brunswick at Raritan estate.

When the War for Independence broke out, Paterson joined the vanguard of the New Jersey patriots. He served in the provincial congress (1775–76), the constitutional convention (1776), legislative council (1776–77), and council of safety (1777). During the last year, he also held a militia commission. From 1776 to 1783 he was attorney general of New Jersey, a task that occupied so much of his time that it prevented him from accepting election to the Continental Congress in 1780. Meantime, the year before, he had married Cornelia Bell, by whom he had three children before her death in 1783. Two years later, he took a new bride, Euphemia White, but it is not known whether or not they had children.

From 1783, when he moved into the city of New Brunswick, until 1787, Paterson devoted his energies to the law and stayed out of the public limelight. Then he was chosen to represent New Jersey at the Constitutional Convention, which he attended only until late July. Until then, he took notes of the proceedings. More importantly, he figured prominently because of his advocacy and co-authorship of the New Jersey, or Paterson, Plan, which asserted the rights of the small states against the large. He apparently returned to the convention only to sign the final document. After supporting its ratification in New Jersey, he began a career in the new government.

In 1789 Paterson was elected to the U.S. Senate (1789–90), where he played a pivotal role in drafting the Judiciary Act of 1789. His next position was governor of his state (1790–93). During this time, he began work on the volume later published as *Laws of the State of New Jersey* (1800) and began to revise the rules and practices of the chancery and common law courts.

During the years 1793–1806, Paterson served as an associate justice of the U.S. Supreme Court. Riding the grueling circuit to which federal judges were subjected in those days and sitting with the full Court, he presided over a number of major trials.

In September 1806, his health failing, the 60-year-old Paterson embarked on a journey to Ballston Spa, N.Y., for a cure but died en route at Albany in the home of his daughter, who had married Stephen Van Rensselaer. Paterson was at first laid to rest in the nearby Van Rensselaer manor house family vault, but later his body was apparently moved to the Albany Rural Cemetery, Menands, N.Y.

William Leigh Pierce

Georgia *(No Portrait Available)*

Very little is known about William Pierce's early life. He was probably born in Georgia in 1740, but he grew up in Virginia. During the Revolutionary War Pierce acted as an aide-de-camp to Gen. Nathanael Greene and eventually attained the rank of brevet major. For his conduct at the battle of Eutaw Springs, Congress presented him with a ceremonial sword.

The year Pierce left the army, 1783, he married Charlotte Fenwick of South Carolina. They had two sons, one of whom died as a child. Pierce made his home in Savannah, where he engaged in business. He first organized an import-export company, Pierce, White, and Call, in 1783, but it dissolved less than a year later. He made a new start with his wife's dowry and formed William Pierce & Company. In 1786 he was a member of the Georgia House of Representatives and was also elected to the Continental Congress.

At the Constitutional Convention Pierce did not play a large role, but he exerted some influence and participated in three debates. He argued for the election of one house of the federal legislature by the people and one house by the states; he favored a 3-year term instead of a 7-year term in the second house. Because he agreed that the Articles had been insufficient, he recommended strengthening the federal government at the expense of state privileges as long as state distinctions were not altogether destroyed. Pierce approved of the resulting Constitution, but he found it necessary to leave in the middle of the proceedings. A decline in the European rice market adversely affected his business. Soon after he returned to Savannah he went bankrupt, having "neither the skill of an experienced merchant nor any reserve capital." Only 2 years later, on December 10, 1789, Pierce died in Savannah at age 49 leaving tremendous debts.

Pierce's notes on the proceedings of the convention were published in the *Savannah Georgian* in 1828. In them he wrote incisive character sketches that are especially valuable for the information they provide about the lesser-known delegates.

Charles Pinckney
South Carolina

Charles Pinckney, the second cousin of fellow-signer Charles Cotesworth Pinckney, was born at Charleston, S.C., in 1757. His father, Col. Charles Pinckney, was a rich lawyer and planter, who on his death in 1782 was to bequeath Snee Farm, a country estate outside the city, to his son Charles. The latter apparently received all his education in the city of his birth, and he started to practice law there in 1779.

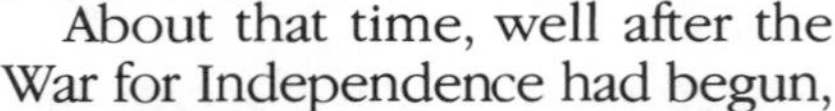

About that time, well after the War for Independence had begun, though his father demonstrated ambivalence about the Revolution, young Pinckney enlisted in the militia, became a lieutenant, and served at the siege of Savannah (September–October 1779). When Charleston fell to the British the next year, the youth was captured and remained a prisoner until June 1781.

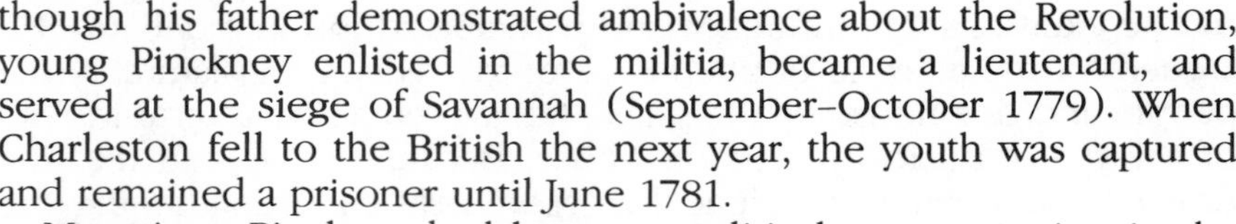

Meantime, Pinckney had begun a political career, serving in the Continental Congress (1777–78 and 1784–87) and in the state legislature (1779–80, 1786–89, and 1792–96). A nationalist, he worked hard in Congress to ensure that the United States would receive navigation rights to the Mississippi and to strengthen congressional power.

Pinckney's role in the Constitutional Convention is controversial. Although one of the youngest delegates, he later claimed to have been the most influential one and contended he had submitted a draft that was the basis of the final Constitution. Most historians have rejected this assertion. They do, however, recognize that he ranked among the leaders. He attended full time, spoke often and effectively, and contributed immensely to the final draft and to the resolution of problems that arose during the debates. He also worked for ratification in South Carolina (1788). That same year, he married Mary Eleanor Laurens, daughter of a wealthy and politically powerful South Carolina merchant; she was to bear at least three children.

Subsequently, Pinckney's career blossomed. From 1789 to 1792 he held the governorship of South Carolina, and in 1790 chaired the state constitutional convention. During this period, he became associated with the Federalist Party, in which he and his cousin Charles Cotesworth Pinckney were leaders. But, with the passage of time, the former's views began to change. In 1795 he attacked the Federalist-backed Jay's Treaty and increasingly began to cast his lot with Carolina back-country Democratic-Republicans against his own eastern aristocracy. In 1796 he became governor once again, and in 1798 his Democratic-Republican supporters helped him win a seat in the U.S. Senate. There, he bitterly opposed his former party, and in the presidential election of 1800 served as Thomas Jefferson's campaign manager in South Carolina.

The victorious Jefferson appointed Pinckney as Minister to Spain (1801–5), in which capacity he struggled valiantly but unsuccessfully to win cession of the Floridas to the United States and facilitated Spanish acquiescence in the transfer of Louisiana from France to the United States in 1803.

Upon completion of his diplomatic mission, his ideas moving ever closer to democracy, Pinckney headed back to Charleston and to leadership of the state Democratic-Republican Party. He sat in the legislature in 1805–6 and then was again elected as governor (1806–8). In this position, he favored legislative reapportionment, giving better representation to back-country districts, and advocated universal white manhood suffrage. He served again in the legislature from 1810 to 1814 and then temporarily withdrew from politics. In 1818 he won election to the U.S. House of Representatives, where he fought against the Missouri Compromise.

In 1821, Pinckney's health beginning to fail, he retired for the last time from politics. He died in 1824, just 3 days after his 67th birthday. He was laid to rest in Charleston at St. Philip's Episcopal Churchyard.

Charles Cotesworth Pinckney
South Carolina

The eldest son of a politically prominent planter and a remarkable mother who introduced and promoted indigo culture in South Carolina, Charles Cotesworth Pinckney was born in 1746 at Charleston. Only 7 years later, he accompanied his father, who had been appointed colonial agent for South Carolina, to England. As a result, the youth enjoyed a European education.

Pinckney received tutoring in London, attended several preparatory schools, and went on to Christ Church College, Oxford, where he heard the lectures of the legal authority Sir William Blackstone and graduated in 1764. Pinckney next pursued legal training at London's Middle Temple and was accepted for admission into the English bar in 1769. He then spent part of a year touring Europe and studying chemistry, military science, and botany under leading authorities.

Late in 1769, Pinckney sailed home and the next year entered practice in South Carolina. His political career began in 1769, when he was elected to the provincial assembly. In 1773 he acted as attorney general for several towns in the colony. By 1775 he had identified with the patriot cause and that year sat in the provincial congress. Then, the next year, he was elected to the local committee of safety and made chairman of a committee that drew up a plan for the interim government of South Carolina.

When hostilities broke out, Pinckney, who had been a royal militia officer since 1769, pursued a full-time military calling. When South Carolina organized its forces in 1775, he joined the First South Carolina Regiment as a captain. He soon rose to the rank of colonel and fought in the South in defense of Charleston and in the North at the Battles of Brandywine, Pa., and Germantown, Pa. He commanded a regiment in the campaign against the British in the Floridas in 1778 and at the siege of Savannah. When Charleston fell in 1780, he was taken prisoner and held until 1782. The following year, he was discharged as a brevet brigadier general.

After the war, Pinckney resumed his legal practice and the management of estates in the Charleston area but found time to continue his public service, which during the war had included tours in the lower house of the state legislature (1778 and 1782) and the senate (1779).

Pinckney was one of the leaders at the Constitutional Convention. Present at all the sessions, he strongly advocated a powerful national government. His proposal that senators should serve without pay was not adopted, but he exerted influence in such matters as the power of the Senate to ratify treaties and the compromise that was reached concerning abolition of the international slave trade. After the convention, he defended the Constitution in South Carolina.

Under the new government, Pinckney became a devoted Federalist. Between 1789 and 1795 he declined presidential offers to command the U.S. Army and to serve on the Supreme Court and as Secretary of War and Secretary of State. In 1796, however, he accepted the post of Minister to France, but the revolutionary regime there refused to receive him and he was forced to proceed to the Netherlands. The next year, though, he returned to France when he was appointed to a special mission to restore relations with that country. During the ensuing XYZ affair, refusing to pay a bribe suggested by a French agent to facilitate negotiations, he is said to have replied "No! No! Not a sixpence!"

When Pinckney arrived back in the United States in 1798, he found the country preparing for war with France. That year, he was appointed as a major general in command of American forces in the South and served in that capacity until 1800, when the threat of war ended. That year, he represented the Federalists as vice-presidential candidate, and in 1804 and 1808 as the presidential nominee. But he met defeat on all three occasions.

For the rest of his life, Pinckney engaged in legal practice, served at times in the legislature, and engaged in philanthropic activities. He was a charter member of the board of trustees of South Carolina College (later the University of South Carolina), first president of the Charleston Bible Society, and chief executive of the Charleston Library Society. He also gained prominence in the Society of the Cincinnati, an organization of former officers of the War for Independence.

During the later period of his life, Pinckney enjoyed his Belmont estate and Charleston high society. He was twice married; first to Sarah Middleton in 1773 and after her death to Mary Stead in 1786. Survived by three daughters, he died in Charleston in 1825 at the age of 79. He was interred there in the cemetery at St. Michael's Episcopal Church.

Edmund Randolph

Virginia

On August 10, 1753, Edmund Randolph was born in Tazewell Hall, Williamsburg, Va. His parents were Ariana Jenings and John Randolph. Edmund attended the College of William and Mary and continued his education by studying the law under his father's tutelage.

When the Revolution broke out, father and son followed different paths. John Randolph, a Loyalist, followed the royal governor, Lord Dunmore, to England in 1775. Edmund then lived with his uncle Peyton Randolph, a prominent figure in Virginia politics. During the war Edmund served as an aide-de-camp to General Washington and also attended the convention that adopted Virginia's first state constitution in 1776. He was the convention's youngest member at age 23. 1776 was also the year of Randolph's marriage to Elizabeth Nicholas.

Randolph continued to advance in the political world. He became mayor of Williamsburg and Virginia's attorney-general. In 1779 he was elected to the Continental Congress, and in November 1786 Randolph became Governor of Virginia. In 1786 he was a delegate to the Annapolis Convention.

Four days after the opening of the federal convention in Philadelphia, on May 29, 1787, Edmund Randolph presented the Virginia Plan for creating a new government. This plan proposed a strong central government composed of three branches, legislative, executive, and judicial, and enabled the legislative to veto state laws and use force against states that failed to fulfill their duties. After many debates and revisions, including striking the section permitting force against a state, the Virginia Plan became in large part the basis of the Constitution.

Though Randolph introduced the highly centralized Virginia Plan, he fluctuated between the Federalist and Antifederalist points of view. He sat on the committee of detail that prepared a draft of the Constitution, but by the time the document was adopted, Randolph declined to sign. He felt it was not sufficiently republican, and he was especially wary of creating a one-man executive. He preferred a three-man council since he regarded "a unity in the Executive" to be the "foetus of monarchy." In a *Letter . . . on the Federal Constitution,* dated October 10, 1787, Randolph explained at length his objections to the Constitution. The old Articles of Confederation were inadequate, he agreed, but the proposed new plan of union contained too many flaws. Randolph was a strong advocate of the process of amendment. He feared that if the Constitution were submitted for ratification without leaving the states the opportunity to amend it, the document might be rejected and thus close off any hope of another plan of union. However, he hoped that amendments would be permitted and second convention called to incorporate the changes.

By the time of the Virginia convention for ratification, Randolph supported the Constitution and worked to win his state's approval of it. He stated his reason for his switch: "The accession of eight states reduced our *deliberations* to the single question of *Union or no Union.*"

Under President Washington, Edmund Randolph became Attorney General of the United States. After Thomas Jefferson resigned as Secretary of State, Randolph assumed that post for the years 1794–95. During the Jefferson-Hamilton conflict he tried to remain unaligned. After retiring from politics in 1795, Randolph resumed his law practice and was regarded as a leading figure in the legal community. During his retirement he wrote a history of Virginia. When Aaron Burr went on trial for treason in 1807, Edmund Randolph acted as his senior counsel. In 1813, at age 60 and suffering from paralysis, Randolph died while visiting Nathaniel Burwell at Carter Hall. His body is buried in the graveyard of the nearby chapel.

George Read

Delaware

Read's mother was the daughter of a Welsh planter, and his Dublin-born father a landholder of means. Soon after George's birth in 1733 near the village of North East in Cecil County, Md., his family moved to New Castle, Del., where the youth, who was one of six sons, grew up. He attended school at Chester, Pa., and Rev. Francis Alison's academy at New London, Pa., and about the age of 15 he began reading with a Philadelphia lawyer.

In 1753 Read was admitted to the bar and began to practice. The next year, he journeyed back to New Castle, hung out his shingle, and before long enlisted a clientele that extended into Maryland. During this period he resided in New Castle but maintained Stonum, a country retreat near the city. In 1763 he wed Gertrude Ross Till, the widowed sister of George Ross, like Read a future signer of the Declaration of Independence. She bore four sons and a daughter.

While crown attorney general (1763–74) for the Three Lower Counties (present Delaware), Read protested against the Stamp Act. In 1765 he began a career in the colonial legislature that lasted more than a decade. A moderate Whig, he supported nonimportation measures and dignified protests. His attendance at the Continental Congress (1774–77) was irregular. Like his friend John Dickinson, he was willing to protect colonial rights but was wary of extremism. He voted against independence on July 2, 1776, the only signer of the Declaration to do so, apparently either bowing to the strong Tory sentiment in Delaware or believing reconciliation with Britain was still possible.

That same year, Read gave priority to state responsibilities. He presided over the Delaware constitutional convention, in which he chaired the drafting committee, and began a term as speaker of the legislative council, which in effect made him vice president of the state. When the British took Wilmington the next fall, they captured the president, a resident of the city. At first, because Read was away in Congress, Thomas McKean, speaker of the lower house, took over as acting president. But in November, after barely escaping from the British himself while he and his family were en route to Dover from Philadelphia, newly occupied by the redcoats, Read assumed the office and held it until the spring of 1778. Back in the legislative council, in 1779 he drafted the act directing Delaware congressional delegates to sign the Articles of Confederation.

During 1779, in poor health, Read resigned from the legislative council, refused reelection to Congress, and began a period of inactivity. During the years 1782–88, he again sat on the council and concurrently held the position of judge of the court of appeals in admiralty cases.

Meantime, in 1784, Read had served on a commission that adjusted New York-Massachusetts land claims. In 1786 he attended the Annapolis Convention. The next year, he participated in the Constitutional Convention, where he missed few if any sessions and championed the rights of the small states. Otherwise, he adopted a Hamiltonian stance, favoring a strong executive. He later led the ratification movement in Delaware, the first state to ratify.

In the U.S. Senate (1789–93), Read's attendance was again erratic, but when present he allied with the Federalists. He resigned to accept the post of chief justice of Delaware. He held it until his death at New Castle 5 years later, just 3 days after he celebrated his 65th birthday. His grave is there in the Immanuel Episcopal Churchyard.

John Rutledge

South Carolina

John Rutledge, elder brother of Edward Rutledge, signer of the Declaration of Independence, was born into a large family at or near Charleston, S.C., in 1739. He received his early education from his father, an Irish immigrant and physician, and from an Anglican minister and a tutor. After studying law at London's Middle Temple in 1760, he was admitted to English practice. But, almost at once, he sailed back to Charleston to begin a fruitful legal career and to amass a fortune in plantations and slaves. Three years later, he married Elizabeth Grimké, who eventually bore him 10 children, and moved into a townhouse, where he resided most of the remainder of his life.

In 1761 Rutledge became politically active. That year, on behalf of Christ Church Parish, he was elected to the provincial assembly and held his seat until the War for Independence. For 10 months in 1764 he temporarily held the post of provincial attorney general. When the troubles with Great Britain intensified about the time of the Stamp Act in 1765, Rutledge, who hoped to ensure continued self-government for the colonies, sought to avoid severance from the British and maintained a restrained stance. He did, however, chair a committee of the Stamp Act Congress that drew up a petition to the House of Lords.

In 1774 Rutledge was sent to the First Continental Congress, where he pursued a moderate course. After spending the next year in the Second Continental Congress, he returned to South Carolina and helped reorganize its government. In 1776 he served on the committee of safety and took part in the writing of the state constitution. That year, he also became president of the lower house of the legislature, a post he held until 1778. During this period, the new government met many stern tests.

In 1778 the conservative Rutledge, disapproving of democratic revisions in the state constitution, resigned his position. The next year, however, he was elected as governor. It was a difficult time. The British were invading South Carolina and the military situation was desperate. Early in 1780, by which time the legislature had adjourned,

Charleston was besieged. In May it fell, the American army was captured, and the British confiscated Rutledge's property. He ultimately escaped to North Carolina and set about attempting to rally forces to recover South Carolina. In 1781, aided by Gen. Nathanael Greene and a new Continental Army force, he reestablished the government. In January 1782 he resigned the governorship and took a seat in the lower house of the legislature. He never recouped the financial losses he suffered during the war.

In 1782–83 Rutledge was a delegate to the Continental Congress. He next sat on the state chancery court (1784) and again in the lower house of the legislature (1784–90). One of the most influential delegates at the Constitutional Convention, where he maintained a moderate nationalist stance and chaired the committee of detail, he attended all the sessions, spoke often and effectively, and served on five committees. Like his fellow South Carolina delegates, he vigorously advocated southern interests.

The new government under the Constitution soon lured Rutledge. He was a presidential elector in 1789 and Washington then appointed him as associate justice of the U.S. Supreme Court, but for some reason he apparently served only a short time. In 1791 he became chief justice of the South Carolina supreme court. Four years later, Washington again appointed him to the U.S. Supreme Court, this time as Chief Justice to replace John Jay. But Rutledge's outspoken opposition to Jay's Treaty (1794), and the intermittent mental illness he had suffered from since the death of his wife in 1792, caused the Federalist-dominated Senate to reject his appointment and end his public career. Meantime, however, he had presided over one term of the Court.

Rutledge died in 1800 at the age of 60 and was interred at St. Michael's Episcopal Church in Charleston.

Roger Sherman

Connecticut

In 1723, when Sherman was 2 years of age, his family relocated from his Newton, Mass., birthplace to Dorchester (present Stoughton). As a boy, he was spurred by a desire to learn and read widely in his spare time to supplement his minimal education at a common school. But he spent most of his waking hours helping his father with farming chores and learning the cobbler's trade from him. In 1743, 2 years after his father's death, Sherman joined an elder brother who had settled in New Milford, Conn.

Purchasing a store, becoming a county surveyor, and winning a variety of town offices, Sherman prospered and assumed leadership in the community. In 1749 he married Elizabeth Hartwell, by whom he had seven children. Without benefit of a formal legal education, he was admitted to the bar in 1754 and embarked upon a distinguished judicial and political career. In the period 1755–61, except for a brief interval, he served as a representative in the colonial legislature and held the offices of justice of the peace and county judge. Somehow he also eked out time to publish an essay on monetary theory and a series of almanacs incorporating his own astronomical observations and verse.

In 1761, abandoning his law practice, Sherman moved to New Haven, Conn. There, he managed a store that catered to Yale students and another in nearby Wallingford. He also became a friend and benefactor of Yale College, functioning for many years as its treasurer. In 1763, or 3 years after the death of his first wife, he wed Rebecca Prescott, who bore eight children.

Meanwhile, Sherman's political career had blossomed. He rose from justice of the peace and county judge to an associate judge of the Connecticut Superior Court and to representative in both houses of the colonial assembly. Although opposed to extremism, he early joined the fight against Britain. He supported nonimportation measures and headed the New Haven committee of correspondence.

Sherman was a longtime and influential member of the Continental Congress (1774–81 and 1783–84). He won membership on the committees that drafted the Declaration of Independence and the Articles of Confederation, as well as those concerned with Indian affairs, national finances, and military matters. To solve economic problems, at both national and state levels, he advocated high taxes rather than excessive borrowing or the issuance of paper currency.

While in Congress, Sherman remained active in state and local politics, continuing to hold the office of judge of the Connecticut Superior Court, as well as membership on the council of safety (1777–79). In 1783 he helped codify Connecticut's statutory laws. The next year, he was elected as mayor of New Haven (1784–86).

Although on the edge of insolvency, mainly because of wartime losses, Sherman could not resist the lure of national service. In 1787 he represented his state at the Constitutional Convention, and attended practically every session. Not only did he sit on the committee on postponed matters, but he also probably helped draft the New Jersey Plan and was a prime mover behind the Connecticut, or Great, Compromise, which broke the deadlock between the large and small states over representation. He was, in addition, instrumental in Connecticut's ratification of the Constitution.

Sherman capped his career by serving in the U.S. House of Representatives (1789–91) and Senate (1791–93), where he espoused the Federalist cause. He died at New Haven in 1793 at the age of 72 and is buried in the Grove Street Cemetery.

Richard Dobbs Spaight, Sr.

North Carolina

Of distinguished English-Irish parentage, Spaight was born at New Bern, N.C., in 1758. When he was orphaned at 8 years of age, his guardians sent him to Ireland, where he obtained an excellent education. He apparently graduated from Scotland's Glasgow University before he returned to North Carolina in 1778.

At that time, the War for Independence was in full swing, and Spaight's superior attainments soon gained him a commission. He became an aide to the state militia commander and in 1780 took part in the Battle of Camden, S.C. The year before, he had been elected to the lower house of the legislature.

In 1781 Spaight left the military service to devote full time to his legislative duties. He represented New Bern and Craven County (1781–83 and 1785–87); in 1785 he became speaker. Between terms, he also served in the Continental Congress (1783–85).

In 1787, at the age of 29, Spaight joined the North Carolina delegation to the Philadelphia convention. He was not a leader but spoke on several occasions and numbered among those who attended every session. After the convention, he worked in his home state for acceptance of the Constitution.

Spaight met defeat in bids for the governorship in 1787 and the U.S. Senate 2 years later. From then until 1792, illness forced his retirement from public life, during which time he visited the West Indies, but he captured the governorship in the latter year (1792–95). In 1793 he served as presidential elector. Two years later, he wed Mary Leach, who bore three children.

In 1798 Spaight entered the U.S. House of Representatives as a Democratic-Republican and remained in office until 1801. During this time, he advocated repeal of the Alien and Sedition Acts and voted for Jefferson in the contested election of 1800. The next year, Spaight was voted into the lower house of the North Carolina legislature; the following year, to the upper.

Only 44 years old in 1802, Spaight was struck down in a duel at New Bern with a political rival, Federalist John Stanly. So ended the promising career of one of the state's foremost leaders. He was buried in the family sepulcher at Clermont estate, near New Bern.

Caleb Strong

Massachusetts

The son of Caleb and Phebe Strong, young Strong was born on January 9, 1745 in Northampton, Mass. He received his college education at Harvard, from which he graduated with highest honors in 1764. Like so many of the delegates to the Constitutional Convention, Strong chose to study law and was admitted to the bar in 1772 and enjoyed a prosperous country practice.

From 1774 through the duration of the Revolution, Strong was a member of Northampton's committee of safety. In 1776 he was elected to the Massachusetts General Court and also held the post of county attorney for Hampshire County for 24 years. He was offered a position on the state supreme court in 1783 but declined it.

At the Constitutional Convention, Strong counted himself among the delegates who favored a strong central government. He successfully moved that the House of Representatives should originate all money bills and sat on the drafting committee. Though he preferred a system that accorded the same rank and mode of election to both houses of Congress, he voted in favor of equal representation in the Senate and proportional in the House. Strong was called home on account of illness in his family and so missed the opportunity to sign the Constitution. However, during the Massachusetts ratifying convention, he took a leading role among the Federalists and campaigned strongly for ratification.

Massachusetts chose Strong as one of its first U.S. senators in 1789. During the 4 years he served in that house, he sat on numerous committees and participated in framing the Judiciary Act. Caleb Strong wholeheartedly supported the Washington administration. In 1793 he urged the government to send a mission to England and backed the resulting Jay's Treaty when it met heated opposition.

Caleb Strong, the Federalist candidate, defeated Elbridge Gerry to become Governor of Massachusetts in 1800. Despite the growing strength of the Democratic party in the state, Strong won reelection annually until 1807. In 1812 he regained the governorship, once again over Gerry, and retained his post until he retired in 1816. During the War of 1812 Strong withstood pressure from the Secretary of War to order part of the Massachusetts militia into federal service. Strong opposed the war and approved the report of the Hartford Convention, a gathering of New England Federalists resentful of Jeffersonian policies.

Strong died on November 7, 1819, 2 years after the death of his wife, Sarah. He was buried in the Bridge Street Cemetary in Northampton. Four of his nine children survived him.

George Washington

Virginia

The eldest of six children from his father's second marriage, George Washington was born into the landed gentry in 1732 at Wakefield Plantation, Va. Until reaching 16 years of age, he lived there and at other plantations along the Potomac and Rappahannock Rivers, including the one that later became known as Mount Vernon. His education was rudimentary, probably being obtained from tutors but possibly also from private schools, and he learned surveying. After he lost his father when he was 11 years old, his half-brother Lawrence, who had served in the Royal Navy, acted as his mentor. As a result, the youth acquired an interest in pursuing a naval career, but his mother discouraged him from doing so.

At the age of 16, in 1748, Washington joined a surveying party sent out to the Shenandoah Valley by Lord Fairfax, a land baron. For the next few years, Washington conducted surveys in Virginia and present West Virginia and gained a lifetime interest in the West. In 1751–52 he also accompanied Lawrence on a visit he made to Barbados, West Indies, for health reasons just before his death.

The next year, Washington began his military career when the royal governor appointed him to an adjutantship in the militia, as a major. That same year, as a gubernatorial emissary, accompanied by a guide, he traveled to Fort Le Boeuf, Pa., in the Ohio River Valley, and delivered to French authorities an ultimatum to cease fortification and settlement in English territory. During the trip, he tried to better British relations with various Indian tribes.

In 1754, winning the rank of lieutenant colonel and then colonel in the militia, Washington led a force that sought to challenge French control of the Ohio River Valley, but met defeat at Fort Necessity, Pa.—an event that helped trigger the French and Indian War (1754–63). Late in 1754, irked by the dilution of his rank because of the pending arrival of British regulars, he resigned his commission. That same year, he leased Mount Vernon, which he was to inherit in 1761.

In 1755 Washington reentered military service with the courtesy title of colonel, as an aide to Gen. Edward Braddock, and barely escaped death when the French defeated the general's forces in the Battle of the Monongahela, Pa. As a reward for his bravery, Washington rewon his colonelcy and command of the Virginia militia forces, charged with defending the colony's frontier. Because of the shortage of men and equipment, he found the assignment challenging. Late in 1758 or early in 1759, disillusioned over governmental neglect of the militia and irritated at not rising in rank, he resigned and headed back to Mount Vernon.

Washington then wed Martha Dandridge Custis, a wealthy widow and mother of two children. The marriage produced no offspring, but Washington reared those of his wife as his own. During the period 1759–74, he managed his plantations and sat in the Virginia House of Burgesses. He supported the initial protests against British policies; took an active part in the nonimportation movement in Virginia; and, in time, particularly because of his military experience, became a Whig leader.

By the 1770s, relations of the colony with the mother country had become strained. Measured in his behavior but strongly sympathetic to the Whig position and resentful of British restrictions and commercial exploitation, Washington represented Virginia at the First and

Second Continental Congresses. In 1775, after the bloodshed at Lexington and Concord, Congress appointed him as commander in chief of the Continental Army. Overcoming severe obstacles, especially in supply, he eventually fashioned a well-trained and disciplined fighting force.

The strategy Washington evolved consisted of continual harassment of British forces while avoiding general actions. Although his troops yielded much ground and lost a number of battles, they persevered—even during the dark winters at Valley Forge, Pa., and Morristown, N.J. Finally, with the aid of the French fleet and army, he won a climactic victory at the Battle of Yorktown, Va., in 1781.

During the next 2 years, while still commanding the agitated Continental Army, which was underpaid and poorly supplied, Washington denounced proposals that the military take over the government, including one that planned to appoint him as king, but supported army petitions to the Continental Congress for proper compensation. Once the Treaty of Paris (1783) was signed, he resigned his commission and returned once again to Mount Vernon. His wartime financial sacrifices and long absence, as well as generous loans to friends, had severely impaired his extensive fortune, which consisted mainly of his plantations, slaves, and landholdings in the West. At this point, however, he was to have little time to repair his finances, for his retirement was brief.

Dissatisfied with national progress under the Articles of Confederation, Washington advocated a stronger central government. He hosted the Mount Vernon Conference (1785) at his estate after its initial meetings in Alexandria, though he apparently did not directly participate in the discussions. Despite his sympathy with the goals of the Annapolis Convention (1786), he did not attend. But, the following year, encouraged by many of his friends, he presided over the Constitutional Convention, whose success was immeasurably influenced by his presence and dignity. Following ratification of the new instrument of government in 1788, the electoral college unanimously chose him as the first President.

The next year, after a triumphal journey from Mount Vernon to New York City, Washington took the oath of office at Federal Hall. During his two precedent-setting terms, he governed with dignity as well as restraint. He also provided the stability and authority the emergent nation so sorely needed, gave substance to the Constitution, and reconciled competing factions and divergent policies within the government and his administration. Although not averse to exercising presidential power, he respected the role of Congress and did not infringe upon its prerogatives. He also tried to maintain harmony between his Secretary of State Thomas Jefferson and Secretary of the Treasury Alexander Hamilton, whose differences typified evolving party divisions, from which Washington kept aloof.

Yet, usually leaning upon Hamilton for advice, Washington supported his plan for the assumption of state debts, concurred in the constitutionality of the bill establishing the Bank of the United States, and favored enactment of tariffs by Congress to provide federal revenue and protect domestic manufacturers.

Washington took various other steps to strengthen governmental authority, including suppression of the Whisky Rebellion (1794). To unify the country, he toured the Northeast in 1789 and the South in 1791. During his tenure, the government moved from New York to Philadelphia in 1790, he superintended planning for relocation to the District of Columbia, and he laid the cornerstone of the Capitol (1793).

In foreign affairs, despite opposition from the Senate, Washington exerted dominance. He fostered United States interests on the North American continent by treaties with Britain and Spain. Yet, until the nation was stronger, he insisted on the maintenance of neutrality. For example, when the French Revolution created war between France and Britain, he ignored the remonstrances of pro-French Jefferson and pro-English Hamilton.

Although many people encouraged Washington to seek a third term, he was weary of politics and refused to do so. In his "Farewell Address" (1796), he urged his countrymen to forswear party spirit and sectional differences and to avoid entanglement in the wars and domestic policies of other nations.

Washington enjoyed only a few years of retirement at Mount Vernon. Even then, demonstrating his continued willingness to make sacrifices for his country, in 1798 when the nation was on the verge of war with France he agreed to command the army, though his services were not ultimately required. He died at the age of 67 in 1799. In his will, he emancipated his slaves.

Hugh Williamson

North Carolina

The versatile Williamson was born of Scotch-Irish descent at West Nottingham, Pa., in 1735. He was the eldest son in a large family, whose head was a clothier. Hoping he would become a Presbyterian minister, his parents oriented his education toward that calling. After attending preparatory schools at New London Cross Roads, Del., and Newark, Del., he entered the first class of the College of Philadelphia (later part of the University of Pennsylvania) and took his degree in 1757.

The next 2 years, at Shippensburg, Pa., Williamson spent settling his father's estate. Then training in Connecticut for the ministry, he soon became a licensed Presbyterian preacher but was never ordained. Around this time, he also took a position as professor of mathematics at his alma mater.

In 1764 Williamson abandoned these pursuits and studied medicine at Edinburgh, London, and Utrecht, eventually obtaining a degree from the University of Utrecht. Returning to Philadelphia, he began to practice but found it to be emotionally exhausting. His pursuit of scientific interests continued, and in 1768 he became a member of the American Philosophical Society. The next year, he served on a commission that observed the transits of Venus and Mercury. In 1771 he wrote *An Essay on Comets,* in which he advanced several original ideas. As a result, the University of Leyden awarded him an LL.D. degree.

In 1773, to raise money for an academy in Newark, Del., Williamson made a trip to the West Indies and then to Europe. Sailing from Boston, he saw the Tea Party and carried news of it to London. When the British Privy Council called on him to testify as to what he had seen, he warned the councilors that the colonies would rebel if the British did not change their policies. While in England, he struck up a close friendship with fellow-scientist Benjamin Franklin, and they cooperated in electrical experiments. Moreover, Williamson furnished to Franklin the letters of Massachusetts Royal Governor Thomas Hutchinson to his lieutenant governor that tended to further alienate the mother country and colonies and created a sensation in America.

In 1775 a pamphlet Williamson had written while in England, called *The Plea of the Colonies*, was published. It solicited the support of the English Whigs for the American cause. When the United States proclaimed their independence the next year, Williamson was in the Netherlands. He soon sailed back to the United States, settling first in Charleston, S.C., and then in Edenton, N.C. There, he prospered in a mercantile business that traded with the French West Indies and once again took up the practice of medicine.

Williamson applied for a medical post with the patriot forces, but found all such positions filled. The Governor of North Carolina, however, soon called on his specialized skills, and he became surgeon-general of state troops. After the Battle of Camden, S.C., he frequently crossed British lines to tend to the wounded. He also prevented sickness among the troops by paying close attention to food, clothing, shelter, and hygiene.

After the war, Williamson began his political career. In 1782 he was elected to the lower house of the state legislature and to the Continental Congress. Three years later, he left Congress and returned to his legislative seat. In 1786 he was chosen to represent his state at the Annapolis Convention but arrived too late to take part. The next year, he again served in Congress (1787–89) and was chosen as a delegate to the Constitutional Convention. Attending faithfully and demonstrating keen debating skill, he served on five committees, notably on the committee on postponed matters, and played a significant part in the proceedings, particularly the major compromise on representation.

After the convention, Williamson worked for ratification of the Constitution in North Carolina. In 1788 he was chosen to settle outstanding accounts between the state and the federal government. The next year, he was elected to the first U.S. House of Representatives, where he served two terms. In 1789 he married Maria Apthorpe, who bore at least two sons.

In 1793 Williamson moved to New York City to facilitate his literary and philanthropic pursuits. Over the years, he published many political, educational, economic, historical, and scientific works, but the last earned him the most praise. The University of Leyden awarded him an honorary degree. In addition, he was an original trustee of the University of North Carolina and later held trusteeships at the College of Physicians and Surgeons and the University of the State of New York. He was also a founder of the Literary and Philosophical

Society of New York and a prominent member of the New-York Historical Society.

In 1819, at the age of 83, Williamson died in New York City and was buried at Trinity Church.

James Wilson

Pennsylvania

Wilson was born in 1741 or 1742 at Carskerdo, near St. Andrews, Scotland, and educated at the universities of St. Andrews, Glasgow, and Edinburgh. He then emigrated to America, arriving in the midst of the Stamp Act agitations in 1765. Early the next year, he accepted a position as Latin tutor at the College of Philadelphia (later part of the University of Pennsylvania) but almost immediately abandoned it to study law under John Dickinson.

In 1768, the year after his admission to the Philadelphia bar, Wilson set up practice at Reading, Pa. Two years later, he moved westward to the Scotch-Irish settlement of Carlisle, and the following year he took a bride, Rachel Bird. He specialized in land law and built up a broad clientele. On borrowed capital, he also began to speculate in land. In some way he managed, too, to lecture on English literature at the College of Philadelphia, which had awarded him an honorary master of arts degree in 1766.

Wilson became involved in Revolutionary politics. In 1774 he took over chairmanship of the Carlisle committee of correspondence, attended the first provincial assembly, and completed preparation of *Considerations on the Nature and Extent of the Legislative Authority of the British Parliament.* This tract circulated widely in England and America and established him as a Whig leader.

The next year, Wilson was elected to both the provincial assembly and the Continental Congress, where he sat mainly on military and Indian affairs committees. In 1776, reflecting the wishes of his constituents, he joined the moderates in Congress voting for a 3-week delay in considering Richard Henry Lee's resolution of June 7 for independence. On the July 1 and 2 ballots on the issue, however, he voted in the affirmative and signed the Declaration of Independence on August 2.

Wilson's strenuous opposition to the republican Pennsylvania constitution of 1776, besides indicating a switch to conservatism on his part, led to his removal from Congress the following year. To avoid the clamor among his frontier constituents, he repaired to Annapolis during the winter of 1777–78 and then took up residence in Philadelphia.

Wilson affirmed his newly assumed political stance by closely identifying with the aristocratic and conservative republican groups, multiplying his business interests, and accelerating his land speculation. He also took a position as Advocate General for France in America (1779–83), dealing with commercial and maritime matters, and legally defended Loyalists and their sympathizers.

In the fall of 1779, during a period of inflation and food shortages, a mob, including many militiamen and led by radical-constitutionalists, set out to attack the republican leadership. Wilson was a prime target. He and some 35 of his colleagues barricaded themselves in his home at Third and Walnut Streets, thereafter known as "Fort Wilson." During a brief skirmish, several people on both sides were killed or wounded. The shock cooled sentiments and pardons were issued all around, though major political battles over the commonwealth constitution still lay ahead.

During 1781 Congress appointed Wilson as one of the directors of the Bank of North America, newly founded by his close associate and legal client Robert Morris. In 1782, by which time the conservatives had regained some of their power, the former was reelected to Congress, and he also served in the period 1785–87.

Wilson reached the apex of his career in the Constitutional Convention (1787), where his influence was probably second only to that of Madison. Rarely missing a session, he sat on the committee of detail and in many other ways applied his excellent knowledge of political theory to convention problems. Only Gouverneur Morris delivered more speeches.

That same year, overcoming powerful opposition, Wilson led the drive for ratification in Pennsylvania, the second state to endorse the instrument. The new commonwealth constitution, drafted in 1789–90 along the lines of the U.S. Constitution, was primarily Wilson's work and represented the climax of his 14-year fight against the constitution of 1776.

For his services in the formation of the federal government, though Wilson expected to be appointed Chief Justice of the Supreme Court, in 1789 President Washington named him as an associate justice. He was chosen that same year as the first law professor at the College of Philadelphia. Two years later he began an official digest of the laws of Pennsylvania, a project he never completed, though he carried on for a while after funds ran out.

Wilson, who wrote only a few opinions, did not achieve the success on the Supreme Court that his capabilities and experience promised. Indeed, during those years he was the object of much criticism and barely escaped impeachment. For one thing, he tried to influence the enactment of legislation in Pennsylvania favorable to land speculators. Between 1792 and 1795 he also made huge but unwise land investments in western New York and Pennsylvania, as well as in Georgia. This did not stop him from conceiving a grandiose but ill-fated scheme, involving vast sums of European capital, for the recruitment of European colonists and their settlement in the West. Meantime, in 1793, a widower with six children, he had remarried, to Hannah Gray; their one son died in infancy.

Four years later, to avoid arrest for debt, the distraught Wilson moved from Philadelphia to Burlington, N.J. The next year, apparently while on federal circuit court business, he arrived at Edenton, N.C., in a state of acute mental stress and was taken into the home of James Iredell, a fellow Supreme Court justice. He died there within a few months. Although first buried at Hayes Plantation near Edenton, his remains were later reinterred in the yard of Christ Church at Philadelphia.

George Wythe

Virginia

George Wythe, the second of Thomas and Margaret Wythe's three children, was born in 1726 on his family's plantation on the Back River in Elizabeth City County, Va. Both parents died when Wythe was young, and he grew up under the guardianship of his older brother, Thomas. Though Wythe was to become an eminent jurist and teacher, he received very little formal education. He learned Latin and Greek from his well-educated mother, and he probably attended for a time a grammar school operated by the College of William and Mary.

Wythe's brother later sent him to Prince George County to read law under an uncle. In 1746, at age 20, he joined the bar, moved to Spotsylvania County, and became associated with a lawyer there. In 1747 he married his partner's sister, Ann Lewis, but she died the next year. In 1754 Lt. Gov. Robert Dinwiddie appointed him as acting colonial attorney general, a position that he held for only a few months. The next year, Wythe's brother died and he inherited the family estate. He chose, however, to live in Williamsburg in the house that his new father-in-law, an architect, designed and built for him and his wife, Elizabeth Taliaferro. They married in 1755, and their only child died in infancy.

At Williamsburg, Wythe immersed himself in further study of the classics and the law and achieved accreditation by the colonial supreme court. He served in the House of Burgesses from the mid-1750s until 1775, first as delegate and after 1769 as clerk. In 1768 he became mayor of Williamsburg, and the next year he sat on the board of visitors of the College of William and Mary. During these years he also directed the legal studies of young scholars, notably Thomas Jefferson. Wythe and Jefferson maintained a lifelong friendship, first as mentor and pupil and later as political allies.

Wythe first exhibited revolutionary leanings in 1764 when Parliament hinted to the colonies that it might impose a stamp tax. By then an experienced legislator, he drafted for the House of Burgesses a remonstrance to Parliament so strident that his fellow delegates modified it before adoption. Wythe was one of the first to express the concept of separate nationhood for the colonies within the British empire.

When war broke out, Wythe volunteered for the army but was sent to the Continental Congress. Although present from 1775 through 1776, Wythe exerted little influence and signed the Declaration of Independence after the formal signing in August 1776. That same year, Wythe, Jefferson, and Edmund Pendleton undertook a 3-year project to revise Virginia's legal code. In 1777 Wythe also presided as speaker of the Virginia House of Delegates.

An appointment as one of the three judges of the newly created Virginia high court of chancery followed in 1778. For 28 years, during 13 of which he was the only chancellor, Wythe charted the course of Virginia jurisprudence. In addition, he was an ex officio member of the state superior court.

Wythe's real love was teaching. In 1779 Jefferson and other officials of the College of William and Mary created the first chair of law in a U.S. institution of higher learning and appointed Wythe to fill it. In that position, he educated America's earliest college-trained lawyers, among them John Marshall and James Monroe. In 1787 he attended the Constitutional Convention but played an insignificant role. He left the proceedings early and did not sign the Constitution. The following year, however, he was one of the Federalist leaders at the Virginia ratifying convention. There he presided over the committee of the whole and offered the resolution for ratification.

In 1791, the year after Wythe resigned his professorship, his chancery duties caused him to move to Richmond, the state capital. He was reluctant to give up his teaching, however, and opened a private law school. One of his last and most promising pupils was young Henry Clay.

In 1806, in his eightieth year, Wythe died at Richmond under mysterious circumstances—probably of poison administered by his grandnephew and heir, George Wythe Sweeney. Reflecting a lifelong aversion to slavery, Wythe emancipated his slaves in his will. His grave is in the yard of St. John's Episcopal Church in Richmond.

Robert Yates

New York *(No Portrait Available)*

The son of Joseph and Maria Yates, Robert Yates was born in Schenectady, N.Y., on January 27, 1738. He received a classical education in New York City and later studied law with William Livingston. Yates was admitted to the New York bar in 1760 and thereafter resided in Albany.

Between 1771 and 1775 Yates sat on the Albany board of aldermen. During the pre-Revolution years Yates counted himself among the Radical Whigs, whose vigilance against corruption and emphasis on the protection of liberty in England appealed to many in the colonies. Once the Revolution broke out, Yates served on the Albany committee of safety and represented his county in four provincial congresses and in the convention of 1775–77. At the convention he sat on various committees, including the one that drafted the first constitution for New York State.

On May 8, 1777 Yates was appointed to New York's supreme court and presided as its chief justice from 1790 through 1798. While on the bench he attracted criticism for his fair treatment of Loyalists. Other duties included serving on commissions that were called to settle boundary disputes with Massachusetts and Vermont.

In the 1780s Robert Yates stood as a recognized leader of the Antifederalists. He opposed any concessions to the federal congress, such as the right to collect impost duties, that might diminish the sovereignty of the states. When he travelled to Philadelphia in May 1787 for the federal convention, he expected that the delegates would simply discuss revising the existing Articles. Yates was on the committee that debated the question of representation in the legislature, and it soon became apparent that the convention intended much more than modification of the current plan of union. On July 5, the day the committee presented its report, Yates and John Lansing (to whom Yates was related by marriage) left the proceedings. In a joint letter to Gov. George Clinton of New York, they spelled out the reasons for their early departure. They warned against the dangers of centralizing power and urged opposition to adopting the Constitution. Yates continued to attack the Constitution in a series of letters signed "Brutus" and "Sydney" and voted against ratification at the Poughkeepsie convention.

In 1789 Yates ran for governor of New York but lost the election. Three years after his retirement from the state supreme court, on September 9, 1801, he died, leaving his wife, Jannetje Van Ness Yates, and four of his six children. Though he had enjoyed a comfortable income at the start of his career, his capital had dwindled away until very little was left. In 1821 his notes from the Constitutional Convention were published under the title *Secret Proceedings and Debates of the Convention Assembled . . . for the Purpose of Forming the Constitution of the United States.*

A P P E N D I X

Framers of the Constitution: THE CONSTITUTION AND ITS HISTORY

We the people of the United States, in Order to form a more perfect Union, establish Justice, insure domestic Tranquility, provide for the common defence, promote the general Welfare, and secure the Blessings of Liberty to ourselves and our Posterity, do ordain and establish this Constitution for the United States of America.

ARTICLE. I.

SECTION. 1. All legislative Powers herein granted shall be vested in a Congress of the United States, which shall consist of a Senate and House of Representatives.

SECTION. 2. The House of Representatives shall be composed of Members chosen every second Year by the People of the several States, and the Electors in each State shall have the Qualifications requisite for Electors of the most numerous Branch of the State Legislature.

No Person shall be a Representative who shall not have attained to the Age of twenty five Years, and been seven Years a Citizen of the United States, and who shall not, when elected, be an Inhabitant of that State in which he shall be chosen.

Representatives and direct Taxes shall be apportioned among the several States which may be included within this Union, according to their respective Numbers, which shall be determined by adding to the whole Number of free Persons, including those bound to Service for a Term of Years, and excluding Indians not taxed, three fifths of all other Persons. The actual Enumeration shall be made within three Years after the first Meeting of the Congress of the United States, and within every subsequent Term of ten Years, in such Manner as they shall by Law direct. The Number of Representatives shall not exceed one for every thirty Thousand, but each State shall have at Least one Representative; and until such enumeration shall be made, the State of New Hampshire shall be entitled to chuse three, Massachusetts eight, Rhode-Island and Providence Plantations one, Connecticut five, New-York six, New Jersey four, Pennsylvania eight, Delaware one, Maryland six, Virginia ten, North Carolina five, South Carolina five, and Georgia three.

When vacancies happen in the Representation from any State, the Executive Authority thereof shall issue Writs of Election to fill such Vacancies.

The House of Representatives shall chuse their Speaker and other Officers; and shall have the sole Power of Impeachment.

SECTION. 3. The Senate of the United States shall be composed of two Senators from each State, chosen by the Legislature thereof, for six Years; and each Senator shall have one Vote.

Immediately after they shall be assembled in Consequence of the first Election, they shall be divided as equally as may be into three Classes. The Seats of the Senators of the first Class shall be vacated at the Expiration of the second Year, of the second Class at the Expiration of the fourth Year, and of the third Class at the Expiration of the sixth Year, so that one third may be chosen every second Year; and if Vacancies happen by Resignation, or otherwise, during the Recess of the Legislature of any State, the Executive thereof may make temporary Appointments until the next Meeting of the Legislature, which shall then fill such Vacancies.

No Person shall be a Senator who shall not have attained to the Age of thirty Years, and been nine Years a Citizen of the United States, and who shall not, when elected, be an Inhabitant of that State for which he shall be chosen.

The Vice President of the United States shall be President of the Senate, but shall have no Vote, unless they be equally divided.

The Senate shall chuse their other Officers, and also a President pro tempore, in the Absence of the Vice President, or when he shall exercise the Office of President of the United States.

The Senate shall have the sole Power to try all Impeachments. When sitting for that Purpose, they shall be on Oath or Affirmation. When the President of the United States is tried, the Chief Justice shall preside: And no Person shall be convicted without the Concurrence of two thirds of the Members present.

Judgment in Cases of Impeachment shall not extend further than to removal from Office, and disqualification to hold and enjoy any Office of honor, Trust or Profit under the United States: but the Party convicted shall nevertheless be liable and subject to Indictment, Trial, Judgment and Punishment, according to Law.

SECTION. 4. The Times, Places and Manner of holding Elections for Senators and Representatives, shall be prescribed in each State by the Legislature thereof; but the Congress may at any time by Law make or alter such Regulations, except as to the Places of chusing Senators.

The Congress shall assemble at least once in every Year, and such Meeting shall be on the first Monday in December, unless they shall by Law appoint a different Day.

SECTION. 5. Each House shall be the Judge of the Elections, Returns and Qualifications of its own Members, and a Majority of each shall constitute a Quorum to do Business; but a smaller Number may adjourn from day to day, and may be authorized to compel the Attendance of absent Members, in such Manner, and under such Penalties as each House may provide.

Each House may determine the Rules of its Proceedings, punish its Members for disorderly Behaviour, and, with the Concurrence of two thirds, expel a Member.

Each House shall keep a Journal of its Proceedings, and from time to time publish the same, excepting such Parts as may in their Judgment require Secrecy; and the Yeas and Nays of the Members of either House on any question shall, at the Desire of one fifth of those Present, be entered on the Journal.

Neither House, during the Session of Congress, shall, without the Consent of the other, adjourn for more than three days, nor to any other Place than that in which the two Houses shall be sitting.

SECTION. 6. The Senators and Representatives shall receive a Compensation for their Services, to be ascertained by Law, and paid out of the Treasury of the United States. They shall in all Cases, except Treason, Felony and Breach of the Peace, be privileged from Arrest during their Attendance at the Session of their respective Houses, and in going to and returning from the same; and for any Speech or Debate in either House, they shall not be questioned in any other Place.

No Senator or Representative shall, during the Time for which he was elected, be appointed to any civil Office under the Authority of the United States, which shall have been created, or the Emoluments whereof shall have been encreased during such time; and no Person holding any Office under the United States, shall be a Member of either House during his Continuance in Office.

SECTION. 7. All Bills for raising Revenue shall originate in the House of Representatives; but the Senate may propose or concur with Amendments as on other Bills.

Every Bill which shall have passed the House of Representatives and the Senate, shall, before it become a Law, be presented to the President of the United States; If he approve he shall sign it, but if not he shall return it, with his Objections to that House in which it shall have originated, who shall enter the Objections at large on their Journal, and proceed to reconsider it. If after such Reconsideration two thirds of that House shall agree to pass the Bill, it shall be sent, together with the Objections, to the other House, by which it shall likewise be reconsidered, and if approved by two thirds of that House, it shall become a Law. But in all such Cases the Votes of both Houses shall be determined by yeas and Nays, and the Names of the Persons voting for and against the Bill shall be entered on the Journal of each House respectively. If any Bill shall not be returned by the President within ten Days (Sundays excepted) after it shall have been presented to him, the Same shall be a Law, in like Manner as if he had signed it, unless the Congress by their Adjournment prevent its Return, in which Case it shall not be a Law.

Every Order, Resolution, or Vote to which the Concurrence of the Senate and House of Representatives may be necessary (except on a question of Adjournment) shall be presented to the President of the United States; and before the Same shall take Effect, shall be approved by him, or being disapproved by him, shall be repassed by two thirds of the Senate and House of Representatives, according to the Rules and Limitations prescribed in the Case of a Bill.

SECTION. 8. The Congress shall have Power To lay and collect Taxes, Duties, Imposts and Excises, to pay the Debts and provide for the common Defence and general Welfare of the United States; but all Duties, Imposts and Excises shall be uniform throughout the United States;

To borrow Money on the credit of the United States;

To regulate Commerce with foreign Nations, and among the several States, and with the Indian tribes;

To establish an uniform Rule of Naturalization, and uniform Laws on the subject of Bankruptcies throughout the United States;

To coin Money, regulate the Value thereof, and of foreign Coin, and fix the Standard of Weights and Measures;

To provide for the Punishment of counterfeiting the Securities and current Coin of the United States;

To establish Post Offices and post Roads;

To promote the Progress of Science and useful Arts, by securing for limited Times to Authors and Inventors the exclusive Right to their respective Writings and Discoveries;

To constitute Tribunals inferior to the supreme Court;

To define and punish Piracies and Felonies committed on the high Seas, and Offences against the Law of Nations;

To declare War, grant Letters of Marque and Reprisal, and make Rules concerning Captures on Land and Water;

To raise and support Armies, but no Appropriation of Money to that Use shall be for a longer Term than two Years;

To provide and maintain a Navy;

To make Rules for the Government and Regulation of the land and naval Forces;

To provide for calling forth the Militia to execute the Laws of the Union, suppress Insurrections and repel Invasions;

To provide for organizing, arming, and disciplining, the Militia, and for governing such Part of them as may be employed in the Service of the United States, reserving to the States respectively, the Appointment of the Officers, and the Authority of training the Militia according to the discipline prescribed by Congress;

To exercise exclusive Legislation in all Cases whatsoever, over such District (not exceeding ten Miles square) as may, by Cession of particular States, and the Acceptance of Congress, become the Seat of the Government of the United States, and to exercise like Authority over all Places purchased by the Consent of the Legislature of the State in which the Same shall be, for the Erection of Forts, Magazines, Arsenals, dock-Yards, and other needful Buildings;—And

To make all Laws which shall be necessary and proper for carrying into Execution the foregoing Powers, and all other Powers vested by this Constitution in the Government of the United States, or in any Department or Officer thereof.

SECTION. 9. The Migration or Importation of such Persons as any of the States now existing shall think proper to admit, shall not be prohibited by the Congress prior to the Year one thousand eight hundred and eight, but a Tax or duty may be imposed on such Importation, not exceeding ten dollars for each Person.

The Privilege of the Writ of Habeas Corpus shall not be suspended, unless when in Cases of Rebellion or Invasion the public Safety may require it.

No Bill of Attainder or ex post facto Law shall be passed.

No Capitation, or other direct, Tax shall be laid, unless in Proportion to the Census or Enumeration herein before directed to be taken.

No Tax or Duty shall be laid on Articles exported from any State.

No Preference shall be given by any Regulation of Commerce or Revenue to the Ports of one State over those of another: nor shall Vessels bound to, or from, one State, be obliged to enter, clear, or pay Duties in another.

No Money shall be drawn from the Treasury, but in Consequence of Appropriations made by Law; and a regular Statement and Account of the Receipts and Expenditures of all public Money shall be published from time to time.

No Title of Nobility shall be granted by the United States: And no Person holding any Office of Profit or Trust under them, shall, without the Consent of the Congress, accept of any present, Emolument, Office, or Title, of any kind whatever, from any King, Prince, or foreign State.

SECTION. 10. No State shall enter into any Treaty, Alliance, or Confederation; grant Letters of Marque and Reprisal; coin Money; emit Bills of Credit; make any Thing but gold and silver Coin a Tender in Payment of Debts; pass any Bill of Attainder, ex post facto Law, or Law impairing the Obligation of Contracts, or grant any Title of Nobility.

No State shall, without the Consent of the Congress, lay any Imposts or Duties on Imports or Exports, except what may be absolutely necessary for executing it's inspection Laws: and the net Produce of all Duties and Imposts, laid by any State on Imports or Exports, shall be for the Use of the Treasury of the United States; and all such Laws shall be subject to the Revision and Controul of the Congress.

No State shall, without the Consent of Congress, lay any Duty of Tonnage, keep Troops, or Ships of War in time of Peace, enter into any Agreement or Compact with another State, or with a foreign Power, or engage in War, unless actually invaded, or in such imminent Danger as will not admit of delay.

ARTICLE. II.

SECTION. 1. The executive Power shall be vested in a President of the United States of America. He shall hold his Office during the Term of four Years, and, together with the Vice President, chosen for the same Term, be elected, as follows

Each State shall appoint, in such Manner as the Legislature thereof may direct, a Number of Electors, equal to the whole Number of Senators and Representatives to which the State may be entitled in the Congress: but no Senator or Representative, or Person holding an Office of Trust or Profit under the United States, shall be appointed an Elector.

The Electors shall meet in their respective States, and vote by Ballot for two Persons, of whom one at least shall not be an inhabitant of the same State with themselves. And they shall make a List of all the Persons voted for, and of the Number of Votes for each; which List they shall sign and certify, and transmit sealed to the Seat of the Government of the United States, directed to the President of the Senate. The President of the Senate shall, in the Presence of the Senate and House of Representatives, open all the Certificates, and the Votes shall then be counted. The Person having the greatest Number of Votes shall be the President, if such Number be a Majority of the whole Number of Electors appointed; and if there be more than one who have such Majority, and have an equal Number of Votes, then the House of Representatives shall immediately chuse by Ballot one of them for President; and if no Person have a Majority, then from the five highest on the List the said House shall in like Manner chuse the President. But in chusing the President, the Votes shall be taken by States, the Representation from each State having one Vote; A quorum for this purpose shall consist of a Member or Members from two thirds of the States, and a Majority of all the States shall be necessary to a Choice. In every Case, after the Choice of the President, the Person having the greatest Number of Votes of the Electors shall be the Vice President. But if there should remain two or more who have equal Votes, the Senate shall chuse from them by Ballot the Vice President.

The Congress may determine the Time of chusing the Electors, and the Day on which they shall give their Votes; which Day shall be the same throughout the United States.

No Person except a natural born Citizen, or a Citizen of the United States, at the time of the Adoption of this Constitution, shall be eligible to the Office of President; neither shall any Person be eligible to that Office who shall not have attained to the Age of thirty five Years, and been fourteen Years a Resident within the United States.

In Case of the Removal of the President from Office, or of his Death, Resignation, or Inability to discharge the Powers and Duties of the said Office, the Same shall devolve on the Vice President, and the Congress may by Law provide for the Case of Removal, Death, Resignation or Inability, both of the President and Vice President, declaring what Officer shall then act as President, and such Officer shall act accordingly, until the Disability be removed, or a President shall be elected.

The President shall, at stated Times, receive for his Services, a Compensation, which shall neither be encreased nor diminished during the Period for which he shall have been elected, and he shall not receive within that Period any other Emolument from the United States, or any of them.

Before he enter on the Execution of his Office, he shall take the following Oath or Affirmation:—"I do solemnly swear (or affirm) that I will faithfully execute the Office of President of the United States, and will to the best of my Ability, preserve, protect and defend the Constitution of the United States."

SECTION. 2. The President shall be Commander in Chief of the Army and Navy of the United States, and of the Militia of the several States, when called into the actual Service of the United States; he may require the Opinion, in writing, of the principal Officer in each of the executive Departments, upon any Subject relating to the Duties of their respective Offices, and he shall have Power to grant Reprieves and Pardons for Offences against the United States, except in Cases of Impeachment.

He shall have Power, by and with the Advice and Consent of the Senate, to make Treaties, provided two thirds of the Senators present concur; and he shall nominate, and by and with the Advice and Consent of the Senate, shall appoint Ambassadors, other public Ministers and Consuls, Judges of the supreme Court, and all other Officers of the United States, whose Appointments are not herein otherwise provided for, and which shall be established by Law: but the Congress may by Law vest the Appointment of such inferior Officers, as they think proper, in the President alone, in the Courts of Law, or in the Heads of Departments.

The President shall have Power to fill up all Vacancies that may happen during the Recess of the Senate, by granting Commissions which shall expire at the End of their next Session.

SECTION. 3. He shall from time to time give to the Congress Information of the State of the Union, and recommend to their Consideration such Measures as he shall judge necessary and expedient; he may, on extraordinary Occasions, convene both Houses, or either of them, and in Case of Disagreement between them, with Respect to the Time of Adjournment, he may adjourn them to such Time as he shall think proper; he shall receive Ambassadors and other public Ministers; he shall take Care that the Laws be faithfully executed, and shall Commission all the Officers of the United States.

SECTION. 4. The President, Vice President and all civil Officers of the United States, shall be removed from Office on Impeachment for, and Conviction of, Treason, Bribery, or other high Crimes and Misdemeanors.

ARTICLE III.

SECTION. 1. The judicial Power of the United States, shall be vested in one supreme Court, and in such inferior Courts as the Congress may from time to time ordain and establish. The Judges, both of the supreme and inferior Courts, shall hold their Offices during good Behaviour, and shall, at stated Times receive for their Services, a Compensation, which shall not be diminished during their Continuance in Office.

SECTION. 2. The judicial Power shall extend to all Cases, in Law and Equity, arising under this Constitution, the Laws of the United States, and Treaties made, or which shall be made, under their Authority;—to all Cases affecting Ambassadors, other public Ministers and Consuls;—to all Cases of admiralty and maritime Jurisdiction;—to Controversies to which the United States shall be a Party;—to Controversies between two or more States;—between a State and Citizens of another State;—between Citizens of different States,—between Citizens of the same State claiming Lands under Grants of different States, and between a State, or the Citizens thereof, and foreign States, Citizens or Subjects.

In all Cases affecting Ambassadors, other public Ministers and Consuls, and those in which a State shall be Party, the supreme Court shall have original Jurisdiction. In all the other Cases before mentioned, the supreme Court shall have appellate Jurisdiction, both as to Law and Fact, with such Exceptions, and under such Regulations as the Congress shall make.

The Trial of all Crimes, except in Cases of Impeachment, shall be by Jury; and such Trial shall be held in the State where the said Crimes shall have been committed; but when not committed within any State, the Trial shall be at such Place or Places as the Congress may by Law have directed.

SECTION. 3. Treason against the United States, shall consist only in levying War against them, or in adhering to their Enemies, giving them Aid and Comfort. No Person shall be convicted of Treason unless on the Testimony of two Witnesses to the same overt Act, or on Confession in open Court.

The Congress shall have Power to declare the Punishment of Treason, but no Attainder of Treason shall work Corruption of Blood, or Forfeiture except during the Life of the Person attainted.

ARTICLE. IV.

SECTION. 1. Full Faith and Credit shall be given in each State to the public Acts, Records, and judicial Proceedings of every other State. And the Congress may by general Laws prescribe the Manner in which such Acts, Records and Proceedings shall be proved, and the Effect thereof.

SECTION. 2. The Citizens of each State shall be entitled to all Privileges and Immunities of Citizens in the several States.

A Person charged in any State with Treason, Felony, or other Crime, who shall flee from Justice, and be found in another State, shall on Demand of the executive Authority of the State from which he fled, be delivered up, to be removed to the State having Jurisdiction of the Crime.

No Person held to Service or Labour in one State, under the Laws thereof, escaping into another, shall, in Consequence of any Law or Regulation therein, be discharged from such Service or Labour, but shall be delivered up on Claim of the Party to whom such Service or Labour may be due.

SECTION. 3. New States may be admitted by the Congress into this Union; but no new State shall be formed or erected within the Jurisdiction of any other State; nor any State be formed by the Junction of two or more States, or Parts of States, without the Consent of the Legislatures of the States concerned as well as of the Congress.

The Congress shall have Power to dispose of and make all needful Rules and Regulations respecting the Territory or other Property belonging to the United States; and nothing in this Constitution shall be so construed as to Prejudice any Claims of the United States, or of any particular State.

SECTION. 4. The United States shall guarantee to every State in this Union a Republican Form of Government, and shall protect each of them against Invasion; and on Application of the Legislature, or of the Executive (when the Legislature cannot be convened) against domestic Violence.

ARTICLE. V.

The Congress, whenever two thirds of both Houses shall deem it necessary, shall propose Amendments to this Constitution, or, on the Application of the Legislatures of two thirds of the several States, shall call a Convention for proposing Amendments, which, in either Case, shall be valid to all Intents and Purposes, as Part of this Constitution, when ratified by the legislatures of three fourths of the several States, or by Conventions in three fourths thereof, as the one or the other Mode of Ratification may be proposed by the Congress; Provided that no Amendment which may be made prior to the Year One thousand eight hundred and eight shall in any Manner affect the first and fourth Clauses in the Ninth Section of the first Article; and that no State, without its Consent, shall be deprived of it's equal Suffrage in the Senate.

ARTICLE. VI.

All Debts contracted and Engagements entered into, before the Adoption of this Constitution, shall be as valid against the United States under this Constitution, as under the Confederation.

This Constitution, and the Laws of the United States which shall be made in Pursuance thereof; and all Treaties made, or which shall be made, under the Authority of the United States, shall be the supreme Law of the Land; and the Judges in every State shall be bound thereby, any Thing in the Constitution or Laws of any State to the Contrary notwithstanding.

The Senators and Representatives before mentioned, and the Members of the several State Legislatures, and all executive and judicial Officers, both of the United States and of the several States, shall be bound by Oath or Affirmation, to support this Constitution; but no religious Test shall ever be required as a Qualification to any Office or public Trust under the United States.

ARTICLE. VII.

The Ratification of the Conventions of nine States, shall be sufficient for the Establishment of this Constitution between the States so ratifying the Same.

DONE in Convention by the Unanimous Consent of the States present the Seventeenth Day of September in the Year of our Lord one thousand seven hundred and Eighty seven and of the Independance of the United States of America the Twelfth. IN WITNESS whereof We have hereunto subscribed our Names.

AMENDMENT I

Congress shall make no law respecting an establishment of religion, or prohibiting the free exercise thereof; or abridging the freedom of speech, or of the press; or the right of the people peaceably to assemble, and to petition the Government for a redress of grievances.

AMENDMENT II

A well regulated Militia, being necessary to the security of a free State, the right of the people to keep and bear Arms, shall not be infringed.

AMENDMENT III

No Soldier shall, in time of peace be quartered in any house, without the consent of the Owner, nor in time of war, but in a manner to be prescribed by law.

AMENDMENT IV

The right of the people to be secure in their persons, houses, papers, and effects, against unreasonable searches and seizures, shall not be violated, and no Warrants shall issue, but upon probable cause, supported by Oath or affirmation, and particularly describing the place to be searched, and the persons or things to be seized.

AMENDMENT V

No person shall be held to answer for a capital, or otherwise infamous crime, unless on a presentment or indictment of a Grand Jury, except in cases arising in the land or naval forces, or in the Militia, when in actual service in time of War or public danger; nor shall any person be subject for the same offence to be twice put in jeopardy of life or limb; nor shall be compelled in any criminal case to be a witness against himself, nor be deprived of life, liberty, or property, without due process of law; nor shall private property be taken for public use, without just compensation.

AMENDMENT VI

In all criminal prosecutions, the accused shall enjoy the right to a speedy and public trial, by an impartial jury of the State and district wherein the crime shall have been committed, which district shall have been previously ascertained by law, and to be informed of the nature and cause of the accusation; to be confronted with the witnesses against him; to have compulsory process for obtaining Witnesses in his favor, and to have the assistance of counsel for his defence.

AMENDMENT VII

In Suits at common law, where the value in controversy shall exceed twenty dollars, the right of trial by jury shall be preserved, and no fact tried by a jury, shall be otherwise re-examined in any Court of the United States, than according to the rules of the common law.

AMENDMENT VIII

Excessive bail shall not be required, nor excessive fines imposed, nor cruel and unusual punishments inflicted.

AMENDMENT IX

The enumeration in the Constitution, of certain rights, shall not be construed to deny or disparage others retained by the people.

AMENDMENT X

The powers not delegated to the United States by the Constitution, nor prohibited by it to the States, are reserved to the States respectively, or to the people.

AMENDMENT XI

The Judicial power of the United States shall not be construed to extend to any suit in law or equity, commenced or prosecuted against one of the United States by Citizens of another State, or by Citizens or Subjects of any Foreign State.

AMENDMENT XII

The Electors shall meet in their respective states, and vote by ballot for President and Vice-President, one of whom, at least, shall not be an inhabitant of the same state with themselves; they shall name in their ballots the person voted for as President, and in distinct ballots the person voted for as Vice-President, and they shall make distinct lists of all persons voted for as President, and of all persons voted for as Vice-President, and of the number of votes for each, which lists they shall sign and certify, and transmit sealed to the seat of the government of the United States, directed to the President of the Senate;—The President of the Senate shall, in the presence of the Senate and House of Representatives, open all the certificates and the votes shall then be counted;—The person having the greatest number of votes for President, shall be the President, if such number be a majority of the whole number of Electors appointed; and if no person have such majority, then from the persons having the highest numbers not exceeding three on the list of those voted for as President, the House of Representatives shall choose immediately, by ballot, the President. But in choosing the President, the votes shall be taken by states, the representation from each state having one vote; a quorum for this purpose shall consist of a member or members from two-thirds of the states, and a majority of all the states shall be necessary to a choice. And if the House of Representatives shall not choose a President whenever the right of choice shall devolve upon them, before the fourth day of March next following, then the Vice-President shall act as President, as in the case of the death or other constitutional disability of the President.—The person having the greatest number of votes as Vice-President, shall be the Vice-President, if such number be a majority of the whole number of Electors appointed, and if no person have a majority, then from the two highest numbers on the list, the Senate shall choose the Vice-President; a quorum for the purpose shall consist of two-thirds of the whole number of Senators, and a majority of the whole number shall be necessary to a choice. But no person constitutionally ineligible to the office of President shall be eligible to that of Vice-President of the United States.

AMENDMENT XIII

SECTION 1. Neither slavery nor involuntary servitude, except as a punishment for crime whereof the party shall have been duly convicted, shall exist within the United States, or any place subject to their jurisdiction.

SECTION 2. Congress shall have power to enforce this article by appropriate legislation.

AMENDMENT XIV

SECTION 1. All persons born or naturalized in the United States, and subject to the jurisdiction thereof, are citizens of the United States and of the State wherein they reside. No State shall make or enforce any law which shall abridge the privileges or immunities of citizens of the United States; nor shall any State deprive any person of life, liberty, or property, without due process of law; nor deny to any person within its jurisdiction the equal protection of the laws.

SECTION 2. Representatives shall be apportioned among the several States according to their respective numbers, counting the whole number of persons in each State, excluding Indians not taxed. But when the right to vote at any election for the choice of electors for President and Vice President of the United States, Representatives in Congress, the Executive and Judicial officers of a State, or the members of the Legislature thereof, is denied to any of the male inhabitants of such State, being twenty-one years of age, and citizens of the United States, or in any way abridged, except for participation in rebellion, or other crime, the basis of representation therein shall be reduced in the proportion which the number of such male citizens shall bear to the whole number of male citizens twenty-one years of age in such State.

SECTION 3. No person shall be a Senator or Representative in Congress, or elector of President and Vice President, or hold any office, civil or military, under the United States, or under any State, who, having previously taken an oath, as a member of Congress, or as an officer of the United States, or as a member of any State legislature, or as an executive or judicial officer of any State, to support the Constitution of the United States, shall have engaged in insurrection or rebellion against the same, or given aid or comfort to the enemies thereof. But Congress may by a vote of two-thirds of each House, remove such disability.

SECTION 4. The validity of the public debt of the United States, authorized by law, including debts incurred for payment of pensions and bounties for services in suppressing insurrection or rebellion, shall not be questioned. But neither the United States nor any State shall assume or pay any debt or obligation incurred in aid of insurrection or rebellion against the United States, or any claim for the loss or emancipation of any slave; but all such debts, obligations and claims shall be held illegal and void.

SECTION 5. The Congress shall have power to enforce, by appropriate legislation, the provisions of this article.

AMENDMENT XV

SECTION 1. The right of citizens of the United States to vote shall not be denied or abridged by the United States or by any State on account of race, color, or previous condition of servitude.

SECTION 2. The Congress shall have power to enforce this article by appropriate legislation.

AMENDMENT XVI

The Congress shall have power to lay and collect taxes on incomes, from whatever source derived, without apportionment among the several States, and without regard to any census or enumeration.

AMENDMENT XVII

The Senate of the United States shall be composed of two Senators from each State, elected by the people thereof, for six years; and each Senator shall have one vote. The electors in each State shall have the qualifications requisite for electors of the most numerous branch of the State legislatures.

When vacancies happen in the representation of any State in the Senate, the executive authority of such State shall issue writs of election to fill such vacancies: *Provided,* That the legislature of any State may empower the executive thereof to make temporary appointments until the people fill the vacancies by election as the legislature may direct.

This amendment shall not be so construed as to affect the election or term of any Senator chosen before it becomes valid as part of the Constitution.

AMENDMENT XVIII

SECTION 1. After one year from the ratification of this article the manufacture, sale, or transportation of intoxicating liquors within, the importation thereof into, or the exportation thereof from the United States and all territory subject to the jurisdiction thereof for beverage purposes is hereby prohibited.

SECTION 2. The Congress and the several States shall have concurrent power to enforce this article by appropriate legislation.

SECTION 3. This article shall be inoperative unless it shall have been ratified as an amendment to the Constitution by the legislatures of the several States, as provided in the Constitution, within seven years from the date of the submission hereof to the States by the Congress.

AMENDMENT XIX

The right of citizens of the United States to vote shall not be denied or abridged by the United States or by any State on account of sex.

Congress shall have power to enforce this article by appropriate legislation.

AMENDMENT XX

SECTION 1. The terms of the President and Vice President shall end at noon on the 20th day of January, and the terms of Senators and Representatives at noon on the 3d day of January, of the years in which such terms would have ended if this article had not been ratified; and the terms of their successors shall then begin.

SECTION 2. The Congress shall assemble at least once in every year, and such meeting shall begin at noon on the 3d day of January, unless they shall by law appoint a different day.

SECTION 3. If, at the time fixed for the beginning of the term of the President, the President elect shall have died, the Vice President elect shall become President. If a President shall not have been chosen before the time fixed for the beginning of his term, or if the President elect shall have failed to qualify, then the Vice President elect shall act as President until a President shall have qualified; and the Congress may by law provide for the case wherein neither a President elect nor a Vice President elect shall have qualified, declaring who shall then act as President, or the manner in which one who is to act shall be selected, and such person shall act accordingly until a President or Vice President shall have qualified.

SECTION 4. The Congress may by law provide for the case of the death of any of the persons from whom the House of Representatives may choose a President whenever the right of choice shall have devolved upon them, and for the case of the death of any of the persons from whom the Senate may choose a Vice President whenever the right of choice shall have devolved upon them.

SECTION 5. Sections 1 and 2 shall take effect on the 15th day of October following the ratification of this article.

SECTION 6. This article shall be inoperative unless it shall have been ratified as an amendment to the Constitution by the legislatures of three-fourths of the several States within seven years from the date of its submission.

AMENDMENT XXI

SECTION 1. The eighteenth article of amendment to the Constitution of the United States is hereby repealed.

SECTION 2. The transportation or importation into any State, Territory, or possession of the United States for delivery or use therein of intoxicating liquors, in violation of the laws thereof, is hereby prohibited.

SECTION 3. This article shall be inoperative unless it shall have been ratified as an amendment to the Constitution by conventions in the several States, as provided in the Constitution, within seven years from the date of the submission hereof to the States by the Congress.

AMENDMENT XXII

SECTION 1. No person shall be elected to the office of the President more than twice, and no person who has held the office of President, or acted as President, for more than two years of a term to which some other person was elected President shall be elected to the office of the President more than once. But this Article shall not apply to any person holding the office of President when this Article was proposed by the Congress, and shall not prevent any person who may be holding the office of President, or acting as President, during the term within which this Article becomes operative from holding the office of President or acting as President during the remainder of such term.

SECTION 2. This article shall be inoperative unless it shall have been ratified as an amendment to the Constitution by the legislatures of three-fourths of the several States within seven years from the date of its submission to the States by the Congress.

AMENDMENT XXIII

SECTION 1. The District constituting the seat of Government of the United States shall appoint in such manner as the Congress may direct:

A number of electors of President and Vice President equal to the whole number of Senators and Representatives in Congress to which the District would be entitled if it were a State, but in no event more than the least populous State; they shall be in addition to those appointed by the States, but they shall be considered, for the purposes of the election of President and Vice President, to be electors appointed by a State; and they shall meet in the District and perform such duties as provided by the twelfth article of amendment.

SECTION 2. The Congress shall have power to enforce this article by appropriate legislation.

AMENDMENT XXIV

SECTION 1. The right of citizens of the United States to vote in any primary or other election for President or Vice President, for electors for President or Vice President, or for Senator or Representatives in Congress, shall not be denied or abridged by the United States or any State by reason of failure to pay any poll tax or other tax.

SECTION 2. The Congress shall have power to enforce this article by appropriate legislation.

AMENDMENT XXV

SECTION 1. In case of the removal of the President from office or of his death or resignation, the Vice President shall become President.

SECTION 2. Whenever there is a vacancy in the office of the Vice President, the President shall nominate a Vice President who shall take office upon confirmation by a majority vote of both Houses of Congress.

SECTION 3. Whenever the President transmits to the President pro tempore of the Senate and the Speaker of the House of Representatives his written declaration that he is unable to discharge the powers and duties of his office, and until he transmits to them a written declaration to the contrary, such powers and duties shall be discharged by the Vice President as Acting President.

SECTION 4. Whenever the Vice President and a majority of either the principal officers of the executive departments or of such other body as Congress may by law provide, transmit to the President pro tempore of the Senate and the Speaker of the House of Representatives their written declaration that the President is unable to discharge the powers and duties of his office, the Vice President shall immediately assume the powers and duties of the office as Acting President.

Thereafter, when the President transmits to the President pro tempore of the Senate and the Speaker of the House of Representatives his written declaration that no inability exists, he shall resume the powers and duties of his office unless the Vice President and a majority of either the principal officers of the executive department or of such other body as Congress may by law provide, transmit within four days to the President pro tempore of the Senate and the Speaker of the House of Representatives their written declaration that the President is unable to discharge the powers and duties of his office. Thereupon Congress shall decide the issue, assembling within forty-eight hours for that purpose if not in session. If the Congress, within twenty-one days after receipt of the latter written declaration, or, if Congress is not in session, within twenty-one days after Congress is required to assemble, determines by two-thirds vote of both Houses that the President is unable to discharge the powers and duties of his office, the Vice President shall continue to discharge the same as Acting President; otherwise, the President shall resume the powers and duties of his office.

AMENDMENT XXVI

SECTION 1. The right of citizens of the United States, who are eighteen years of age or older, to vote shall not be denied or abridged by the United States or by any State on account of age.

SECTION 2. The Congress shall have power to enforce this article by appropriate legislation.

HISTORY OF THE DOCUMENT

The veneration of the American people for the parchment, or engrossed, copies of the Declaration of Independence (1776), the Constitution (1787), and the Bill of Rights (1789) has been reflected in the painstaking care bestowed on them. After long odysseys, part of which they shared, today they are enshrined in Exhibition Hall of the National Archives Building. The Constitution and Bill of Rights, which were not regularly exhibited to the public until 1924 and 1952 respectively, are in far better physical condition than the Declaration, which has been displayed continuously since 1841 except for one period of three decades.

On September 20, 1787, Maj. William Jackson, secretary of the Constitutional Convention, delivered the engrossed copy of the Constitution to his counterpart in the Continental Congress, Charles Thomson, who already was responsible for safeguarding the Declaration of Independence. He likely stored the two documents first in New York's City Hall, where Congress was meeting, and then between October 1788 and April 1789 at the two-room office on the southeast corner of Broad and Pearl Streets that Secretary for Foreign Affairs John Jay vacated for temporary use by the Continental Congress while City Hall (which became Federal Hall) was being renovated.

Although the new government was formally launched when George Washington was inaugurated on the balcony of Federal Hall on April 30, 1789, Confederation officers maintained continuity until the executive branch could be organized, and Thomson probably moved into the hall with the new Congress. When he resigned on July 23, at Washington's request he turned over the Constitution and Declaration to Roger Alden, who had been deputy secretary of the Continental Congress.

The legislation creating the Department of State (September 15, 1789) charged it with the protection of important state papers. Accordingly, Acting Secretary John Jay, who was in charge until appointee Thomas Jefferson could return from France and take over early in 1790, assumed jurisdiction over the Declaration, the Constitution, and within a couple of weeks the newly issued parchment copy of the Bill of Rights. During this period, they were undoubtedly stored in the department's temporary offices on lower Broadway.

In late 1790 the government moved to Philadelphia. Except possibly for brief intervals when they may have been among the state papers evacuated to Trenton, N.J., during yellow-fever epidemics, the three documents remained there for a decade in successive State Department offices on Market Street, the southeast corner of Arch and Sixth Streets, on North Alley, and the northeast corner of Fifth and Chestnut Streets.

In 1800 the documents were shipped by sea to the new capital, Washington, D.C. They were apparently kept for a couple of months in the department's temporary offices in the old, or first, Treasury Building, just east of the White House at 15th Street and Pennsylvania Avenue NW., on the southern end of the site of the present Treasury Building; and then for a time they were kept at another temporary location, in one of the "Six Buildings," between 21st and 22d Streets on Pennsylvania Avenue NW. Likely in 1801 the department relocated to the War Office Building, just west of the White House at 17th Street and Pennsylvania Avenue NW. The state papers remained there until late in August 1814, during the War of 1812, when British troops invaded the capital. Shortly before they arrived, at the direction of Secretary of State James Monroe, the papers were packed in linen sacks and transported in carts to an unused gristmill belonging to an Edgar Patterson, on the Virginia side of the Potomac River about 2 miles above Chain Bridge. Before long, because a nearby cannon factory made the site a likely military target, a State Department clerk borrowed wagons from farmers in the neighborhood and moved the papers to an empty house in Leesburg, Va., about 35 miles away. It was locked and the keys were given to a Reverend Littlejohn for safekeeping.

Within a few weeks, after the British had departed and the threat had subsided, in September 1814 the documents were brought back to Washington and temporarily kept at a private residence on the south side of G Street near 18th Street NW. that the State Department temporarily occupied until the fire-scarred War Office Building was ready for reoccupancy in April 1816.

In September 1819, the department moved the Declaration, Constitution, and Bill of Rights to its new headquarters at 15th Street and Pennsylvania Avenue NW., on the north end of the site of the present Treasury Building. There they remained together until 1841, when the Declaration was taken away and displayed to the public at the new Patent Office Building.

In 1866 the Constitution and Bill of Rights were moved to premises the department leased on 14th Street near S Street NW. In July 1875 they made their final move within the department, to the partially completed State, War and Navy Building (present Old Executive Office Building), at 17th Street and Pennsylvania Avenue NW. Two years later, the Declaration, which had just been exhibited in Philadelphia (1876–77) as part of the centennial celebration of independence, rejoined the Constitution and Bill of Rights in the State, War and Navy Building, though the Declaration continued to be displayed. By this time, its long exposure to sunlight, the making of various facsimiles, handling, and greater age had faded its ink considerably. In contrast, the Constitution and Bill of Rights, benefiting from their longtime obscurity, were in relatively good condition.

As a matter of fact, during the first century of existence of the parchment copy of the Constitution, it had attracted virtually no public attention. Only in a few instances was it even inspected. For example, in 1823 Secretary of State John Quincy Adams and others examined it during a political dispute concerning its punctuation. A few years later, James Madison, "Father of the Constitution" and its onetime custodian as Secretary of State (1801–9), expressed uncertainty as to its location. In 1846 a publisher used it to prepare a book on the Constitution. When historian J. Franklin Jameson examined the parchment in 1883, he found it folded in a small tin box in the bottom of a closet at the State, War, and Navy Building.

In 1894, noting the deterioration in the Declaration, the State Department sealed it and the Constitution between two glass plates and locked them in a safe or steel case in the basement, apparently along with the Bill of Rights. There they lay, except on rare occasions, unobserved and in darkness for a quarter of a century. In 1921, in response to a presidential executive order, which reflected the findings of a special committee, the department, though it retained control of the Bill of Rights, relinquished the Constitution and Declaration to the Library of Congress, where they could receive expert care and be safely exhibited to the public.

Librarian Herbert Putnam, personally made the transfer in a library mail truck, a Model T Ford. At first, he kept the documents in a safe in his office. In 1924, however, he put them on public display on the second floor of the present main building in a bronze and marble shrine. Placed over special moisture-absorbing cellulose paper, they were sealed between double panes of insulated plate glass, from which the air was expelled and just under which gelatin film kept out harmful rays of light.

The Constitution and Declaration remained there until December 26, 1941, just 19 days after Japan attacked Pearl Harbor. Packed in acid-free paper and rock wool in a hermetically sealed bronze container, they left Washington by train in a pullman compartment under Secret Service guard en route to the United States Bullion Depository, Fort Knox, Ky. They arrived there the following day and were placed in a vault. Taking advantage of the opportunity, specialists cleaned and restored the documents to the maximum degree. On September 29, 1944, with the approval of the Joint Chiefs of Staff, they were returned to the Library of Congress and on October 1 were reexhibited.

In February 1924 President and Mrs. Calvin Coolidge dedicated the newly completed shrine in the Library of Congress that contained the Constitution and the Declaration of Independence. Dr. Herbert Putnam, Librarian of Congress, is at the left.

In 1951, based on the results of a long study that the National Bureau of Standards had initiated at the request of the Librarian of Congress to determine the best possible protection from the atmosphere, insects, mold, and light, each of the six leaves of the two instruments were sealed in separate cases fitted with glass and special filters that screened out damaging light rays. The helium atmosphere was inert and properly humidified.

In December 1952 the two documents were transported in wooden boxes atop mattresses in an armored troop carrier under military escort to their permanent home, the National Archives Building. It had been completed in 1935 as the repository for official governmental records, which are under the jurisdiction of the National Archives and Records Administration. A special hall had been designed to safeguard and exhibit the most famous of the nation's documents. The Bill of Rights had already been shipped to the National Archives Building from the State, War and Navy Building in 1938; during the interim, it was not permanently displayed.

Still enshrined at the National Archives Building today, along with thousands of other priceless national records, are the parchment copies of the Declaration, Constitution, and Bill of Rights. The massive bronze doors at the Constitution Avenue entrance to the building lead to the circular Exhibition Hall. At its rear center stands a marble shrine containing the Declaration; the first and fourth, or signature, pages of the Constitution; and the Bill of Rights. Every

National Archives Building, where the Constitution reposes today.

Constitution Day (September 17) the first four pages of the Constitution are all displayed together in a portable exhibit case in the center of the rotunda.

At other times, the second and third pages, as well as the rarely displayed fifth and last page of the Constitution (known as the "Resolution of Transmittal to the Continental Congress"), are safeguarded in the vault below. The fifth page, signed by Washington, detailed the steps required for adoption of the new plan of government, including the ratification process.

The Bill of Rights on display, which lists the first 12 proposed constitutional amendments, only the last 10 of which the states ratified, is the enrolled parchment copy of the congressional resolution of September 25, 1789, engrossed by Clerk of the House William Lambert. Thirteen other parchment copies, differing only in such details as handwriting, capitalization, and lineation, were transmitted to the states for ratification; only a few of these have survived.

When not exhibited, the nation's most precious documents are secured in a fireproof, shockproof, bombproof vault, which is constructed of steel and reinforced concrete and is located below the

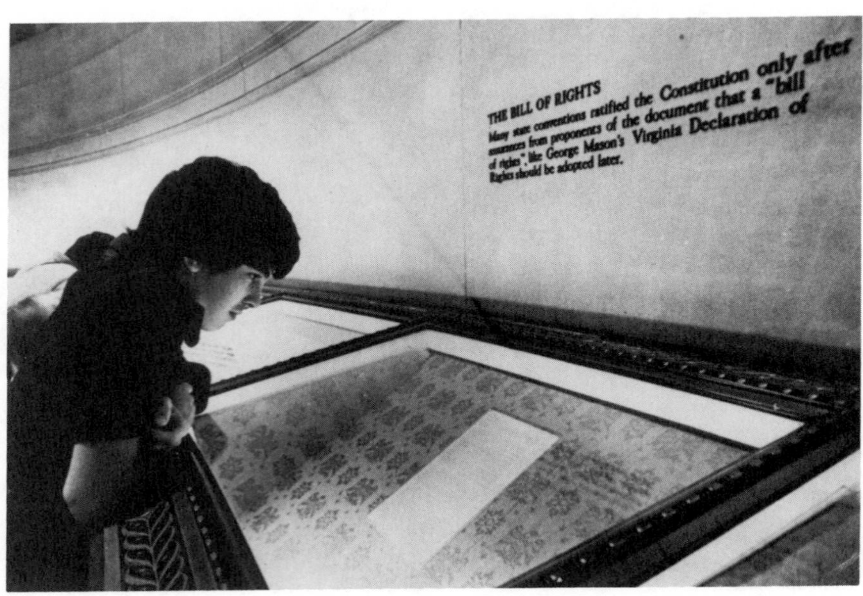

Each year hundreds of thousands of school children visit the National Archives to view the nation's great documents.

shrine under the floor of Exhibition Hall. An electrical mechanism automatically lowers them into the vault and raises them back to their positions in the shrine. Other machinery then closes a massive lid of metal and concrete over the vault. These mechanisms can be activated in the event of danger, and, during a power failure, they can be operated manually.

Along both sides of the bulwark charters is a "Formation of the Union" display. It consists of documents illustrating the evolution of the U.S. government from 1774 until 1791. Included are the Articles of Association (1774), the Articles of Confederation (1778), the Treaty of Paris (1783), and Washington's inaugural address (1789).

On each wall above the exhibit is a mural. In one, Jefferson and the drafting committee are presenting the Declaration to John Hancock, President of the Continental Congress. In the other, James Madison, accompanied by various members of the Constitutional Convention, is submitting the Constitution to George Washington, the convention's presiding officer.

Mentioning the National Archives readily evokes the image of the neoclassical rotunda that enshrines the Declaration of Independence and the Constitution of the United States. Less familiar are the volume and variety of the millions of documents preserved from the days of the First Continental Congress through the 20th century and entrusted to the National Archives and its branches.

The bicentennial anniversaries of the Constitution and the Bill of Rights invite both novice and veteran scholars to examine more closely the records relating to the Constitution and its history. Any attempt to completely describe these records would fill a volume or more. This small space allows for only a cursory mention of the major sources. After examing the most frequently used records, researchers may decide to make more extensive investigations of the National Archives' voluminous holdings.

Many records from the Revolutionary and early federal period have been microfilmed to allow for easy access while preserving the original documents from harm. The collection most relevant to this volume is the Records of the Constitutional Convention.

The *Records of the Constitutional Convention of 1787* (filmed as microfilm publication M866) consist of four parts: the official records of the convention, the papers of David Brearley (Brearly), the delegates' credentials, and a motion in the hand of Elbridge Gerry.

The official records are those papers that the convention directed its secretary, William Jackson, to turn over to its president, George Washington. Although Jackson burned some loose scraps of papers, he turned over four volumes of journals and various other papers. On March 16, 1796, Washington deposited these official records with Timothy Pickering, the secretary of state. The records remained in the custody of the State Department until they were transferred to the Library of Congress in 1922. The National Archives obtained the convention's official records in June 1952, the same year it received the Articles of Confederation, the Declaration of Independence, and the Constitution from the Library of Congress.

The proceedings and votes William Jackson recorded from May 14 through September 17, 1787, became known as the Journal of the Constitutional Convention. The journal comprises the formal journal of the convention, the journal of proceedings of the committee of the whole, and two voting records. In addition to the journal, Jackson saved two copies of the Virginia Plan as amended by the convention; the first printed draft of the Constitution, annotated by Washington; a draft of a letter from the convention to the Continental Congress to accompany the Constitution; and other letters to the convention.

In 1818 the Department of State received the papers of David Brearly, a delegate to the convention, from his estate. Though not considered part of the official records, these papers contain valuable documents relating to the convention, some of which are not among those collected by William Jackson. The Brearly Papers include population estimates of the states, copies of the Virginia Plan and the New Jersey Plan, Hamilton's plan of government, the committee report on the Great Compromise, and two annotated printed drafts of the Constitution.

The convention's records also include transcribed copies of the delegates' credentials and a motion written by Elbridge Gerry. The credentials provided authority and instructions from each state to its delegates. Gerry's motion concerned the method of electing the "supreme Executive."

The largest body of records from the Revolutionary and early federal era on microfilm are the *Papers of the Continental Congress, 1774–89* (M247). The Continental Congress was not only active during the Revolutionary War, but it also was the governing body of the United States under the Articles of Confederation. Most of the 50,000 documents are arranged in a numerical sequence of 196 items. Included are copies of the Declaration of Independence, the Articles of Confederation, the Northwest Ordinance, the Constitution, and other documents intrumental in forming the new government. The papers concern many subjects, the major ones being military and fiscal affairs and foreign relations. The types of documents include journals of proceedings, letters and reports, claims, and diplomatic despatches. The National Archives published a five-volume name and subject index to all the papers except the Journals of the Congress.

Additional information on microfilm concerning the early foreign relations of the United States may be found in *Domestic Letters of the Department of State, 1784–1861* (M40) and *Foreign Letters of the Continental Congress and the Department of State, 1785–1790* (M61). The *Miscellaneous Papers of the Continental Congress* (M322) and records relating to Revolutionary War accounts and pensions, Indian affairs, the first Post Office department, and the first censuses are also valuable for research about the early years of the U.S. government.

Since the adoption of the Constitution, questions have arisen as to what is and is not permissible under its provisions. For studying questions of constitutionality, a logical place to start is Record Group 267, the Records of the Supreme Court of the United States.

Among the Supreme Court records, one may trace the course of judicial review from the establishment of the court in 1789 through the 20th century. The National Archives has maintained the records as the Court arranged them. The kinds of records include case files, minutes, dockets, journals, opinions, correspondence, and fiscal records. Case files constitute the largest volume of records, and some files are especially rich. However, most files contain just the basic documentation of each case, including petitions, orders, decrees, and judgments. Other possible sources for constitutional research are Justice Department records, congressional committee records, and the records of government agencies.

The largest body of court records in the custody of the National Archives is that of the U.S. district and circuit courts (RG 21). The Judiciary Act of 1789, which established the Supreme Court, also divided the United States into 13 districts, each with a district court and judge, and then grouped the districts into circuits. A circuit court, consisting of a district judge and any two Supreme Court justices, was to convene in each district twice a year. The 11 Archives field branches hold the records of courts that sat within their regions.

District courts had original jurisdiction over most federal cases. The circuit courts, in addition to limited original jurisdiction, heard cases appealed from the district courts. In 1891 the U.S. Court of Appeals (its records are in RG 276) took over the appellate jurisdiction, and in 1911 the circuit courts were abolished.

The earliest documents in Record Group 21 date from 1685, and the holdings extend through the 20th century. The cases concern admiralty law, bankruptcy, naturalization, land grants, and criminal offenses. Records of the Confederacy's district courts are also in this record group.

The vast holdings of the National Archives offer countless opportunities for discovering more about the origins and evolution of the Constitution. Those who delve into the records in the custody of the National Archives and Records Administration will encounter a veritable treasure trove of material relating to an array of subjects. It is hoped that the interest in the Constitution inspired by the occasion of its bicentennial may lead to a fruitful association between the National Archives and researchers in many disciplines.

SUGGESTED READING

BEARD, CHARLES A. *An Economic Interpretation of the Constitution of the United States.* New York: Macmillan, 1913.

———. *The Republic: Conversations on Fundamentals.* New York: Viking Press, 1943.

BOWEN, CATHERINE D. *Miracle at Philadelphia: The Story of the Constitutional Convention, May to September 1787.* Boston: Little, Brown, 1966.

FARRAND, MAX. *The Fathers of the Constitution: A Chronicle of the Establishment of the Union.* New Haven, Conn.: Yale University Press, 1921.

———. *The Framing of the Constitution of the United States.* New Haven, Conn.: Yale University Press, 1913.

———, ed. *The Records of the Federal Convention of 1787.* 3 vols., New Haven, Conn.: Yale University Press, 1911; rev. ed., 4 vols., 1937.

HAMILTON, ALEXANDER, JOHN JAY, and JAMES MADISON. *The Federalist [Papers]: A Collection of Essays Written in Favour of the New Constitution, As Agreed Upon by the Federal Convention, September 17, 1787.* [1788]. Available in many complete and abridged editions, including paperback.

JENSEN, MERRILL. *The Making of the American Constitution.* Princeton, N.J.: Van Nostrand, 1964.

LEVY, LEONARD WILLIAMS, ed. *Essays on the Making of the Constitution.* New York: Oxford University Press, 1969.

McGEE, DOROTHY H. *Framers of the Constitution.* New York: Dodd, Mead, 1968.

MAIN, JACKSON TURNER. *The Antifederalists: Critics of the Constitution, 1781–1788.* Chapel Hill, N.C.: University of North Carolina Press, 1961.

———. *Political Parties Before the Constitution.* Chapel Hill, N.C.: University of North Carolina Press, 1973.

NATIONAL ARCHIVES. *The Formation of the Union.* Washington: National Archives and Records Service (Pub. No. 70-13), 1970.

ROSSITER, CLINTON. *1787: The Grand Convention.* New York: Macmillan, 1966.

RUTLAND, ROBERT A. *The Birth of the Bill of Rights, 1776–1791.* Chapel Hill, N.C.: University of North Carolina Press, 1955.

SZATMARY, DAVID P. *Shays' Rebellion: The Making of an Agrarian Insurrection.* Amherst, Mass.: University of Massachusetts Press, 1980.

TANSILL, CHARLES, ed. *Documents Illustrative of the Formation of the Union of the American States.* 69th Congress, 1st Session, House Doc. No. 398. Washington: Government Printing Office, 1927.

UNITED STATES CONSTITUTION SESQUICENTENNIAL COMMISSION. *History of the Formation of the Union Under the Constitution.* Washington: Government Printing Office, 1940.

UNITED STATES HOUSE OF REPRESENTATIVES. *The Constitution of the United States, As Amended Through July 1971.* 93d Congress, 2d Session, House Doc. No. 93-215. Washington: Government Printing Office, 1974.

UNITED STATES SENATE. *The Constitution of the United States of America: Analysis and Interpretation—Annotations of Cases Decided by the Supreme Court of the United States to June 29, 1972.* 92d Congress, 2d Session, Senate Doc. No. 92-82. Washington: Government Printing Office, 1973.

VAN DOREN, CARL. *The Great Rehearsal: The Story of the Making and Ratifying of the Constitution of the United States.* New York: Viking Press, 1948.

WARREN, CHARLES. *The Making of the Constitution.* Boston: Little, Brown, 1928.

WHITNEY, DAVID C. *Founders of Freedom in America: Lives of the Men Who Signed the Constitution and So Helped to Establish the United States of America.* Chicago: J. G. Ferguson, 1965.

WOOD, GORDON S. *The Creation of the American Republic, 1776–1787.* Chapel Hill, N.C.: University of North Carolina Press, 1969.

ART AND PICTURE CREDITS

The National Archives and Records Administration gratefully acknowledges the assistance of agencies and individuals furnishing illustrations and granting permission to reproduce them.

5 National Archives (Hugh Talman, ca. 1979).

10 National Archives.

12 Drawing and engraving (1800) by William Birch & Son. Library of Congress.

15 National Archives.

17 *Pennsylvania Journal* (Philadelphia), May 19, 1787. Library of Congress.

19 Engraving (undated) by an unknown artist, in *Columbian Magazine* (1789). Library of Congress.

21 National Archives.

23 *Jefferson*, detail from oil (1786) by Mather Brown, Charles Francis Adams, Lexington, Mass.; *Adams*, detail from oil (1788) by Mather Brown, Library of the Boston Athenaeum.

24 *Lee*, detail from oil (1784) by Charles Willson Peale, Independence National Historical Park, Pa.; *Henry*, detail from miniature, watercolor on ivory (late 19th century), Herbert DuPuy Collection, Museum of Art, Carnegie Institute, Pittsburgh; *Jay*, detail from oil (1795–96) by Raphaelle and Rembrandt Peale, after Charles Willson Peale, Maryland Historical Society, Baltimore; *Chase*, detail from oil (ca. 1773) by Charles Willson Peale, Independence National Historical Park.

26 Engraving (ca. 1787) by James Trenchard, after a drawing (1778) by Charles Willson Peale, in *Columbian Magazine* (1787). Library of Congress.

27 Drawing and engraving (ca. 1799) by William Birch & Son. Independence National Historical Park.

31 Detail from drawing and engraving (ca. 1800) by William Birch & Son. Library of Congress.

32 *Pennsylvania Packet* (Philadelphia), May 11, 1787. Library of Congress.

33 Engraving (early 19th century) by Mumford, in John F. Watson, *Annals of Philadelphia* (1879–81). Library Company of Philadelphia.

34 *Pennsylvania Journal* (Philadelphia), May 30, 1787.

36 National Archives (148–CCD–14).

37 National Archives.

39 National Archives.

42 Historic Buildings Survey, National Park Service (Jack E. Boucher, 1974).

48 Watercolor (1887) by Benjamin R. Evans, after a drawing (1833) by Gen [Alfred?] Sully. The Historical Society of Pennsylvania.

51 National Archives.

55 National Archives.

60 The Historical Society of Pennsylvania.

68 Library of Congress.

70 Library of Congress.

72 National Archives.

74 Library of Congress.

75 Library of Congress.

77 *Pennsylvania Packet* (Philadelphia), September 18, 1787. Library of Congress.

78 National Archives.

79 National Archives.

80 National Archives.

81 National Archives.

82 National Archives.

84 Library of Congress.

87 Library of Congress.

90 The Historical Society of Pennsylvania.

95 National Archives.

97 Library of Congress.

98 The Historical Society of Pennsylvania.

100 National Archives.

101 Oil (late 19th century) by L. M. Cooke. Gift of Edgar William and Bernice Chrysler Garbisch, National Gallery of Art.

102 Engraving (ca. 1790) by Amos Doolittle, after a drawing by Peter Lacour. I.N. Phelps Stokes Collection, New York Public Library.

104 National Archives.

106 National Archives.

108 Library of Congress.

110 National Archives.

113 Library of Congress (Harris & Ewing).

114 Library of Congress.

121 Engraving (undated) by Henry Dawkins, after W. Tennant, in *An Account of the College of New Jersey* (1764). Library of Congress.

123 Ink and gouache drawing (undated) by Emanuel Leutze, after Robert Fulton. The Historical Society of Pennsylvania.

124 Crayon drawing (undated) by Charles B.J. Fevret de Saint-Memin. The Baltimore Museum of Art: Bequest of Helen H. Bayard.

125 Detail from oil (1787) by Charles Willson Peale. Architect of the Capitol.

127 National Archives (148–GW–533b).

128 Detail from oil (prior to 1858) by Washington B. Cooper. Tennessee State Museum, Tennessee Historical Society (Stephen D. Cox, 1986).

129 Reproduced from a portrait by an unknown artist in Hamilton Schuyler, *St. Michael's Church, Trenton* (1926). Trentoniana Collection, Trenton Public Library.

132 National Archives (148–CCD–81a).

133 Oil (ca. 1758) by John Wollaston. Maryland Historical Society, Balitmore.

134 Detail from oil (ca. 1807–10) by Charles Willson Peale. National Portrait Gallery, Smithsonian Institution. Gift of Shubrick Clymer.

136 Detail from miniature, oil on ivory, by Eliza L. Mirbel, Independence National Historical Park.

138 National Archives (148–CC–7–1).

139 Oil (1782) by Charles Willson Peale. Independence National Historical Park.

142 Detail from pastel (ca. 1796) attributed to James Sharples, Sr. Independence National Historical Park.

144 National Archives (148–CP–157).

147 Detail from oil (1789) by Charles Willson Peale. The Historical Society of Pennsylvania.

149 Detail from watercolor (ca. 1823) by James Barton Longacre, after John Vanderlyn. National Portrait Gallery, Smithsonian Institution.

152 Lithograph (1900) by Albert Rosenthal, after his oil painting. Phillips Exeter Academy, Exeter, N.H.

153 Detail from oil (ca. 1793–94) by Charles Willson Peale. Boston Museum of Fine Arts. Gift of Edwin H. Abbot, Jr., in memory of his brother, Philip Stanley Abbot.

154 Detail from oil (1806) by John Trumbull. National Gallery of Art, Andrew W. Mellon Collection.

158 Detail from oil (1791) by Archibald Robertson. From the collection of the Georgia Historical Society.

159 National Archives (148–CP–130).

160 Detail from oil (1760–70) by John Hesselius. National Portrait Gallery, Smithsonian Institution.

161 Detail from oil (ca. 1814) by John Wesley Jarvis. National Portrait Gallery, Smithsonian Institution.

163 Oil (1792) by John Trumbull. Yale University Art Gallery.

165 Detail from pastel (ca. 1795–1800) attributed to James Sharples, Sr. Independence National Historical Park.

168 Detail from oil (undated) by John Wollaston. Fraunces Tavern Museum, New York CIty.

170 Detail from oil (ca. 1810) attributed to Cephas Thompson, Julia Wickham Porter (Mrs. Charles W. Porter III).

171 Detail from pastel (ca. 1795–1800) attributed to James Sharples, Sr. Independence National Historical Park.

172 Oil (1792) by Charles Willson Peale. The Thomas Gilcrease Institute of American History and Art, Tulsa, Oklahoma.

175 Detail from pastel (ca. 1796) by James Sharples, Sr. Independence National Historical Park.

177 Detail from oil (ca. 1835) by Henry Hoppner Meyer, after unidentified artist. National Portrait Gallery, Smithsonian Institution.

179 National Archives (148–CP–121).

181 Detail from oil (1901) by Albert Rosenthal, after a miniature by Robert Field. Independence National Historical Park.

182 Oil (1784) by Charles Willson Peale. Independence National Historical Park.

183 Engraving (1783) by B. B. Ellis. National Portrait Gallery, Smithsonian Institution.

185 Detail from oil (ca. 1782) by Charles Willson Peale. Independence National Historical Park.

187 Detail from pastel (1794) by James Sharples, Sr. United States Supreme Court.

190 National Archives (148–CCD–54).

192 Detail from engraving (undated) by Cornelius Tiebout. National Portrait Gallery, Smithsonian Institution.

194 National Archives (148–CCD–40).

196 Detail from oil (ca. 1796) by Robert Edge Pine. National Portrait Gallery, Smithsonian Institution.

198 Oil on wood (1791) by John Trumbull. Yale University Art Gallery.

200 Detail from oil (undated) by Ralph Earl. Yale University Art Gallery. Gift of Roger Sherman White.

202 Detail from pastel (ca. 1798–1800) attributed to James Sharples, Sr. Independence National Historical Park.

203 National Archives (148-CP-156).

204 Detail from oil (undated) by Robert Edge Pine. National Portrait Gallery, Smithsonian Institution.

208 National Archives (148-CCD-70a).

210 Miniature, watercolor on ivory (ca. 1795) by Jean Pierre Henri Elouis. National Museum of American Art, Smithsonian Institution. Catherine Walden Myer Fund.

213 Detail from watercolor (ca. 1825) by James Barton Longacre after unidentified artist. National Portrait Gallery, Smithsonian Institution.

238 National Archives (148-CCD-93a).

239 National Archives (64-NA-5674).

240 National Archives (64-NA-5583).

I N D E X

Adams, John, 11, 23, 84, 101, 125, 129, 137, 149, 151, 156, 172
Adams, John Quincy, 164, 237
Adams, Samuel, 23, 95, 149, 150
Age of delegates, 30, 121
Alabama, 13
Alden, Roger, 235
Alison, Rev. Francis, 196
Allen, Ethan, Ira, and Levi, 13
Alsop, Mary, 163
Amendments, 85, 107–115; procedures for, 63, 66–67, 69, 83, 102–103, 115. *See also* Bill of Rights
American Revolution. *See* Revolutionary War
Annapolis Convention, 19–21, 126, 131, 141, 155, 173, 180, 186, 194, 206, 209
Antifederalists: ratification debates, 8, 86–97
Antislavery. *See* Slaves and slavery
Apthorpe, Maria, 209
Army. *See* Military affairs
Articles of Association, 241
Articles of Confederation: draft, 141, 201; exhibited, 241–242, New Jersey plan for revision, 42–43; shortcomings, 9–20; signers, 119; source of ideas for Constitution, 52, 54–56, 63–64; support for, 8, 88–94
Attendance of delegates at Convention, 29

Bachelor delegates, 121–122
Baldwin, Abraham: biography, 120, 121–122, 123–124; Convention activities, 29, 46, 64, 123, 158
Baldwin, Henry, 123
Baldwin, Ruth, 123
Balfour, Jean, 127
Barbary States, 13
Barlow, Joel, 123
Barlow, Ruth Baldwin, 123
Bartram, John, 27
Bassett, Ann Ennals, 125
Bassett, Richard: biography, 20, 119, 120, 121, 122, 124–125; Convention activities, 29, 124
Beach, Anne, 161
Beach, Mary Brewster, 162
Bedford, Col. Gunning, 125
Bedford, Gunning Jr.: biography, 119, 120, 122, 125–126; Convention activities, 29, 46, 126
Bedford, Jane Parker, 125
Bell, Cornelia, 188
Bill of Rights: Convention postponement, 67; exhibited, 235–240; factor in ratification, 67, 86, 95–96, 99, 105; provisions, 103–107
Bird, Rachel, 210
The Black Horse (tavern), 26
Blacks, 109–111, 113–115. *See also* Slaves and slavery
Blackstone, Sir William, 192
Blair, James, 127
Blair, Jean Balfour, 127
Blair, John: biography, 119, 120, 122, 127; Convention activities, 29, 127
Blair, John (father), 127
Blount, Mary Grainger, 128
Blount, Thomas, 128
Blount, William: biography, 119, 122, 128–129; Convention activities, 29, 73, 128
Braddock, Gen. Edward, 205
Brearly, David: biography, 119, 120, 121, 122, 129–130; Convention activities, 29, 47, 64, 130; papers, 242, 243
Brearly, Elizabeth Higbee, 130
Brearly, Elizabeth Mullen, 129
Brent, Sarah, 180
Broom, Jacob: biography, 119, 120, 131; Convention activities, 29, 131
Broom, Rachel Pierce, 131
Bruff (Mrs. Richard Bassett), 125
Burgoyne, Gen. John, 165
Burr, Aaron, 138–139, 156, 178, 195
Burwell, Nathaniel, 195
Butler, Mary Middleton, 132
Butler, Pierce: biography, 119, 120, 122, 132–133; Convention activities, 29, 47, 64, 132
Butler, Sir Richard, 132

Cabinet, 62, 83, 84–85
Caldwell, Margaret Allison, 171
Call, Rebecca, 153
Canals, 69
Carpenter's Hall, 27
Carroll, Charles (of Carrollton), 22, 133
Carroll, Daniel: biography, 119, 120, 122, 133–134; Convention activities, 29, 47, 64, 73, 133–134
Carroll, Eleanor, 133

Carroll, Bishop John, 133
Census, 47, 48, 54
Centennial celebration, 1876, 236
Chase, Samuel, 24, 89, 178
Citizenship, 57
City Tavern, 26, 31, 76
Civil rights, 6, 62, 92-93, 105–107, 109, 111
Clark, Abraham, 20, 22, 138
Clay, Henry, 214
Claypoole, David C., 52
Clinton, George, 47, 89, 96, 167, 184, 215
Clymer, Elizabeth Meredith, 135
Clymer, George: biography, 119, 122, 134–135; Convention activities, 29, 135
Colleges: national university proposal, 69–71. *See also* Education
Commerce. *See* Economic affairs
Commerce clause, 92-93
Committee of detail, 52–56, 62
Committee of style, 66–71
Committee of the whole, 39–41, 153
Committee on postponed matters, 64–66
Confederation. *See* Articles of Confederation
Congress, U.S.: Bill of Rights, 67, 99, 105; Convention costs, 35; first meeting, 101. *See also* House of Representatives, U.S.; Legislative branch; Senate, U.S.
Connecticut, 20; Convention votes, 40, 44, 45, 49; ratification, 94–95, 143, 162, 201
Connecticut Compromise. *See* Great Compromise
Constitution, U.S.: bibliography, 245–246; centennial, 1887, 114; engrossing and signing, 71–73, 78–82; exhibited, 235–241; first draft, 52–53; research opportunities, 242–244; sources, 76, 83; text, 219–234. *See also* Amendments; Bill of Rights; Constitutional Convention; Ratification
Constitutional Convention: aims, 4–8; authorization, 22; costs, 35; proceedings, 33–76; officers, 35; records, 35, 73, 242–243; rules, 35–36, 73; session characteristics, 35, 45, 57; state participation, 34–35. *See also* Delegates
Constitutionality. *See* Supreme Court
Continental Congress (First), 103
Continental Congress: authorizes Convention, 6, 22, 35; role in ratification, 64, 85, 86, 99–101, 235, 242; Convention period activities, 52, 59; members at Philadelphia, 29, 86, 89, 119; model for Convention procedures, 35, 48; records, 243; shortcomings of Confederation, 9–20
Courts. *See* Judiciary; Supreme Court
Cresap, Maria, 177
Currency. *See* Economic affairs
Custis, Martha Dandridge, 205

Davie, Archibald, 136
Davie, Sarah Jones, 136
Davie, William Richardson: biography, 119, 120, 122, 136–137; Convention activities, 29, 46, 136–137
Dayton, Elias, 138
Dayton, Jonathan: biography, 30, 119, 122, 138–139; Convention activities, 29, 138
Dayton, Susan Williamson, 139
Debt. *See* Economic affairs
Declaration of Independence: exhibited, 235-242; signers, 22–23, 29, 89, 95, 119, 121, 141, 151, 183, 187, 196, 198, 201, 210–211, 214; source of Constitution ideas, 103
Delaware, 20; Convention votes, 40, 44, 45, 49, 61; delegate instructions, 23; ratification, 94, 95, 126, 197
Delegates: age, 30, 121; aims, 4–8; Antifederalists later, 89; attendance, 29; economic backgrounds and occupations, 4, 30, 119–120, 122; education, 30, 120–121; instructions, 22–23; list, 28–29; members of Continental Congress, 86, 89; national origins and family, 120, 121–122; pay, 23, 34–35, 165–166; political experience, 29-30, 32–33, 119, 120, 122; prominent omissions, 22–23; signature ceremony, 73, 76; work and recreation in Philadelphia, 25–28, 56–57, 76
Democracy, 3–4, 7, 8, 89

INDEX

Dickinson, John: Annapolis Convention, 20, 141; biography, 119, 120, 139–141, 210; Convention activities and leadership, 29, 31, 46, 64, 73, 141, 196
Dickinson, Mary Cadwalader, 139
Dickinson, Mary Norris, 139
Dickinson, Samuel, 139
Dinwiddie, Robert, 213
District of Columbia, 113, 134
"Due process" clause. *See* Fourteenth amendment
Dunlap, John, 52, 86
Dunlap & Claypoole, 52, 70, 86
Dunmore, Lord, 194

Economic affairs, class and occupations of delegates, 4–8, 119–120; factors in ratification, 88–89, 91, 92–94; sanctity of contracts, 69; shortcomings of Confederation, 10–11, 14–18, 20. *See also* Taxation
Education of delegates, 30, 120–121
Eighteenth amendment, 112
Eighth amendment, 105
Eilbeck, Anne, 179
Eisenhower, Dwight D., 115
Electoral college, 65
Eleventh amendment, 107–109
Ellsworth, Abigail Wolcott, 142
Ellsworth, David, 142
Ellsworth, Jemima, 142
Ellsworth, Oliver: biography, 120, 122, 142–143; Convention activities, 29, 30, 46, 52, 60, 142–143
Emancipation Proclamation, 109
Ennals, Ann, 125
Executive branch. *See* Cabinet; Presidency
Export taxes. *See* Import and export taxes

Fairfax, Lord, 205
Family life of delegates, 22, 26–28, 121–122
Federal Convention. *See* Constitutional Convention
Federal Hall, 101–102, 235
Federalism, 40, 88, 178
The Federalist, 96, 98, 155, 173
Federalists: ratification debates, 86–97
Fenwick, Charlotte, 189
Few, Catherine Nicholson, 145
Few, William: biography, 120, 121, 122, 144–145; Convention activities, 29, 144–145
Fifteenth amendment, 111
Fifth amendment, 105–106
Finance. *See* Economic affairs
First amendment, 105
Fitzsimons, Catherine Meade, 145
Fitzsimons, Thomas: biography, 119, 120, 121, 122, 145–146; Convention activities, 29, 145–146
Florida, 13
Foreign affairs: constitutional provisions, 92, 93–94; records, 243; shortcomings of Confederation, 7, 11–14
Fourteenth amendment, 109–111
Fourth amendment, 105
France, 12
Franchise. *See* Voting rights
Franklin, Benjamin: age, 30, 121; biography, 119, 120, 122, 147–149, 184; Convention attendance and leadership, 29, 30, 45, 149; political experience and views, 29, 69, 71–73, 89, 119; relation to other delegates, 27, 140, 208–209; representation compromise, 45, 46; "rising sun" remark, 76
Franklin, James, 147
Franklin, state of, 13
French, Susanna, 168
Founding Fathers. *See* Delegates

Gage, Gen. Thomas, 162
Gates, Gen. Horatio, 182
"General welfare" clause, 83
The George (tavern), 26
Georgia, 13, 20; Convention votes, 44, 45, 49; ratification, 89, 94, 145
Gerry, Ann Thompson, 150
Gerry, Elbridge: biography, 119, 122, 149–151, 204; Convention attendance and leadership, 26, 29, 30, 46, 57, 150–151; Declaration of Independence, 29, 119; objections and antifederalism, 67, 73, 89, 95, 150–151; papers, 242, 243
Gilman, Nicholas: biography, 119, 120, 121–122, 152; Convention activities, 29, 34, 64, 152, 165–166

Girard, Stephen, 159–160
Gladstone, William, 85
Gorham, Nathaniel: biography, 119, 120, 122, 153–154; Convention activities and leadership, 29, 30, 40, 52, 153; ratification, 95, 153; representation compromise, 46, 73
Gorham, Rebecca Call, 153
Grainger, Mary, 128
Gray, Hannah, 212
Great Britain, 11–14, 18, 93–94
Great (or Connecticut) Compromise, 45–50, 51, 58, 123, 126, 137, 141, 142, 150, 162, 201, 209, 243
Greene, Nathanael, 136, 189, 199
Grimké, Elizabeth, 198

Hamilton, Alexander: Annapolis Convention, 20, 155; biography, 120, 121, 122, 154–156; Convention attendance and status, 23, 29, 35, 47, 73; Convention leadership, 9, 30, 45, 66; *The Federalist* and ratification, 89, 96–99, 155, 173; journal, 35; plan of government, 43–44, 243; political associates and opponents, 124, 134, 138, 143, 146, 163, 172, 173, 197, 207
Hamilton, Elizabeth Schuyler, 155
Hancock, John, 23, 95, 150, 241
Harrison, Benjamin, 89
Hartwell, Elizabeth, 200
Henry, Patrick, 7, 22, 24, 89, 92, 96, 170, 173
Higbee, Elizabeth, 130
House of Representatives, U.S.: characteristics and powers, 53, 58, 62, 66, 73, 110; delegates who served in, 122
Houston, Archibald, 157
Houston, Jane, 157
Houston, Margaret, 157
Houston, William C.: biography, 20, 121, 157; Convention activities, 29, 47, 157
Houstoun, Sir Patrick, 158
Houstoun, William, 29, 119, 120, 158
Hutchinson, Thomas, 209

Illinois, 112
Impeachment, 53, 56, 63, 64
Import and export taxes, 54, 58, 59, 61–62, 71, 93
Income taxes, 111
Indian Queen Tavern, 26, 48, 49
Indians, 9, 11, 13–14, 89, 110, 128, 135, 154, 168, 205
Ingersoll, Elizabeth Pettit, 159
Ingersoll, Jared Jr., 29, 120, 159–160
Ingersoll, Jared Sr., 159, 162
Interpretation of Constitution. *See* Supreme Court
Iredell, James, 212

Jackson, Andrew, 174
Jackson, William, 35–37, 51, 71, 72, 85, 235, 242–243
Jameson, J. Franklin, 237
Jay, John: diplomatic posts, 13, 149; Federalist leadership, 24, 89, 96, 155, 173; political posts, 184, 199, 235
Jefferson, Thomas, 241; and delegates, 23, 29, 84; diplomatic posts, 184, 235; political associates and opponents, 124, 146, 152, 156, 166, 173, 178, 181, 191, 204, 207, 213, 214
Jenifer, Daniel of St. Thomas: biography, 119, 120, 121–122, 160–161; Convention activities, 29, 161
Johnson, Anne Beach, 161
Johnson, Mary Brewster Beach, 162
Johnson, Samuel, 161
Johnson, William Samuel: biography, 120, 121, 122, 161–162; Convention activities, 29, 30, 66, 162
Joint Chiefs of Staff, U.S., 237
Jones, Allen, 136
Jones, Sarah, 136
Judicial review, 84. *See also* Supreme Court
Judiciary: characteristics and powers, 38, 40, 50, 53, 56, 62–63, 107–109, 244; delegates who served on, 122. *See also* Supreme Court
Justice Department, U.S., 244

Kennedy, John F., 115
King, Mary Alsop, 163
King, Rufus: biography, 119, 122, 163–164; Convention activities and leadership, 29, 30, 64, 66, 163; journal, 35, 73, 163; ratification

debates, 95; representation compromise, 46, 47, 73; sanctity of contracts, 69
Lafayette, Marquis de, 138, 139, 155, 171, 181
Lambert, William, 240
"Lame duck" amendment, 112
Langdon, Elizabeth Sherburne, 165
Langdon, John: biography, 119, 122, 165–166; Convention activities, 29, 34, 165–166
Lansing, Cornelia Ray, 166
Lansing, Gerrit Jacob, 166
Lansing, Jannetje, 166
Lansing, John Jr.: biography, 166–167; Convention activities, 29, 43, 44, 47, 167, 215; journal, 35; objections and antifederalism, 89, 99, 167
Laurens, Henry, 22
Laurens, Mary Eleanor, 190
Lawson, Peter, 124
Lawyers, 30
Leach, Mary, 202
Lee, Charles, 181
Lee, Richard Henry, 22, 24, 89, 90, 170, 173, 210
Legislative branch: characteristics and powers, 38–40, 50, 53–54, 56, 57, 62, 83; representation formula, 41–50, 57. *See also* Congress, U.S.; Great Compromise
L'Enfant, Pierre Charles, 186
Letters From the Federal Farmer to the Republican (Lee), 89, 90
Letters . . . on the Federal Constitution (Randolph), 195
Letters of a Landholder (Ellsworth), 143
Lewis, Ann, 213
Library Company of Philadelphia, 27
Library of Congress, 237–238, 242
Lincoln, Abraham, 109
Littlejohn, Reverend, 236
Livingston, Robert R., 184
Livingston, Susanna French, 168
Livingston, William: biography, 120, 122, 168–169; Convention activities, 29, 31, 169; political associates and experience, 119, 155, 215
Locke, John, 83

McClurg, Elizabeth Seldon, 170
McClurg, James, 29, 119, 120, 170
McHenry, James: biography, 120, 122, 171–172; Convention activities, 29, 171; journal, 35, 171
McHenry, Margaret Allison Caldwell, 171
McKean, Thomas, 141, 197
McLean, John, 86
Madison, Dolley Payne Todd, 173
Madison, James: admission of new states, 63; Bill of Rights, 105; biography, 30, 120, 121, 122, 172–174, 237; Convention attendance and leadership, 29, 30, 34, 40, 57, 64, 66, 173, 211, 241; defects of Confederation, 9, 20, 45, 173; election of President, 63–64; *The Federalist* and ratification, 89, 96, 98, 105, 155, 173; internal improvements, 71; journal, 35, 173; national university, 69–71; political associates and opponents, 124, 125, 132, 137, 141, 151, 156, 163, 170; ratification requirements, 63; representation compromises, 46, 47, 49, 50, 57; Virginia Plan, 38, 41, 44
Marshall, John, 84, 96, 151, 214
Martin, Alexander, 29, 119, 121–122, 175–176
Martin, Hugh, 175
Martin, Jane, 175
Martin, Luther: biography, 120, 122, 177–178; Convention activities and leadership, 29, 31, 44–45, 46, 59, 178; objections and antifederalism, 89, 178
Martin, Maria Cresap, 177
Maryland, 20; Convention votes, 44, 45, 49; ratification, 95, 96, 134, 171, 178
Mason, Ann Thomson, 179
Mason, Anne Eilbeck, 179
Mason, George: biography, 119, 121, 179–180; Convention activities and leadership, 29, 30, 46, 59, 61, 63, 180; objections to Constitution, 67, 68, 73, 89, 96, 173, 180
Mason, George (father), 179
Mason, Sarah Brent, 180
Massachusetts, 20; Convention votes, 40, 44, 45, 49; economic affairs, 16, 22; ratification, 91, 95–96, 150, 153, 203
Meade, Catherine, 145
Meade, George, 145
Meade, Robert, 145

Mercer, Ann, 181
Mercer, John (father of John Francis Mercer), 181
Mercer, John (uncle of George Mason), 179
Mercer, John Francis: biography, 120, 122, 181; Convention activities, 29, 89, 178, 181
Mercer, Sophia Sprigg, 181
Meredith, Elizabeth, 134
Middleton, Mary, 132
Middleton, Sarah, 193
Mifflin, Sarah Morris, 182
Mifflin, Thomas: biography, 119, 120, 122, 182–183; Convention activities, 28, 29, 31, 85, 183
Military affairs: constitutional powers, 92, 93–94; opposition to standing army, 8; shortcomings of Confederation, 13–14; state militias, 59; records, 243. *See also* Revolutionary War
Ministers, 120
Mississippi, 13
Mississippi River, 13, 14, 93
Moland, John, 139
Monetary policy. *See* Economic affairs
Money bills, origination of, 46, 53, 58, 64, 66
Montesquieu, Baron Charles D., 83
Monroe, James, 89, 96, 164, 214, 236
Morris, Anne Cary Randolph, 185
Morris, Gouverneur: admission of new states, 63; biography, 119, 120, 122, 183–185, 187; borrowing power, 58; Convention attendance and leadership, 29, 31, 56, 64, 66, 184, 211; representation compromises, 46, 47, 48, 49; signing by state, 71–73; speeches, 173, 184
Morris, Lewis, 183, 184
Morris, Mary White, 185
Morris, Robert: associates, 184, 211; biography, 119, 120, 122, 135, 146, 185–187; Convention activities and leadership, 26, 27, 28, 29, 31, 33, 85, 186; Declaration of Independence, 29, 119, 186
Morris, Sarah, 182
Mount Vernon Conference, 19–20, 161, 173, 180, 206
Mullen, Elizabeth, 129
National Archives Building, 5, 8, 235, 239–241; research opportunities, 242–244
National Bureau of Standards, 238
National origins of delegates, 120
Nationalism, 38, 40, 44, 46, 88
Navigation acts. *See* Import and export taxes
Nelson, Thomas Jr., 22
New Hampshire, 13, 20, 22; Convention participation, 8, 23, 34–35; ratification, 96, 99, 152
New Jersey, 20; Convention votes, 44, 45, 49, 61; ratification, 94, 130, 169, 188. *See also* New Jersey Plan
New Jersey Plan, 38–44, 53, 130, 169, 188, 201, 243
New Orleans, La., 13
New York, 13, 20; constitution, 52, 54; Convention participation and votes, 8, 23, 40, 44, 45, 47, 73; ratification, 89, 91, 96–99, 155, 167, 215
Newspapers: reports of Convention and ratification, 32, 34, 77, 85–87, 96–98
Nicholas, Elizabeth, 194
Nicholson, Catherine, 145
Nineteenth amendment, 112
Ninth amendment, 106
Norris, Mary, 139
North Carolina, 13, 20; Convention votes, 40, 44, 45, 49; ratification, 99, 104, 105, 137, 202, 209
Northwest Ordinance, 59, 103, 243

Occupations of delegates, 4, 30, 119–120
Ohio, 13
Ohio Company, 179
Ordinances of 1784, 1785, 11

Paine, Thomas, 186
Parker, Jane B., 125
Parties, political, 109
Paterson, Cornelia Bell, 188
Paterson, Euphemia White, 188
Paterson, William: biography, 119, 120, 121, 122, 187–188; Convention activities, 29, 46, 60, 130; journal, 35, 188; New Jersey Plan, 41, 42, 43, 188
Patowmack Company, 20, 133
Patterson, Edgar, 236

Peale, Charles Willson, 28
Peale's Museum, 27
Pendleton, Edmund, 96, 214
Penn, William, 25
Pennsylvania, 20; Convention participation and votes, 23, 40, 44, 45, 49, 61; ratification, 91, 94–95, 209
Pennsylvania State House, 26, 34, 42, 85
Pettit, Elizabeth, 159
Phelps, Oliver, 154
Philadelphia, Pa., 12, 25–28
Pickering, Timothy, 242
Pierce, Charlotte Fenwick, 189
Pierce, Rachel, 131
Pierce, William Leigh: biography, 119, 122, 189; Convention activities, 29, 189; journal, 35, 189
Pinckney, Charles; biography, 120, 122, 190–191; Convention attendance and leadership, 29, 31, 69–71, 190; office-holding requirements, 57; plan of government, 40, 52–53; representation, 43, 49
Pinckney, Col. Charles, 190
Pinckney, Charles Cotesworth: biography, 119, 120, 121, 122, 151, 164, 190, 192–193; Convention activities, 29, 31, 47, 193
Pinckney, Mary Eleanor Laurens, 190
Pinckney, Mary Stead, 193
Pinckney, Sarah Middleton, 193
Pinckney, William, 178
Pitt, William, 85
Poll taxes, 111, 113–115
Prescott, Rebecca, 200
Presidency: characteristics and powers, 38, 40, 41, 50–54, 62, 64–66, 69, 85, 109, 112, 115; delegates nominated for, 122; first election, 99–101
Printing of Constitution, 35, 52, 67, 69, 71, 85. *See also* Newspapers
Prohibition, 112
Property qualifications, 6, 57, 123
Providence Plantations, 99
Pulaski, Casimir, 136
Putnam, Herbert, 237

Randolph, Anne Cary, 185
Randolph, Ariana Jenings, 194
Randolph, Edmund: biography, 20, 119, 120, 122, 194–195; Convention attendance and leadership, 29, 30, 34, 46, 49, 53, 61; ratification debates, 67, 71, 73, 89, 96, 195; Virginia Plan, 38, 40, 43, 44, 194
Randolph, Elizabeth Nicholas, 194
Randolph, John, 194
Randolph, Peyton, 194
Ratification process: debates, 67, 86–97; requirements, 7, 56, 63
Ray, Cornelia, 166
Read, Deborah, 147
Read, George: biography, 20, 119, 120, 122, 196–197; Convention activities, 29, 73, 144, 197
Read, Gertrude Ross Till, 196
Read, Joseph, 125
Reconstruction period, 109–111
Reed, Joseph, 159
Religious affiliation of delegates, 122
Religious freedom, 6, 57, 105
Representation. *See* Legislative branch
Republicanism, 4, 150
Revolutionary War: debt assumption, 58, 93–94; records, 243; state militias, 59
Revenue. *See* Money bills; Taxation
Rhode Island, 16, 20; Convention nonparticipation, 6, 8, 22, 34; ratification, 99
Richardson, William, 136
Roosevelt, Franklin D., 112
Ross, George, 196
Rush, Benjamin, 89, 171
Rutledge, Edward, 198
Rutledge, Elizabeth Grimké, 198
Rutledge, John: biography, 119, 120, 122, 198–199; Convention activities and leadership, 29, 31, 46, 47, 52, 54, 199

Schuyler, Elizabeth, 155
Schuyler, Gen. Philip, 166
Scientists, 120
Second amendment, 105
Secrecy, 36, 92, 177
Secret Proceedings . . . of the Convention (Yates), 216
Secret Service, U.S., 237
Seldon, Elizabeth, 170
Senate, U.S.: characteristics and powers, 53, 64–66, 111–112; delegates who served in, 122

Seventeenth amendment, 111–112
Seventh amendment, 106
Shallus, Jacob, 71, 73
Shays, Daniel, 16
Shays' Rebellion, 8, 16–18
Sherburne, Elizabeth, 165
Sherman, Elizabeth Hartwell, 200
Sherman, Rebecca Prescott, 200
Sherman, Roger: admission of new states, 63; Bill of Rights, 67; biography, 119, 120, 121, 122, 200–201; Convention attendance and leadership, 29, 30, 45, 64, 201; Declaration of Independence, 29, 119, 201; election of president, 66; New Jersey Plan, 41, 42; representation, 46, 47, 67
Sixteenth amendment, 111
Sixth amendment, 105
Slaves and slavery: Convention debates, 4, 7, 8, 59, 67; emancipation, 109, 111; extradition of fugitives, 61, 63; owned by delegates, 30, 119–120, 132, 137; representation-taxation issue, 46, 47–49, 61, 142, 166, 169, 178; slave trade, 54, 59–62, 143, 193
Society of the Cincinnati, 28
South Carolina, 20; Convention votes, 40, 44, 45, 49, 73; ratification, 96, 132, 190, 193
Sovereignty, 41–42, 69
Spain, 13, 14, 89, 93
Spaight, Mary Leach, 202
Spaight, Richard Dobbs Sr.: biography, 120, 121, 122, 202–203; Convention activities, 29, 202
Sprigg, Sophia, 181
Stanly, John, 203
Stark, Gen. John, 165
State Department, U.S., 235–239, 242–243
States: admission of new, 11, 40, 49, 59, 63, 83; constitutional powers and limitations, 6, 54–56, 58–59, 63, 106–109; constitutions as source of ideas, 103; delegate participation, 34–35; representation issue, 38, 41–50; Revolutionary War, 18, 58; shortcomings of Confederation, 9–19
Stead, Mary, 193
Stockton, Richard, 187
Stone, Thomas, 22
Strong, Caleb: biography, 95, 119, 122, 203–204; Convention activities, 29, 203
Strong, Sarah, 204
Suffrage. *See* Voting rights
Supreme Court, U.S.: characteristics and powers, 53, 56, 62, 63, 64, 83, 84; constitutional interpretation, 62–63, 84, 107, 111, 115; delegates who served on, 122; records, 243–244
Sweeney, George Wythe, 214

Taliaferro, Elizabeth, 213
Talleyrand, 151
Tariffs. *See* Import and export taxes
Taxation: power to levy, 8, 42–43, 53, 54; shortcomings of Confederation, 9; 16th amendment, 111; slavery issues, 47, 48, 59–62. *See also* Import and export taxes
Tenth amendment, 106–107
Third amendment, 105
Thirteenth amendment, 109
Thompson, Ann, 150
Thomson, Charles, 85, 235
Till, Gertrude Ross, 196
Todd, Dolley Payne, 173
Trade. *See* Economic affairs
Treaty of Paris, 9, 12, 13, 19, 149, 180, 241
Trenton Iron Works, 28
Truman, Harry S., 113
Twelfth amendment, 109
Twentieth amendment, 112-113
Twenty-fifth amendment, 115
Twenty-first amendment, 112
Twenty-fourth amendment, 111, 113–115
Twenty-second amendment, 85, 112–113
Twenty-sixth amendment, 115
Twenty-third amendment, 113

Van Ness, Jannetje, 215
Van Rensselaer, Stephen, 188
Vergennes, Comte de, 12
Vermont, 13
Veto power, 40, 41, 54, 62, 67
Vice Presidency: characteristics and powers, 65, 109, 112–113, 115; delegates nominated for, 122
Virginia, 20; Convention leadership, 34,

38; Convention votes, 40, 44, 45, 49, 61; ratification, 91, 96–97, 99, 127, 173, 195, 214. *See also* Virginia Plan
Virginia Plan, 38–44, 52, 173, 177–178, 194, 242, 243
Voting rights, 6, 56, 65, 111–115

Walton, George, 22, 135
War of 1812, 236
War of Independence. *See* Revolutionary War
Washington, George: Bill of Rights, 105; biography, 120, 122, 204–207; Convention leadership, 29, 30, 35, 40, 55, 73, 74, 206, 241, 242; military and political associates and appointments, 126, 127, 128, 130, 131, 133–134, 155, 156, 160, 170, 171, 182, 184, 186, 194, 195, 199, 204, 212; presidential election and inaugural, 30, 101–102, 105, 206–207, 235, 241; ratification, 63, 65, 89, 96; reception in Philadelphia, 26, 28; representation, 73; shortcomings of Confederation, 9, 14, 20; transmittal letter, 85, 94, 240
Washington, Lawrence, 204–205
Washington, Martha Dandridge Custis, 205
Webster, Daniel, 178
West Indies, 11, 14, 16
White, Euphemia, 188
White, Mary, 185
Williamson, Hugh: biography, 120, 121, 122, 176, 208–210; Convention activities, 29, 31, 45, 47, 62, 64
Williamson, Maria Apthorpe, 209
Williamson, Susan, 139
Willing, Thomas and Charles, 185
Wilson, Hannah Gray, 212
Wilson, James: authority of Convention, 43; biography, 119, 120, 121, 122, 132, 210–212; Convention attendance and leadership, 29, 31, 52, 57, 211; Declaration of Independence 29, 119, 210–211; election of President, 63–64; ratification requirements, 63; representation compromise, 46, 49; speeches, 71, 173
Wilson, Rachel Bird, 210
Wilson, Woodrow, 115
Wirt, William, 178
Wolcott, Abigail, 142
Women, 112–113
World War II, 237
Wythe, Ann Lewis, 213
Wythe, Elizabeth Taliaferro, 213
Wythe, George: biography, 119, 120, 121, 127, 213–214; Convention activities, 29, 30, 96, 214; Declaration of Independence, 29, 119, 214
Wythe, Margaret, 213
Wythe, Thomas (Jr.), 213
Wythe, Thomas (Sr.), 213

Yates, Jannetje Van Ness, 215
Yates, Joseph, 215
Yates, Maria, 215
Yates, Robert: biography, 119, 215–216; Convention attendance, 29, 47, 167; journal, 35, 216; objections and antifederalism, 44, 89, 99, 215; representation compromise, 46, 47